Implacable, Indefatigable

"Onslow" class

"Dido" class

"Hunt" class

"Battle" class

"Algerine" class

"Castle" class

"T" class

"S" class (shape of C.T. varies slightly)

"V" class

AYE, AYE, SIR!

Overleaf: Submarine depot ships *Montclare* and *Forth* at Devonport in March, 1947. *Montclare* is secured to the port side of *Forth* which has the gangplank in place for access to both ships.

AYE, AYE, SIR!

AN AUTOBIOGRAPHY
OF A NATIONAL SERVICE SAILOR 1946-1948

by

ANTHONY J. WALKER

W. H. WALKER & BROTHERS LIMITED
RICKMANSWORTH   2000

Published by
W.H. Walker & Brothers Limited
ISBN 0-9517923-2-6
© Anthony J. Walker, 2000

British Library Cataloguing-in-Publication Data

A catalogue record for this book is
available from the British Library

All rights reserved. No part of this book may be reproduced,
stored in a retrieval system, or transmitted in any form or by
any means, electronic, mechanical, photocopying, recording
or otherwise without the prior permission of the publishers.

Printed in Great Britain by
The Wolsey Press, Ipswich, Suffolk.

CONTENTS

Foreword by Commander Ian Hamilton, RN(Retd).		vii
Introduction		xiii
Acknowledgements		xv
Apologies		xxv
Prologue		xxvii
1	Enlistment	1
2	Training Days - HMS *Royal Arthur*	9
	HMS *Glendower*	21
	HMS *Scotia*	33
3	Submarine Depot Ship HMS *Forth* (S/m3)	39
4	Home Fleet Autumn Manoeuvres	69
5	Submarine Depot Ship HMS *Montclare* (S/m3)	103
6	The Clyde Naval Review	123
7	Rothesay Ashore	169
8	Discharge	199
Epilogue		202
Sequel		220
Appendix one		223
Appendix two		229
Appendix three		235
Appendix four		237
Appendix five		239
Copyright Holders		242
Bibliography		243
Index		245

To everyone I met, the friendships made,
and to the town of Rothesay.

Foreword

This beautifully produced volume is Anthony Walker's third production and tells the interesting story of his period of National Service in the Royal Navy, largely based on the small town of Rothesay on the Island of Bute in the Firth of Clyde, in the immediate post-war period, 1946–1948.

Not only does it tell of the life and experiences of a National Serviceman in the Royal Navy but it fills a gap in the naval and military history of the area. Bute has a fairly well-documented—and interesting— naval and military history.

Rothesay Castle was occupied for a time by the Norsemen, who only withdrew after their defeat at the Battle of Largs. Bute men marched to join Wallace's army before the Battle of Falkirk, and at the time of the 1715 Rebellion a militia regiment was raised under the command of James, Earl of Bute, 'Our Right Trusty and Right Entirely Beloved Lieutenant of the Shire of Bute'.

In 1298 the King of Scots appointed his eldest son Duke of Rothesay. In 1998 the Prince of Wales visited Rothesay Castle in his capacity as Duke of Rothesay—the title by which he was always known and addressed by the Gordon Highlanders.

During the Napoleonic Wars, in addition to those who served on Regular engagements in the Royal Navy and the Army and those press-ganged from among the seafaring inhabitants, the County of Bute provided Quota-Men for the Royal Navy, the Argyll & Buteshire Militia, the Buteshire Battalion of Volunteer Infantry (including an Artillery Section), the Bute Volunteer Cavalry and the Buteshire Regiment of Local Militia. There is mention, too, that 'Two special collections (in the Parish Church) for parishioners, while Prisoners of War in France, realized £115'—a very considerable sum in those days.

Under the Quota Acts of 1795, magistrates were called upon to produce men for the Royal Navy from the counties, cities and towns. In his *A Social History of the Navy*, Michael Lewis quotes the figures; examples are 'Yorkshire 1,081, Rutland 23; London 5,704 and Radnor 26.' Bute was particularly hard hit, being called on to produce 168, but only '94 men who were accepted in full'— this from a population of around 5,000.

The Artillery Detachment of The Buteshire Battalion of Volunteer Infantry had a shore battery of five 18-pdr. guns at what is still known as Battery Place. These remained in place until 1914.

It is recorded that in 1804 the local minister would not permit the Volunteers the use of the schoolroom for a Saturday night dance. In retaliation, the Captains of Companies marched their men the following morning past the Church 'with the fifes playing a reel before them'—a proceeding abhorrent to the Scottish Kirk of that day. Again, on Thursday, 5th December, 1805, on the occasion of the general thanksgiving for Lord Nelson's victory at Trafalgar, the Volunteers marched to Church in the afternoon 'to a Gaelic service, and comparatively few of them knew Gaelic, with their fifes playing, and attended by a mob of children and rabble'.

Again, in the late 1850s, when there was once more a threat of invasion by the French, a Rifle Corps was formed, later to become a Company of a Volunteer Battalion of the Argyll & Sutherland Highlanders, and also a Coast Artillery Battery of the Royal Garrison Artillery.

On the disbandment of the Volunteers and the formation in 1908 of the Territorial Force, later the Territorial Army, a Bute Battery was formed as part of the 4th (Highland) Mountain Artillery Brigade, Royal Garrison Artillery. This was the only Mountain Artillery unit in the Territorial Army, and was unique in the Imperial Forces in that both gunners and drivers were British. In all other such units, mostly serving on the North-West Frontier of India, the drivers were exclusively native. This Mountain Artillery Brigade had a distinguished record, being the first artillery to land on Gallipoli and the first artillery to enter Bulgaria at the end of the war.

In 1939 the Bute Battery had become 202 Anti-Tank Battery, which went to France in January, 1940, with the 51st (Highland) Division and, with most of the Division, were lost at St. Valery. Their replacement unit, 241 Anti-Tank Regiment, had a distinguished record, serving from Alamein to the Rhine.

To turn to the Royal Navy and Bute, the submarine depot ship H.M.S. *Cyclops* arrived at Rothesay from the Mediterranean early in 1940 to become depot ship of the 7th Submarine Flotilla. Rothesay became probably the most important submarine base in the United Kingdom, to which, it is claimed, 95% of all British submarines came for 'working-up' and for so-called 'rest periods' between patrols. Allied submarines, Norwegian, Dutch and Polish, were based on *Cyclops*.

Underway here, powered by Pressurised Water-Cooled Nuclear Reactor, is *Spartan*, one of a small number of Nuclear Powered Fleet submarines (SSN) in the "Swiftsure" class, built by Vickers Shipbuilding and Engineering Ltd (VSEL), Barrow. *Spartan* was laid down 26 April, 1976, launched 7 April, 1978, and commissioned 22 September, 1979. Displacement 4,400 tons surfaced, length 82.90m, and beam 10.1m. Her speed is 30+ knots submerged, and has a complement of 116. October, 1992

Kames Hydropathic at Port Bannatyne, named H.M.S. *Varbel*, was taken over as the initial Training Establishment for the midget submarines of the 12th Submarine Flotilla. The memorial to the men of the flotilla who lost their lives in the war is in the village of Port Bannatyne. One submarine of the flotilla was lost here during training and the men who lost their lives are buried in a local cemetery. Also lost nearby, between Arran and Ardrossan, was the American-built escort carrier H.M.S. *Dasher* which blew up as a result of an accident on 27th March, 1943, and sank with the loss of 379 lives. A considerable amount of debris and papers was washed upon the shores of Bute.

The saga of the tanker *San Demetrio*, torpedoed in the Atlantic but eventually making her way home to be beached on Bute, and of the Dutch liner *Volendam*, torpedoed when carrying some of the first child evacuees to Canada and U.S.A., but struggling back to be beached in Kames Bay, will live long in the annals of the Merchant Navy. In the North Bute Cemetery lie the bodies of 36 R.A.F. pilots drowned when on their way to Canada for pilot training in the S.S. *Coronda*.

Our two small boatyards produced between them six harbour defence motor launches, and we had, of course, our own H.M.S. *Rothesay*, a minesweeping sloop of 656 tons, built in 1941.

Our closest connection with the Royal Air Force was when a unit of the R.A.F. Regiment was stationed across Rothesay Bay at Toward in Argyll.

A number of military units trained on the island, and the small island of Inchmarnock, lying off the west coast of Bute, was turned over in its entirety to military training. Among the units that were here were the 9th (Scottish) Commando and the North Nova Scotia Highlanders and Le Regiment de La Chaudiere, both in the 3rd Canadian Division, whose claim it is that they made more progress than any other division on D-Day.

A decoy village was built on the little-inhabited north end of the island with the intention of diverting German bombers from Greenock and towns on the Upper Clyde. It consisted of a series of lights on poles replicating street lights. When an 'alert' was sounded these were switched on as the blackout intensified on the mainland. Parts of the structures remained in place until the 1980s.

Early in May, 1941, in two nights' bombing raids on Greenock, 246 people were killed and 625 were injured, 290 of them seriously. Another 52 were listed as 'missing, believed killed'. The fires could be seen clearly from Bute, but the island escaped with a few bombs falling harmlessly in the fields.

The Clyde and the Mersey were our most important ports during the Second World War. Over 500 million tons of shipping entered and left the Clyde during the war, 52 million tons of cargo were handled and about four million troops were embarked or disembarked. During 1942, 3,960 merchant ships and 6,650 coastal vessels entered the Clyde.

Another good view of *Spartan* with the crew at work on the casing. February, 1993 "RN Photographs".

A Boat Company of the Royal Army Service Corps arrived at Rothesay in 1943, and on its departure at the end of the war Bute lost its connection with the Royal Artillery, which had lasted since 1859, the re-formed units of the Territorial Army being an Amphibious Company and a Fast Launch Company of the Royal Army Service Corps. These lasted until the early 1960s, when there was imposed a mass reduction in the strength of the Territorial Army.

The submarines and their depot ship also departed, and Bute's only link with the Royal Navy now is our two affiliated ships, the Swiftsure class submarine H.M.S. *Spartan* and the mine countermeasures vessel H.M.S. *Walney*, which have been adopted by the town of Rothesay.

When H.M.S. *Rothesay* was broken up her trophies, cups, silver salvers, etc, which had been presented by the town, went into the Trophy Store at Portsmouth. They were then brought back to the Bute Museum, and when *Spartan* was adopted the trophies were lent to her. When she went into Rosyth for a two-year refit they went to *Walney*. The ships pay an occasional visit here and the ships' companies are entertained, football matches are organised, and they are invited to the golf clubs, etc.

I have a personal interest in H.M.S. *Walney*, or rather in her predecessor which, together with H.M.S. *Hartland*, made a "suicide" attack into the harbour at Oran in November, 1942. My ship, the battleship H.M.S. *Malaya*, was the first British ship to go to an American yard for repair under the "Lease-Lend" agreement. We went to the Brooklyn Yard.

The "Sandown" class Mine Counter-Measures Vessel (MCMV) *Walney*, built by Vosper Thorneycroft in 1992. These vessels known as mine hunters are built of Glass Reinforced Plastic (GRP) and are equipped with sophisticated sonar mine detecting equipment. *Walney* has a displacement of 500 tons, length 52.5m, and beam 10.5m. She has a speed of 13 knots and a complement of 34. September, 1992

Whilst there we had the job of taking over and manning ten U.S. Coastguard cutters for service in the Royal Navy. I was Captain's Secretary at the time and we applied to the Admiralty for instruction on the new names for these vessels, which were to be named after American coastguard stations. We heard nothing. Captain Palliser decided that if we did not receive a reply from the Admiralty we would name them after British coastguard stations at the hand-over ceremony, which was to be quite an important function. The trouble was that the combined efforts of the Wardroom could not come up with ten such names.

Eventually I remembered a 1932 Admiralty Fleet Order instructing ships that before a practice firing they must inform the coastguard station in whose area the firing was to take place; there followed a list of all the coastguard stations and the areas for which they were responsible.

The Admiralty had a Ships' Names Committee whose job it was to propose ships' names for H.M. approval, so we had a midshipman sitting on the end of a telephone in the British Naval Mission's office in New York waiting for the names to come through. Nothing happened, so Captain Palliser named the ships from MY list, including H.M.S. *Walney*.

We are fortunate in now having Anthony Walker's book as a permanent record of those final years of the Navy in Bute and of life as a National Serviceman in the Royal Navy during the immediate post-war period.

Commander Ian Hamilton, RN(Retd), Rothesay, 2000.

Commander I Hamilton, RN(Retd).

Anthony Walker, officially photographed on enlistment into the Royal Navy as an Ordinary Seaman C/JX 791680, at HMS *Royal Arthur*, Skegness, on 7 February, 1946.

Introduction

This book is, more than anything else, a personal record of my National Service days in the Royal Navy between 7th February, 1946, and 3rd January, 1948. The details, timing of events, names and dates, are all from my own records which I preserved at the time, and which I have retained over all these past years. Some of the details are from notes on the back of photographs, jottings in my photograph album, various documents, personal letters, scraps of paper, notebooks, drafting reports and Service Records. All of these have remained intact since 1948 and have enabled me to relive the life of those times as it was for me, and to recount faithfully the circumstances and events as they occurred.

Over the past 50 years and more the files I had accumulated during my Navy days have lain dormant. The photographs I was able to take during my Service days I had carefully displayed in an album, and appended names, dates and places. My uniform, which has been moved numerous times over the years, still remains in pretty good shape, and the brown standard issue attache case containing all these papers and records from that period has been lying undisturbed in the loft. All this information has served to provide an almost complete and detailed account of what life was like for me personally, a young man in the Royal Navy a few months after the ending of the Second World War.

Delving through all these old records has been rather like returning to a time zone now non-existent. Researching every detail has been extraordinarily nostalgic, as I have re-lived the days and months of my short Naval career. There have been several moments when I wished I could have jumped on my time-machine and been whisked back to those memorable days, which have never forsaken me. With every scrap of information retained, together with the help of photographs from my own collection, it has been possible to remember particular events, moments and occasions, enabling me to account for my experiences and lifestyle in surprising detail during my short time in the Royal Navy.

Apart from my own photographs and journals which have formed the basis of my researches, I have relied heavily on several professional sources in supplying me with additional material, particularly by way of some superb photographs and newspaper reports. These have greatly assisted me in illustrating and strengthening graphically and comprehensively the various chapters in this book. I am extremely grateful for the assistance I have been given in this respect, and I have expressed my appreciation in more depth elsewhere.

Life in the Royal Navy was a completely new world for me, a fascinating, lively and exciting one, a world which after the first few months involved me wholeheartedly. I thoroughly enjoyed life at sea and ashore, and never for a moment did I have any desire or wishful thinking that it would all soon come to an end so I could return home. I wanted to know more about the ships and submarines that I saw or was with from time to time, and I have endeavoured to provide a limited background to these, as far as it is possible and necessary to do so. The camera I had with me was small enough to pack into any available space in my kitbag, and fortunately I was able to make use of this to advantage on several occasions.

There are many excellent and informative reference books available on all types and classes of ships and submarines in the Royal Navy, at any particular time. These books are written by experts who have had an on-going involvement through the years, and have acquired the knowledge and ability to detail accurately shipbuilding programmes, armaments, adaptations, modifications, refits, change of names, and so on. This subject is very complex, and without consistent research and informed knowledge it would be impossible to follow this through with accuracy. It is not the intention, therefore, to re-state such information in this book; to do so would not only be unnecessary but repetitive. My interest did extend, however, to those ships and submarines in which I was involved in one way or another, and I have investigated some background to these since they were very much a part of my Service life.

I have confined my research to the ships and submarines either as they were built, or at their launch or completion dates, and I have not generally followed through, as interesting as it may be, with any detailed information on such matters as streamlining, improvement in design and firepower which took place perhaps in the latter stages of building or after commissioning.

It has taken me a very long time even to think about writing this book, over fifty years in fact. After having trained with the Army Cadet Force as a schoolboy and the Air Training Corps as a youth, my chosen preference in the event of being called up for the Forces was the Royal Navy. Having experienced life to the full in the Senior Service, I am convinced I made the right choice.

My Service days have always remained an important period in my life, and one I look back on with pleasure and pride. A volunteer I was not, but as a conscript I experienced pleasure, satisfaction and fulfilment in having been just the right age to serve in the peacetime operations of the Royal Navy, as it was in 1946, when hammocks and rum issue were still the order of the day.

There were several variations of the following, but these particular words I emblazoned on the inside lid of my attache case, and we were expected to live up to them:

IT IS UPON THE NAVY AND THE GOOD PROVIDENCE OF GOD THAT THE WEALTH, SAFETY AND STRENGTH OF THE UNITED KINGDOM DO CHIEFLY DEPEND.

Acknowledgements

This account of service in the Royal Navy spans a very short period in my life; as with so many other young people of my age at the time it lasted just under two years.

Writing about it has been totally absorbing and extraordinarily nostalgic. I have recalled forgotten memories, relived happy moments, and reminisced in a period, now long past, lasting not only during my Navy days but for the few years leading up to it, and those immediately following.

To begin with, I had an attache case bulging with photographs and all sorts of old records, none of which has seen the light of day for more than fifty years. Poring over these photographs, scrutinising old papers, manuals, reports of all kinds, and reading old letters, provided the foundation for my story, but I needed much more information to supplement my own. On obtaining the historical records I sought, of every kind, I have not only been able to afford the reader with detailed coverage but have learnt far more from all this new material than I ever knew at the time, although I was involved and taking part.

I have not stinted in my pursuit for material relevant to my chapters, and in consequence I have leant heavily on a number of professional sources, and have drawn from these such information as I considered essential.

Everyone I contacted, without exception, has been most friendly and willing to give the time necessary to research my insatiable demands and to offer further help if I needed it. I would like to thank all of them individually for the considerable assistance they gave me in so many ways.

A good view of the battleship *King George V* (C.in.C Home Fleet) as she is about to set sail 29 October, 1946.

Associated Press

I was thrilled when Matthew Faber of Associated Press Photo Library was able to provide me with photographs mainly concerning the Home Fleet Autumn Manoeuvres of 1946. These, together with others, have assisted me greatly and I much appreciate all the co-operation and time he gave me. I also wish to make a special mention of the continuous help I have been given by Debbie Corner of the Royal Navy Submarine Museum, Gosport. I thank her for the friendly and efficient way she has dealt with all my enquiries over many months. The photographs I have been able to include of ships and submarines, together with essential data taken from their numerous Service History Sheets, are invaluable. In thanking Debbie Corner, I would like to add the name Margaret Bidmead, and generally the Royal Navy Submarine Museum Photograph Archive (RNSM), Gosport, for the most interesting and rewarding service I received during the whole of the time I was working on this book.

Without the unique service afforded me by Ron Forrest of Wright and Logan in supplying me with prints of pretty well every ship and submarine I asked him for my book would be sadly lacking in pictorial content. Ron Forrest has been able to provide me with complete coverage wherever I needed it, and I thank him for his friendship and the personal service he gave me throughout.

I became really excited when Imogen Gibbon of the National Maritime Museum, London, said she could supply me with the original building plans of my two submarine depot ships *Forth* and *Montclare*. These drawings are superb, and in the case of *Forth* are date-stamped John Brown & Co. Ltd., Clydebank, Shipbuilding Department, 30th November, 1938. With *Montclare* the building plans indicate in green, modifications that were carried out at Portsmouth Yard in September, 1946, in readiness for our transfer to her in May, 1947. These, together with detailed profile plans of the A-class submarines *Affray* and *Aeneas* and the T-class *Teredo* and *Talent* are excellent in quality, and I am very grateful to the National Maritime Museum, London, for permission to use them.

After launching in September, 1946, the A-class submarine *Ambush* was transferred to the 3rd Submarine Flotilla at Rothesay. She was built by Vickers-Armstrong, Barrow. This picture was taken in 1946 as she was leaving H.M.S. *Dolphin*. Source unknown.

(RNSM)

xvii

I also extend my grateful thanks to *Warship World* for including a help letter in their Summer 1999 issue with regard to my continuous researches in compiling an accurate schedule of vessels attending the Clyde Naval Review in 1947. My letter, together with the Editor's personal plea 'can anyone help Mr Walker?' brought ready responses from A. Eyre of Hull, J. Spurrier of Portsmouth, E. Fountain of London, E. Rycroft of East Sussex and E. Jones, and also from Michael Dryland of Huntingdon, who was serving on H.M.S. *Lennox*, an Algerine-class minesweeper in the Fishery Protection Flotilla which was anchored off Helensburgh. He recalls 'What an enormously impressive sight it was'. I would also like to thank C. Larter of Burton-on-Trent for willingly posting to me a copy of the Clyde Visit Order Berthing Plan, with so many vessels' names printed on it. This proved invaluable in compiling my Ship List.

In this connection I would like to extend my thanks and deep appreciation to Mike Cox of Manchester for all the time and trouble he went to in researching this for me, and for being thorough enough to carefully schedule Commands, Squadrons, Flotillas and Escorts in Admiralty files. This, together with the Berthing Plan, enabled me to compile a complete schedule with a very high degree of accuracy. I enlisted his help again with the Home Fleet Autumn Manoeuvres, and here again he produced all the details and information I was hoping for. I am most appreciative of everything he has done for me, and it is with pleasure I acknowledge the assistance of Mike Cox. Orbatinfo/M. Cox Information Services.

I would like to thank Miss J. A. Newman on behalf of MOD Copyright Administrator for allowing me to reproduce material from *A Seaman's Pocket-Book* (June, 1943), which was issued to me on enlistment to the Service, and formally extend my thanks in the following

Fleetwood, was a sloop in the "Aberdeen" class, built at Devonport Dockyard in 1936, and photographed here in May, 1946. Displacement 990 tons, length 266 feet overall, beam 36 feet. She carried 280 tons fuel oil, and had a complement of 100. Later, she was employed as a Radar Experimental Ship attached to a Signal School with additional accommodation provided.

Wright & Logan

manner – ©British Crown Copyright/MOD. Reproduced with the permission of Her Majesty's Stationery Office. I am extremely grateful also to David A. Belson, Crown Copyright Administrator, Ministry of Defence, for freely giving me permission to reproduce some superb photographs of ships and submarines which were taken at the Clyde Naval Review in July, 1947, and which have been in my possession for over 50 years. Granting permission to use these on behalf of the Controller of Her Majesty's Stationery Office is most generous and much appreciated; these are identified as "RN Photographs".

Thanks to the continued efforts of others, I have been fortunate in obtaining reports and accounts of various events covered in this book. I would like to thank The Newspaper Library of The British Library for their extensive researching of newspapers on my behalf for coverage of special and particular events. Their findings have been particularly rewarding, and my thanks are due for their interest and time in producing such excellent results.

I am very much indebted to Natalie Bushe, Photo library of Scottish Media Newspapers, who has been exceptionally generous in allowing me to reproduce text published in the *Glasgow Herald* covering the Clyde Naval Review in July, 1947. The reporting of this event in such detail has assisted me enormously not only by informing me of the programme of events during the days of the Review and the royal visit by King George VI and the Royal Family, but by mentioning the names of so many of the vessels taking part.

Emma Sollis has been particularly helpful in granting permission on behalf of Ewan MacNaughton Associates to reproduce reports published in the *Daily Telegraph* – 'DIVERS TRY TO SOLVE THE RIDDLE OF THE AFFRAY' and 'R.A.F. FOUND BLIND SPOT IN NAVY'S RADAR'. In this connection also, I would like to thank Tammi Iley, Syndication Department, International Publishing Corporation, for granting permission to reproduce the article 'His Majesty's Submarines' by Hamilton Fyfe. This vivid account of life in a submarine in wartime was published in the *War Illustrated* in August, 1943.

I also want to thank Jack Davis, Departmental Librarian, History and Glasgow Room, Glasgow City Council, for his time in researching my enquiries, and also Mrs. J. M. Wraight and Mrs. A. W. Bailey at the Ministry of Defence Admiralty Library for helping me with my enquiries and pointing me in the right direction.

I very much appreciate the assistance given me by Fiona Pitt, Keeper of Human History at the City of Plymouth Museum and Art Gallery, in sending me photographs showing in part the terrible damage suffered by blanket bombing on the city, Devonport and surrounding areas. My thanks also to the *Western Morning News* for giving me permission to reproduce a particular photograph depicting bombed out buildings in the City of Plymouth area, and also to Deborah Watson of the City of Plymouth Archives and Records for her interest and for the trouble she went to in locating and providing

Life goes on in the aftermath of the bombing of the City of Plymouth and Devonport. Everywhere one looked there were vast areas of destruction and emptiness. The actual date and address of this photograph is unknown, and is reproduced here with the kind permission of the Western Morning News.

me with this picture. Martha Spearpoint was particularly helpful in supplying me with the photograph entitled 'Western Wall of London', showing the devastated area of Cripplegate after the London blitz. This picture appeared in *The Times* newspaper on Wednesday 23rd July, 1947, and my grateful thanks go to her and to News International Syndication for permission to use this.

My special thanks also go to Paul Rodger, Random House UK Limited, who has been particularly generous in allowing me to use the profiles of various naval craft published in the original edition of *Jane's Fighting Ships 1946–1947*. In compiling detailed information on various vessels throughout this book, I have continually referred to this volume of Jane's which has been invaluable. Without this being constantly by my side, my book would be sadly lacking in definition and detail.

My appreciation and thanks go to Lt. Cdr. M. A. Critchley, RN(Retd), of Maritime Books for freely granting me permission to extract relevant information from *Shore Establishments of the Royal Navy* by Lt. Cdr. B. Warlow, RN(Retd). These details have been of great assistance. I would also like to acknowledge the information given me by the Book Trust and the Association of Publishers, and to Deborah Gill of John Murray (Publishers) Ltd who were kind enough to give permission to include a page entitled 'SHIPBUILDING' from *Royal Navy at War*, by Vice Admiral J. E. Harper, CB, MVO. I was more than pleased to hear from Lt. Cdr. B. Warlow, assistant editor, *Warship World*, in connection with my enquiries concerning the Clyde Naval Review. He has been exceptionally kind in showing considerable interest in my endeavours, and I would like to extend to him my grateful thanks for freely loaning me photographs and for making me aware of important last-minute changes to the Clyde Visit Orders, and other data which has been invaluable in ensuring my Ship List is as accurate as it could possibly be.

Among the records of my Navy days was the wartime booklet *Ranks & Medal Ribbons of the Fighting Services*, published by the *Daily Mirror*. This assisted me greatly during my training days with the ranks, markings and trades of the Royal Navy, and has proved invaluable also during the writing of this book.

During many visits to numerous second-hand book shops, I came across *A Little Book of Naval Wisdom*, a collection of passages and aphorisms compiled by Harold F. B. Wheeler, F.R.Hist.S., aided by Admiral Sir Rosslyn Wemyss, Admiral Lord Beresford, Rear-Admiral Sir Lionel Halsey, and other eminent officers. The book is undated, and was published by George Harrap & Co. Ltd, Kingsway, London. Reading this little book, which cost me £1, has given me much pleasure, and it is appropriate to include some of these passages throughout my book. The book appears to be Second World War vintage; unfortunately it has not been possible to trace the publishers, but it gives me much pleasure in acknowledging the source.

There are several people in Rothesay I would like to acknowledge, and my special thanks go to Iain L. MacLeod of Bute Newspapers for all the time and trouble he went to on my behalf, in many different ways. I am so appreciative of everything he has done for me, particularly with regard to the concentrated effort put in by himself and his wife Helen in searching for relevant articles, reports, extracts and the like from 1946–1948 copies of *The Rothesay Express* and *The Buteman* newspapers. All these are relevant to my story, and have added considerably to the information I already had of my own. I would also like to thank him for the trouble he went to in providing me with certain photographs, and for various introductions which helped considerably in pursuing my objectives. Freedom to use all or any of these extracts and reports was very kindly granted by Bernard E. Karpinski, Chairman, Bute Newspapers Ltd. and I am extremely grateful to Mr. Karpinski, and indeed to everyone connected with Bute Newspapers, for all the information I have obtained relevant to my time at Rothesay. To Alex Bennett, Bennetts Newsagents in Montague Street, I extend my grateful thanks for his willingness to assist in many ways, for sending me a selection of postcards, back copies of *The Buteman* and other items of special interest, and for several most interesting telephone conversations. For his helpful and friendly approach to all my enquiries, I offer my sincere thanks.

My special thanks are due also to Donald Ferguson, Port Manager of Caledonian MacBrayne at Rothesay Pier, for providing me with a wealth of information. In this respect, also, I would like to extend my thanks to Mike Blair, Marketing Manager of Caledonian MacBrayne at Gourock, for allowing me to reproduce relevant information appearing in *Calmac's Gazette*. Martin Whitelaw of Printpoint in Watergate was kind enough to send me a beautifully produced street and road map of Rothesay, with his kind permission to use them for which I am very grateful.

I have made numerous on-going demands of Kathleen Clegg of the Bute Museum for various historical information, and put her to considerable trouble over several months. I very much appreciate the enthusiasm and interest she has shown, and thank her for the time and trouble she went to on my behalf. I would also like to pass my thanks to the Tourist Information Centre at Rothesay, for answering numerous and varied questions put to them over the space of several telephone calls. I am grateful to them for the spontaneous information given which has been most helpful.

I cannot thank Dr J. McKendrick of Waverley Excursions Limited, Anderston Quay, Glasgow, enough for his generous offering of photographs of the Clyde Steamers. I was thrilled to be able to include these and just looking at these splendid views of them have brought back many happy memories of the time I travelled on them. It is very gratifying to know that *Waverley*, the world's last sea-going paddle steamer, now owned by the Paddle Steamer Preservation Society, is still very much in service and looks just as good today as she did on her maiden voyage in 1947. I was also really pleased when Ian McCrorie was kind enough to loan me the splendid photograph of the paddle steamer *Jupiter* steaming into Rothesay, and passing on her way my ship *Montclare*. My sincere thanks to the Ian McCrorie Collection.

P.S. *Waverley*. Built 1946.

Edward W. Paget-Tomlinson.

A general view of Rothesay from Chapelhill, showing the pier, espanade, sweep of the bay, and part of the town itself, as I remember it in 1946.

I would also like to thank Mr. Duncan M. White of Whiteholme (Publishers) Ltd., of Dundee, for allowing me to reproduce various coloured postcards of Rothesay, and also Dennis Hardley Photography, of Benderloch by Oban in Argyll, for granting permission to reproduce a coloured postcard of Rothesay, and also his picture taken in recent times of the loading ramp at Wemyss Bay Pier. His kindness is much appreciated.

I had never met Commander Ian Hamilton until my wife and I spent a few days at Rothesay in July, 1999. Before this we were complete strangers, the only common link between us being the fact that we both served time in the Royal Navy. In my case as a National Service sailor, rising from Ordinary Seaman to Ordinary Signalman and then to Signalman, a totally different scenario from that of Commander Hamilton, who joined the RNVR in August, 1932, transferring to the Royal Navy in 1937 and retiring in 1955, having risen to the rank of Commander.

Since being introduced to him by Iain MacLeod many months before our meeting, a single telephone call developed into a continual flow of exchanges during which I sought from him answers to questions and queries on numerous Naval matters concerning procedures, correctness and accuracy. When writing to him, I continually had the notion that I should address him as 'Sir', and that somewhere along the way I should slip in an 'Aye, Aye, Sir', but I quickly discovered there was no barrier to his friendship.

Commander Hamilton has enjoyed a distinguished Naval career, volunteering for service with the Royal Navy in 1937 during the period of the Italian invasion of Abyssinia, and was on active service in support of the Army in Palestine. During the Second World War Commander Hamilton was engaged in the Atlantic, Mediterranean and Arctic convoys: the bombardment of Fort Capuzzo, Bardia, Rhodes, Genoa, Messina, Salerno, Anzio and Alderney: the battles of Taranto and Matapan and the D-Day Normandy landings. Always

xxiii

In this 1946 postcard of Rothesay Bay, a steamer comes into view between the Church spires as she approaches Rothesay pier.

interested in Naval and Military history, Commander Hamilton has written at length on this and other subjects, much of which is in the Bute Museum.

Now living at Rothesay, Commander Hamilton has kindly written the foreword to my book, but I have much else to thank him for over the many months I have been writing to him seeking clarification on numerous matters which continually arose. His replies have always been factual, clear and comprehensive, and his contribution throughout has always been significant in content, precise in detail and authoritative by nature.

All the watercolours, drawings and sketches in this book were drawn for me specially by Edward W. Paget-Tomlinson who contributed so much to my two previous publications, *Walkers' of Ricky* in 1991, recording the history of my family company, and in

Plenty of activity here in this view of Rothesay in 1946, but the crowds were not nearly so dense then as they were in 1947.

xxiv

This striking photograph shows *Adamant*, Submarine Depot Ship, with the Second Submarine Squadron at Falmouth in 1962. *Adamant*, built by Harland & Wolff at Belfast, was launched November, 1940, and completed 28 February, 1942. Her displacement was 12,500 tons, length 646 feet overall. After completion, *Adamant* served in the Eastern Fleet until late 1944, and then serviced her flotilla in Australian waters. In June, 1950, she became Flagship Senior Officer, Reserve Fleet, Portsmouth, and in October, 1954, was commissioned as parent ship to the Third Submarine Flotilla based at Rothesay, taking the place of *Montclare*, until 1964, when she bacame parent ship to the Second Submarine Squadron at Devonport. When *Adamant* left Rothesay, the connection between Rothesay and the Royal Navy finally ended. *Adamant* was listed for disposal in March, 1966, and arrived at Inverkeithing in September, 1970, to be broken up. Source unknown.

I am grateful to Kathleen Clegg, Bute Museum, for additional background information, and to (RNSM) for suppling the photograph.

(RNSM)

1993 *The Grand Junction Canal*, on the building of the canal now known as the Grand Union. His authority as an author and his mastery as an artist are well known in this country, and I am much indebted to him for willingly assisting me again with *Aye, Aye, Sir*.

Apologies

WITH all the photographs in this book, every effort has been made to ensure that each one has been appropriately acknowledged and that permissions have been sought from copyright holders. To a great extent we have been successful, but there are several where the copyright holder is unknown and we have been unable to trace the source of ownership. We have taken this matter seriously and continued our investigations over the duration of preparing this book, without success. The photographs in question are especially relevant to my particular time period in the Royal Navy, and I offer my sincere apologies for including them without obtaining the permissions to use them.

There are a number of obvious reasons for this, since the majority of these photographs are from a period of over fifty years ago, and it has been impossible to recall the source, or how I came by them. It is made the more difficult since there is no identity on the backs of these photographs.

In addition to this, there are a number of photographs which have been supplied by various sources who do not own the copyright, and where the copyright holder is unknown. The Ministry of Defence have advised me that photographs taken around 1940 are probably Crown Copyright, given that only official photographs were allowed to be taken on military units during wartime. This being so, the copyright holder of all of the photographs included during the wartime period in this book could be 'RN Photographs', with the kind permission of the Controller of Her Majesty's Stationery Office; I am extremely grateful to the MOD Crown Copyright Administrator for being so flexible on this particular point.

I have been successful in obtaining many photographs taken during my particular time in the Navy, and appropriate dates have been added to the captions. There are a number of photographs, however, of which the dates are unknown; some of them were taken before I joined the Service in 1946 and others after I left in 1948. In order to provide the reader with as complete coverage as possible throughout, I have selected those photographs as near to my Service days as possible, in order that these particular ships and submarines are represented.

I would like to refer to one particular photograph, and that is the view of the Home Fleet at anchor off Gourock, at the time of the Clyde Naval Review in July, 1947. This picture was taken at midnight from Lyle Hill, above Greenock, with the Cross of Lorraine in the foreground. We know the photographer was James Hall, but we have not been able to trace either him or his family to seek permission to reproduce this. It is such a striking picture, and one that means a great deal to me since I was very much involved in this great assembly

Alderney, another of the A-class boats, entered service on 2 November, 1946, and was attached to the 3rd Submarine Flotilla on *Forth* in 1946, and *Montclare* in 1947, at Rothesay, where she became very much a part of the daily scene. This photograph was taken in May, 1947.

of ships. It is my hope that whoever owns this picture will be pleased to see it reproduced again after all these years, and understand my reasons for wanting to include it.

Every endeavour has been made also to ensure that this book is factual and correct in the many details contained within it, regarding specifications, launch and completion dates, fleet strengths and building programmes, and so on, and the numerous other details of a specific nature throughout.

We have leant heavily on various sources for the specific details, and on several occasions information has varied, only perhaps by a very little, but these small variations have caused some concern. We have, therefore, had to use the best judgement we could on these differences, and we can only apologise to everyone who may be knowledgeable on these matters, if some of the details are incorrectly stated.

Fleet Aircraft Carrier - "Illustrious" class

Jane's Fighting Ships, 1946/1947, with the kind permission of Random House UK Limited.

Prologue

The war in Europe ended on 8th May, 1945, and with the cessation of hostilities in the Far East, World War II officially ended on 15th August, 1945. Six months later, on 7th February, 1946, I found myself as a raw recruit in His Majesty's Royal Navy.

Like many of my contemporaries during the war years I was fit, able and keen enough to join in the action, albeit at the same time becoming increasingly aware of the possible legacy of taking part. News reports of actions by our armed forces on land and sea and in the air, resulting in terrible injuries or loss of life, coupled with the prospect of spending months away from home, perhaps in bleak and cold, or dry and sweltering climate, did not dampen my enthusiasm.

I was growing up during these war years from being a schoolboy to becoming a young man approaching 18, and I had grown used to living in wartime conditions, and accustomed to donning one uniform or another whilst undergoing preliminary training with the Army Cadet Force, the Air Training Corps and the Civil Defence. Had the war continued for just a few more months, I could have found myself on active service.

I was obviously much aware of this, so too were my parents, and all parents with sons and daughters of eligible age. 'Let's hope and

A spell of rough weather made heavy going for British warships and aircraft carriers which took part in the manoeuvres of the combined British fleets and the British Fleet Air Arm. The exercises were transferred to the South Atlantic from the Mediterranean Sea, to avoid danger in Spanish waters. Mountains of foam wash the sides of the British aircraft carrier *Glorious* as she ploughs through the turbulent waters of the South Atlantic ocean during the Naval and Air Arm manoeuvres. *Glorious* was built in 1915, under emergency war programme as a shallow-draught cruiser, with a view to Baltic operations. Converted into an aircraft carrier in 1930, at a cost of over £2,000,000, she displaced 22,500 tons on a length of 786 feet, and had a speed of 30.5 knots. She carried 48 aircraft, and was armed with sixteen 4.7 inch. guns, and four 3-pounders. This picture was taken from the aircraft carrier *Couragious* on 13 March, 1937. *Couragious* was sunk by a U-boat in September, 1939, and *Glorious* by gunfire at Narvik in June, 1940.

pray the war will be over before he's called up,' I heard my mother say to my father. Similar hopes and prayers were said by the parents of those already in the front line, that the war would be over before further lives were lost.

The way things were going, it was almost certain that once I reached 18 in December, 1945, I would be called up, although one just did not know. In 1944, Churchill stated that the country had equipment and resources but was short of manpower, and on 22nd December, 1944, the Government announced a call-up of a further 250,000 men. Six months later, with the war in Europe over, group releases from the Army commenced. On 18th June, 1945, releases from service were at the rate of 30,000 a week, increasing to 60,000 a week in August. Demobilisation increased after the cessation of hostilities in the Far East, and by December, 1945, as many as 95,000 men were passing through Civilian Clothing Depots every week.

However, in spite of the war having ended and of the large numbers of service personnel returning to civvy street, conscription was still going on. Everyone was asking 'how many more of us will be wanted, and for how long?'. We received news from time to time of several local young men being called up, and it seemed only a matter of time before I would be receiving my call-up papers. During my preliminary training days, I had had the opportunity of making a choice as to which of the services I would prefer to join, if and when the time came, and although I had gained some experience with the ACF and the ATC, my underlying preference had always been the Royal Navy.

So it was that my Enlistment Notice to join the Royal Navy arrived at last in the final days of January, 1946, giving me just 10 days to prepare myself and report for the start of my basic disciplinary training at H.M.S. *Royal Arthur*, Skegness, on 7th February, 1946.

The battleship *Rodney,* was built by Cammell Laird, laid down 28 December, 1922, and completed August, 1927. Her sister ship *Nelson,* was completed two months earlier. Displacement 33,900 tons (full load about 38,000 tons), length 710 feet overall, beam 106 feet. *Rodney* had a wartime complement of 1,640 officers and men, and a speed of 23 knots. *Rodney* cost £7,617,799 to build. She served throughout the war and was placed in reserve in 1946, pending a refit. This picture was taken in September, 1937.

King George VI visits H.M.S. *Rodney* at Rosyth on 28 September, 1945 - his first visit to his fleet after the end of W.W.II. (left to right) Admiral Sir Henry R. Moore, KCB., CVO., DSO., (Commander-in-Chief, Home Fleet), King George VI, Captain R.O. Fitzroy, Queen Elizabeth (now Queen Mother), Princess Margaret, Commander R. Jonas.

Photograph kindly supplied by Commander I. Hamilton, RN(Retd).

With the basic and technical training over, I really began to enjoy Navy life to the full. I was so fortunate in being drafted to Rothesay on the Island of Bute, in those days the premier Scottish holiday resort. Not only that, life on board *Forth* and then *Montclare*, two submarine depot ships, was an experience not to be missed. The location lent itself to enjoying oneself pretty well on a daily basis, and the environment was exciting and rewarding with submarines berthing alongside as well as numerous other craft frequenting Rothesay Bay.

During my short naval career I was very fortunate in being in the right place at the right time to see so many of our splendid ships, many of which were laid down before and during the war, and formed part of an extensive and continuous building programme. A number of these were completed in time to take their place in the firing line, whilst others arrived at various stages at the end of the war and shortly afterwards. It was thought-provoking to realise that I was looking at these marvellous warships which were in the front line during the war, and here they were in all their glory for me to marvel at their sheer size and splendour.

For example, the fleet aircraft carrier *Illustrious* and her sister ship *Formidable* were completed in 1940, as was the battleship *King George V*, while 1941 saw the completion of the fleet carriers *Indomitable* and *Victorious*, with the battleship *Duke of York*. In 1942 the battleships *Howe* and *Anson* were completed, and in 1944 the fleet carriers *Implacable* and *Indefatigable*. More carriers arrived in 1945, these being the light aircraft carriers *Glory, Ocean, Vengeance* and *Venerable*, followed by *Theseus*, and *Triumph* in 1946, at the same time as Britain's last battleship *Vanguard*, completed in April that year. Further examples of the building programme could include the Swiftsure-class cruiser *Superb*, the Battle-class destroyer *Aisne* and the C-class destroyer *Crispin*, as well as a number of A-class submarines, all completed in 1945. Obviously all these completions are only an example of many which emerged from a huge on-going construction programme which covered many classes of all types of ships and submarines. The building of these huge ships was a feat of engineering and construction involving several years' work and considerable manpower. This is best described in the following extract from *Royal Navy at War* (1941) by Vice-Admiral J. E. Harper, CB, MVO, published by John Murray (Publishers) Ltd.

SHIPBUILDING

A modern warship is a marvel of complicated machinery, guns, armour, and a thousand devices.

The class of ship required having been decided, the design is worked out in detail by the Royal Corps of Naval Constructors. Consideration must be given to seaworthiness, speed, armament, armour, fuel capacity, and other details. The constructor's job is to go as far as possible in meeting the requirements of each of the technical departments concerned, without exceeding the total tonnage allowed him.

Warships are usually designed and built in "classes," the same design, with modifications, sufficing for four, six or eight ships. The design completed, tenders are invited from shipbuilding firms, engine makers, gun and armour manufacturers, electrical firms and others. The cost of a ship varies according to design, as well as owing to size. The only comparison which can be made is the cost per ton. In 1900 a battleship cost about £60 per ton; in 1916, £80 to £90; to-day it is probably over £200 per ton. Nearly eighty per cent. of this cost goes in wages, and in whatever yard the ship is built there is not a county in England which does not benefit by making, or supplying, material used before the ship is completed.

The time taken to build, say, a battleship from the time the keel-plate is laid to the date of launch, may vary from one to two years, and then there is another year's work to complete the ship for sea.

The people of these islands have to thank not only the Navy for protecting their food supplies, but also every labourer and mechanic in the naval or mercantile shipbuilding yards. If any of the work is scamped, if rivets are carelessly driven in, if any detail is neglected, it may cause a disaster at sea. The sailor puts his trust in the shipbuilder, and that trust is not misplaced. A ship is launched when about half the total weight has been built into her.

The ceremony at the launch of a warship includes a religious service and the christening, or "hallowing," as it was called a century ago.

"May God protect this ship and all who sail in her," is said as the ship starts to move. As she takes the water the ship becomes, to the sailor and to the builders, a living thing; and we may leave it to her godfathers, St. George, St. Andrew and St. Patrick, whose crosses form the Union Jack, to help her to uphold the honour of that flag which she will bear.

The battle-cruiser *Hood*, completed in 1920, cost £6,000,000, equivalent to £145 per ton. The battleships *Nelson* and *Rodney* in 1927

The "battle"-cruiser *Hood* was the largest war vessel in the world, and was built by John Brown, Clydebank. Laid down in September, 1916, she was launched in August, 1918, and completed March, 1920. Standard displacement 42,100 tons (46,200 tons full load), length overall 860 feet 7 inches. Beam 105 feet 2.5 inches, and speed 31 knots. Her main armament included 8-15 inch. guns. Forming the secondary battery were 12-5.5 inch. guns, each being nearly 23 feet in length and weighing over 6 tons, fire shells weighing 85lb.each. She also had extensive protected areas with strong framing and heavy armour. *Hood* was due for a major refit and modernisation in 1939, but this never came about. She was shelled below her armour belt when in action against the German battlehip *Bismarck*, which caused a massive explosion, and she sank on 23 May, 1941, taking all but three of her crew of 1419 down with her.

cost £6,400,000 and £6,200,000 respectively. The last battleship, *Vanguard*, completed in April, 1946, cost £9,000,000, excluding the cost of her heavy guns.

During my time in the Navy I saw many of these fine warships, a number of them almost new. Bearing in mind the time required to complete them, I realised they must have been laid down when I was at school, and to a large extent were programmed as replacements for those prestigious ships that were lost during the war. Among the many were the carrier *Courageous*, sunk by a U-boat as early as September, 1939, off Ireland with 514 dead out of a crew of 1,200, and the battleship *Royal Oak*, sunk by a U-boat at Scapa Flow in October the same year. The carrier *Glorious* was sunk by gunfire at

The *Ark Royal*, so often sunk by the Nazi propoganda machine, supplying a British destroyer with bread. The destroyer needed these meagre rations, as it was carrying over 150 Lascars, picked up after their ship had been sunk by a German U-boat. Shortly after this picture was taken, *Ark Royal* was torpedoed and sunk in November, 1941, only 40 km E. of Gibraltar.

xxxii

Associated Press

This great new battleship, *Prince of Wales*, commissioned March, 1941, steams into action against the big German battleship *Bismarck*. Flinging spray from her bows in great waves and with her guns raised for action, she speeds after the German warship in a chase which ended in the great British naval victory. Others taking part in the sinking of the *Bismarck*, were the battleships *King George V* and *Rodney*, together with air strikes mounted from the carriers *Victorious* and *Ark Royal*. Involved in the action also were destroyers and cruisers including the cruiser *Dorsetshire*, which finally torpedoed and sunk the *Bismarck* on 27 May, 1941, with the loss of 2,200 lives.

Narvik in June 1940, whilst carrying a load of land-based fighter planes on deck, and the carrier *Eagle* was torpedoed while escorting a Malta convoy in August. The battle-cruiser *Hood* was sunk in May, 1941, with only three survivors out of a crew of 1,419 whilst in action against the German battleship *Bismarck* in the Denmark Strait, East of Greenland. The battleship *Prince of Wales* and the battle-cruiser *Repulse* were lost in December, 1941, off Singapore, when they were attacked by 88 Japanese bombers and torpedo planes, resulting in the death of 730 men. In May, 1941, the cruiser *Gloucester* was sunk in the Aegean with 693 lives lost, and the cruiser *Fiji* was crippled and abandoned. The carrier *Ark Royal* was torpedoed in November, 1941, and the carrier *Hermes* dive-bombed by Japanese aircraft off the coast of Ceylon in April, 1942.

During September, 1939, German submarines sank 25 British merchant ships in the Atlantic, and 1942 was a particularly bad year, when in the last six months alone, almost 600 merchant ships were sunk. March, 1943, was the worst month of the war for the allies in the Atlantic, with 97 ships sunk in the first 20 days of the month.

When I joined the Navy in 1946 it was rather like arriving after the party was over. I had missed all the action, the excitement and adventure of taking part in such tumultuous world events. Like most of us who were not in the front line, I had no conception of what it must have been like in those terrifying sea-battle conditions, being frightened to death and white with fear of it all when trying to escape perhaps from explosion and fire, and abandoning ship or submarine.

Joining my first ship, H.M.S. *Forth*, within months of the ending of the war, there was still a feeling of resentment amongst a small number of the longer-serving members of the crew against new entrants to the Service, joining their ship and taking over the roles previously held by their colleagues. This was never a serious problem, and their feelings only surfaced occasionally, but nevertheless, one was aware of a feeling sometimes of exclusion and intimidation against us, the new boys who had arrived after all the work had been done. We appreciated their feelings on this, as they did ours, that although the majority of us had hoped we would join the action before the war ended, we were just not old enough, and no-one could blame us for that.

Our predecessors were old enough to join a wartime Navy; I and my colleagues joined a peacetime one.

> The sea is our life
> By the use of it, the Empire was formed
> By holding it, the Empire was preserved
> If we fail to appreciate its value, the Empire will perish
>
> Admiral Lord Jellicoe

The battlehip *Prince of Wales* served in Home waters and the Atlantic before being sent to the Far East. This photograph shows the last moments of her as sailors clamber down ropes against the badly listing battleship, to be taken off by a destroyer. On 10 December, 1941, both the *Prince of Wales* and the *Repulse* were sunk north east of Singapore by 88 Japanese bombers and torpedo planes, with the loss of 730 lives.

Illustrious, photographed here in March, 1947, was a frequent visitor to Rothesay Bay, and was one of three built in the "Illustrious" class of Fleet Aircraft Carriers, the others being *Victorious* and *Formidable*. *Illustrious* began building at Vickers-Armstrong, Barrow, in April, 1937, and was completed 21 May, 1940. Displacement 23,000 tons, length overall 753 feet, and beam 95 feet. Joining the Mediterranean Fleet in 1940, *Illustrious* played a leading role throughout the war covering convoys and supporting air strikes.

Wright & Logan

Enlistment 1

IT WAS the beginning of August, 1946, and after all the training I had undergone I found myself standing on the pier at Wemyss Bay awaiting the ferry for the half-hour crossing to the Island of Bute. The ship I was to join was lying at anchor in Rothesay Bay.

It was one of those most perfect of days, with a clear blue sky and a cool gentle breeze blowing off the waters of the Clyde. It was indeed invigorating being amongst what to me was a completely new and exciting environment, and it was not long before I was leaning against the rail of the ferry *Duchess of Montrose*, straining for the first sight of my ship as we sped towards our destination.

'Are you joining *Forth*?' an elderly man said to me. 'Yes,' I replied, 'my first ship.'

'You'll be all right,' he said, 'you'll enjoy yourself at Rothesay, plenty of girls as well.' We both chuckled.

As we drew nearer to Bute, I saw the ship I was joining, H.M.S. *Forth*, with two submarines berthed alongside. She seemed to me to be a ship of enormous proportions.

Wemyss Bay and the Firth of Clyde, sometime in the early 1960's, but this is how I remember it in 1946 - my "Gateway to Paradise". From the train, we walked through this building and out onto the pier to board the ferry for the half-hour crossing to Rothesay. Just waiting on the pier I always experienced a strong sense of freedom here, which became the starting point for me of many jubilant arrivals and sad departures. My thanks to Donald Ferguson, Caledonian MacBrayne, for this postcard.

After completing my training, and as an Ordinary Signalman, I was drafted to my first ship, H.M.S. Forth depot ship of the 3rd Submarine Flotilla, in Rothesay Bay, Isle of Bute, on 2 August, 1946. She looked enormous when I saw her for the first time.

'There she is,' my new friend said to me, 'that's H.M.S. *Forth*— marvellous sight, isn't she?' 'She looks enormous,' I said in awe. 'I'll be completely lost on her.'

'Oh, you'll get used to her in no time,' he told me reassuringly. 'The townsfolk like her being here, good for trade, and brings the visitors in.'

My naval career had begun six months earlier when I had arrived with a group of about 20 other new entrants at H.M.S. *Royal Arthur*, a Shore Establishment at Skegness that had been commissioned on 22nd September, 1939, as the Initial Training Base for new entrants to the Royal Navy. Before the outbreak of the Second World War it had been a Butlin's holiday camp.

That, of course, was not the beginning of my military training. As a schoolboy at Watford Grammar School for Boys during the war years I shared with my generation an enthusiasm to join in the action. On reaching the age of fourteen in 1941 I became eligible to join the Army Cadet Force (ACF), the school unit of which was commanded by one of our teachers, J. C. Stevenson, with the rank of Lieutenant, and I enlisted on 1st May, 1942, Cadet No. 43389 with the 24th Herts cadets.

Apart from regular sessions of physical training and drill in the gymnasium and on the playground, our technical training was varied and interesting, and some of this was under instruction from the Home Guard. Other lectures and training included the operations of our modern army. There was also instruction and practical exercises on signalling and map reading, tanks, guns and gunners, shells, fuses, machine-guns, rifles, bayonets and bombs, armoured cars, anti-aircraft guns and steel helmets. Regular sessions and practical training was on the understanding and use of the Short Magazine Lee-Enfield Rifle, which was approved in 1903 and was known as the

Mark I. Improved patterns of the Mark I had been made over the years, and the Mark III on which we received our training was then in general use. We were also expected to gain qualifications in various aspects of our training for which we were issued with notes for Certificate A Examinations for the use of O.T.C.s and Cadet Corps only.

My brother David had by that time graduated from the Grammar School and had become a member of No. 1280 (Rickmansworth) Squadron, Air Training Corps (ATC). I followed him on 29th July, 1943, the membership card which I received bearing on its reverse the words:

> It is with a view to preparing myself for wartime service with either the Royal Air Force or the Fleet Air Arm or the Royal Navy (cross out which does not apply) that I am joining the Air Training Corps. I hereby promise on my honour to serve this Unit loyally, and to be faithful to my obligations as a member of the Air Training Corps. I further promise to be a good Citizen, honouring my King, my Country and its Flag.

The enrolment officer was W. J. Maurice Last, Pilot Officer, R.A.F.V.R. who was also known to us as a friend of our family. I cannot speak too highly of Maurice Last, who was second-in-command of the Squadron. He was highly efficient and consistently on top of his job. He never failed to encourage members of the Squadron in any way he could, and it was largely due to his efforts and ability that 1280 (Rickmansworth) Squadron was interesting, rewarding and successful for everyone involved with it.

The Air Training Corps was started to prepare young men before calling-up age. The Royal Air Force had work to do in every part of the world, as the Navy had always had, and in consequence it was hard to find enough men of the right standard for crews of the R.A.F. and the Fleet Air Arm, and as Glider Pilots of the Army. The medical standards were high and the educational tests not easy for those who desired to fly with the Fighting Services.

My brother David in the uniform of 1280 (Rickmansworth) Squadron, Air Training Corps, and myself wearing the uniform of The Army Cadet Force, in the 24th Herts Cadets, No 43389, which was a Cadet Unit enrolled under the British National Cadet Association. This photograph was taken in May, 1942.

Early days in the formation of 1280 (Rickmansworth) Squadron, Air Training Corps, in 1943. Pilot Officer W.J.Maurice Last, R.A.F.V.R, leading, with my brother David as one of the squad during a Sunday morning parade.

When a man reached calling up age, it was usually too late to start bringing him up to this standard if he was below it. Before 18 was the time to learn and develop one's physique. The ATC gave young men training in air subjects before being called up, and had the effect of increasing the number of men who were fit to become members of air crew.

The age limit was $15\frac{1}{4}$ to $17\frac{3}{4}$ for recruits. You were not a full member and not entitled to a uniform until you had completed three months on probation, and reached the age of $15\frac{1}{2}$. You were expected to attend at least four hours a week, and could do more if you wanted to. Parades were mostly in the evenings and at weekends.

Local talent to the fore in this Variety Show, staged by the Rickmansworth Civil Defence in 1944/45. At the end of the war in Europe, a small number of us re-grouped and called ourselves The Rickmansworth Players, since when the Society has produced plays and musical shows continuously ever since.

Training consisted of Drill, Physical Training, Mathematics, Morse Code and lectures of general interest. Specialised training was divided into two main categories, (I) Air Crew—comprising Mathematics, Navigation and Morse Code, Aircraft Identification and Administration; (II) Technical—comprising courses for Wireless Operators and Wireless Mechanics, Flight Mechanics, Instrument Repairers, Electricians, M.T. Mechanics, and other trades.

Boys for air crew training were preferably to be of a sturdy but intelligent type, and likely to be up to the high standard of physical fitness laid down. They had to be of a sufficient standard of education to be able to absorb the special training, particularly in mathematics, required of air crews in the service. Certificates of Proficiency were introduced, and Cadets were required to pass oral and written examinations.

During this time I also volunteered to join the Rickmansworth division of the Civil Defence (CD), where my responsibilities with others were involved as a fire-watcher, aeroplane spotter and messenger attached to the Air Raid Precautions (ARP) Headquarters in Rickmansworth. My official enrolment care read as follows:

Rickmansworth Urban District Council

This is to certify that Mr. A. J. Walker is a duly accredited member of 'Messenger' Service and must not be detained under any circumstances.

signed A. Peebles, ARP Officer, 12 September, 1944.

I remained a member of the Air Training Corps and the Civil Defence until I was called up for National Service. At this time, my brother David was a Sergeant and myself a Corporal, and both of us were buglers in the Squadron band.

It was a requirement during those war years for all boys and girls of sixteen to be Registered, and for this I attended the Ministry of Labour and National Service on 29th January, 1944.

Recruits waiting for call-up into the armed forces at this time usually had a choice of preference for either the Army, Navy, Fleet Air Arm, Royal Marines or Air Force. I felt that as a schoolboy, I already had some previous experience of Army manoeuvres, and although I was enjoying my time with the Air Training Corps, I was not sure I was keen enough to spend my National Service years with either. Having savoured both, I considered I would be more suited to the Royal Navy in the event of being called up. With this in mind, I investigated the Navy 'Y' Scheme.

The objective of the 'Y' Scheme was threefold, a) to pick out in advance the young men who were considered likely to do well in the Navy, b) to enable them to get into the service of their choice, and c) to make sure that until they were old enough to be called up, they received the best available type of pre-entry training for the job which they were going to do in the Navy

Candidates for the Seaman's Branch had to be between 16½ and 17 years 8 months. Physical Standard had to be Grade 1, good vision, and not colour blind. They had to have had a good education, and either a School Certificate or recommendation from the Commanding Officer of a recognised pre-entry training corps to the effect that the new entrant was of good education, and possessed good personality and powers of leadership. I felt sure I had some of the necessary qualifications for being accepted into the Royal Navy, particularly since I had received training with the Army Cadet Force as a schoolboy, and was still under training with the Air Training Corps.

At Edgware I completed a preliminary interview and examination, and indicated the Royal Navy as my first choice. At the same time, I was required under National Service Acts to attend Holloway Medical Board No. 2 for a medical examination on 7th November, 1945, and passed as Grade 1. The reverse of the Grade Card was stamped 'selected for RN (RM) subject to vacancies'.

My eighteenth birthday duly arrived, and it seemed a foregone conclusion that it would only be a matter of a few weeks before I received my calling-up papers. Without a doubt, all the preliminary training I had received during my time with the Army

National Service Acts Enlistment Notice dated 28 January, 1946, giving me just ten days to prepare myself, and report to the Royal Navy Training Establishment at H.M.S. Royal Arthur, Skegness, to commence my basic training.

Cadets, Air Training Corps and the Civil Defence was going to be of enormous benefit, in having acquired at least some basic training in marching, standing to attention, saluting, to name but a few, as well as conforming to routine and regulations, and in addition, wearing a uniform and being well turned out. The discipline instilled in all of us would also prove beneficial in having given us a sense of time-keeping, obeying instructions, carrying out duties efficiently and to a high standard, and learning to get on with fellow recruits. I felt I had received sufficient training with the organisations I had joined, which would put me in good stead and provide me with the ability to cope with the real thing when it came.

And so it was, the day finally arrived when my call-up papers landed on the doormat. The Enlistment Notice under National Service Acts dated 28th January, 1946, informed me I was called upon for Service in the Royal Navy and I had to present myself on Thursday, 7th February, 1946, to H.M.S. *Royal Arthur*, Royal Navy, Skegness, Lincs., between 9 am and 12 noon, or as soon as possible thereafter. The notes on the reverse of the Notice were explicit and clear: I had to take with me the following items— Enlistment Notice together with Envelope N.S.124 completed as directed. Also, razor, gas mask, Certificate of Registration, Medical Grade Card, National Registration Identity Card, and ALL ration books, including Clothing Book and ALL unused coupons.

There were other instructions as well. Where applicable one had to take Marriage Certificate and Birth Certificate of any children to claim allowances for them. A uniform would be issued after joining HM Forces. Any kit taken with you should not exceed 15 lbs in total weight and should be limited to overcoat, change of underclothes, and personal kit such as hair-brush, tooth-brush, soap and towel.

Heavily underlined was a warning:

> You must understand that you will be deemed to have enlisted from the date on which you are required to present yourself to your Unit and unless you have obtained sick leave or leave of absence as explained above, failure to join your Unit on the appointed date will make you an absentee and you will then be liable to be arrested and brought before a Court of Jurisdiction.

There was much to do in the few days before I had to leave. I was involved in numerous and varied social activities, all of which had to end. I made my apologies to the Youth Training Service (YTS), and requested leave of absence from the Air Training Corps and Civil Defence. I had to abandon piano lessons, a part in a play with the Rickmansworth School of Drama and Art, and amateur dramatics with The Rickmansworth Players, and of course, last but not least, the temporary job I had with Barclays Bank which I had taken whilst waiting for call-up.

This group photograph, taken sometime in 1946 after I had left the Squadron to join the Royal Navy, shows the strength of 1280 (Rickmansworth) Squadron at this time.

The full reality of it all began to have some meaning; everything in which I was involved socially had to come to an abrupt end, and I was leaving home for the very first time on my own. I had everything to look back on, and nothing to look forward to, except uncertainty and the unknown. The following few days flew past with saying goodbye to family and friends and tidying up my personal affairs.

I rose early the next morning with an urge to get going, and systematically packed everything that I had carefully laid out ready the previous evening. My mother ensured I had a good breakfast before leaving, and then it was time to say our emotional goodbyes. My father drove me to the local railway station, and in no time at all I was boarding the train to London. I was on my way.

'Small measures produce only small results.'

Nelson, 10th July, 1804.

Battleship - *Renown*.

Jane's Fighting Ships, 1946/1947, with the kind permission of Random House UK Limited.

Training days   2

H.M.S. *Royal Arthur*, **Skegness, Lincolnshire**
7 February–18 February 1946

I WAS in good time to catch the train from Euston. On arrival at Skegness station I met up with a group of around 20 other new entrants, similarly placed as myself, and together we caught a bus to take us to *Royal Arthur*.

H.M.S. *Royal Arthur* was a Shore Establishment, commissioned 22nd September, 1939, as the Royal Navy's Initial Training Base for new entrants to the Royal Navy where more than 4,500 men were under training at any given time. During my training days, I underwent training in one form or another at three, *Royal Arthur, Glendower* and *Scotia*. All were run on exactly the same lines as a ship; for example, the main driveway was the Quarter Deck, with the White Ensign flying from the mast.

Basic Disciplinary Training covered many subjects, including marching and parades, handling weapons, drill, knots, splices, hitches and bends, physical training, gymnasium and games, disciplinary procedures, Naval organisation, kit maintenance, health and hygiene, and so on. Not all recruits underwent all this training at *Royal Arthur*, this depended upon the technical course selected.

Writing in the *Sea Cadet* in July, 1945, a young entrant to *Royal Arthur* expressed his views on the Establishment:

> First impression of life in the Royal Navy—I haven't any regrets on joining up, the food here is good, the Navy does not allow you a lot of time to masticate your food, but all in all I've never been hungry yet, and I like my stomach.
>
> The things I have enjoyed most so far have been the Divisions. Each time the flag, or rather Ensign, is hoisted it gives me a feeling of pride to think that I am English and belong to His Majesty's Navy.
>
> We have a reason for being extra smart because in addition to Englishmen, there are Belgian, Dutch, Danish and Norwegian trainees here, and they try hard to show us up, we don't mind them trying.
>
> You can assure Cadets that they are not pushed into any job when they get here. The Officers who give you your final job before you start your course, ask you what you want to do, and if you pick a job which they think you have a possible chance of making a success of, they let you have it. They use the psycho list results as a guide to your adaptability.

On arrival at *Royal Arthur*, one couldn't help noticing the large prominent letters spread across the front of two large buildings, which read "BUTLIN'S SKEGNESS HOLIDAY CAMP OUR TRUE INTENT IS ALL FOR YOUR DELIGHT." Well, this was a good start, we thought, we might be in with a chance here.

H.M.S. Royal Arthur, previously the Butlin's holiday camp at Skegness, became the Royal Navy's Initial Training Base for new entrants, in September, 1939. Although the words of welcome across the buildings was most encouraging, we found little of a holiday atmosphere inside.

Sentries on guard examined our passes and directed us through to a Reception Room for new arrivals. We were welcomed to *Royal Arthur*, offered a mug of tea, and given some verbal instructions as to what we could expect from now on. We were told that we had joined HMS *Royal Arthur* to find a suitable job in the Navy, that we would be kitted out, and would remain in the 'ship' for two weeks, with the exception of a few specialised categories who would carry out their disciplinary training here. Those who remained for two weeks only would proceed to another Establishment for disciplinary training, prior to the commencement of the technical course for the particular branch in which they were entered.

It was late in the day when I arrived at *Royal Arthur* and there was only time left to be allocated a bunk in one of the huts, issued with a *Royal Arthur* handbook and *Seaman's Guide*, told where and when to attend mess and given instructions when and where to report the next morning for further enrolment procedures. I employed any free time left to me that day before lights out in making a start on familiarising myself with the layout of the camp—I mean 'ship'—and where everything was.

I was glad to climb into my bunk that night. It had been quite a full day, and as I lay there rolling everything over in my mind, I began reading the rules, regulations and instructions in the handbook. But after ten minutes or so tiredness overcame me, and I fell asleep.

The *Royal Arthur* handbook told us that in joining His Majesty's Navy we had joined a service which our own country and the whole world admired and respected. We would be wearing a uniform to be extremely proud of, and wherever we were we should remember that we represented THE ROYAL NAVY, which had a reputation for efficiency, smartness, loyalty and justice. Never, by any of our actions, whether on duty or off, should we 'let down' that sacred trust which our country put in us.

The first ship with the name *Royal Arthur* was laid down in 1889 and named after H.R.H. The Duke of Connaught. She was a protected cruiser of 7,700 tons, and carried an armament of one 9.2in. and twelve 6in. guns.

The White Ensign was hoisted every morning at Divisions, and hauled down at sunset. Should we not be 'fallen in' during both these ceremonies, we were to stand to attention, face the Ensign and salute. If 'fallen in' only the officer or rating in charge saluted. The Quarter Deck, a strip of road in front of the mast, was marked at each end by a white line. We had to salute as we came on to it, and cross it at the double..

In 1946, H.M.S. *Royal Arthur* was commanded by Captain I. M. Palmer, D.S.C., R.N., and immediately under him was the Commander, second-in-command of the Establishment, who was responsible for the organisation, discipline, maintenance, welfare and training.

While in the ship we were encouraged to observe our religious privileges, and there were Chaplains for members of the Church of England, of the Free Churches and for Roman Catholics. There was no censorship in force at *Royal Arthur*, but all letters in the post were liable to be censored, and we were told to take great care not to mention anything in our letters which might have been of military importance.

The general organisation at *Royal Arthur* was, that all new entrants were placed in a class, in charge of which was an Instructor. His job was to help us in every way he could, and he was the man to go to whenever we were in doubt or difficulty. Above him was our Divisional Officer, who was responsible for our welfare, and he directed our activities while we were under training.

Classes were in one of three Divisions named after the parts of a ship: Forecastle (F.X.); Top; and Quarter Deck (Q.D.). Each Division was in the charge of a Lieutenant-Commander, assisted by junior officers. The Division was divided by Classes into two halves known as Port and Starboard Watches, and each Watch was again divided into two parts, 1st and 2nd. I was placed in Port 2nd.

Each Division had its own Mess Deck (dining hall): F.X. *York*; Top *Gloucester*; Q.D. *Kent*; and also its own lines of chalets where we slept. We were responsible also for the cleanliness of an area of the Establishment.

As regards saluting, we had to salute all officers of all three services, in the first case when passing them, and when addressed by one. If you happened to be sitting down, you had to stand up before saluting, and it you had a cigarette in your mouth, you took it out. If you were not wearing a cap, then you did not salute, but stood to attention, or, if you were passing by, you turned your head and eyes smartly in the direction of the officer. If you were inside a building, you did not salute, but stood to attention, making way for the officer.

You stood to attention whenever the National Anthem was played, whether on board or ashore, and, if you were wearing a cap, you saluted.

Officers and Instructors were always called 'Sir'. The right way to show you understood an order was to say 'Aye, Aye, Sir'. On no account were you to say 'Very good, Sir', 'Righto', or 'O.K.'.

Discipline was always very strict. Discipline simply meant immediate and willing obedience to all orders and regulations, and 'good discipline' was something to be extremely proud of. All 'pipes' were to be carried out at the double. Orders and instructions usually 'piped' on board ship were 'broadcast' in *Royal Arthur*.

Whenever we were given an order, it was expected that we carry it out smartly and without comment. It was out of order to answer back. If we thought an order was unjust, we had to carry it out just the same, but when we had done so we could request to see the Commander. There was a laid-down procedure for this, and complaints first had to be submitted to your Instructor. We were reminded that there was no excuse for disobeying or refusing to carry out an order, and to do so had very serious consequences.

If you wanted to put forward a request, you had to make out a request form, with your Instructor, and your Divisional Officer helped here, but if you wanted advice or help about a private matter you could request to see your Divisional Officer privately. You couldn't see him privately about a Service matter, and it was never permitted to approach him direct, but always through your Instructor.

There were numerous other matters which new recruits were expected to take on board. For example, smoking was not permitted in 'working hours' or at any time in the chalets. Detailed orders were placed on the Divisional Notice Boards about this. We were allowed to buy Service tobacco duty free through the Paymaster's Stores, but you could not buy more than was necessary for your own personal use.

In 1946, and until the 1947 Budget, cigarettes and tobacco were sold in the NAAFI canteen, where a packet of 20 cigarettes ('coffin nails') could be bought for around one shilling. It was emphasised upon us that these reductions in price were a great privilege, and if it was abused it was likely it would be withdrawn. There were, obviously, certain restrictions to do with smoking, for instance, you could not sell or give away duty free tobacco to anyone. Nor could you send any tobacco or cigarettes through the post. You could only take ashore for each night's leave 1 oz of tobacco or 20 cigarettes. If you went on seven days' leave or more, you could not take more than ½lb of tobacco or 160 cigarettes. If you were in *Royal Arthur* for 14 days only, Service tobacco was not issued. If we broke any of these rules, we could be found guilty of smuggling, a very serious offence, leading to heavy penalties.

No alcoholic drinks of any kind were allowed to be brought into the Establishment. The sale of beer inside the Establishment was permitted, but this had to be consumed in the canteen premises, and bottles of beer were never permitted to be taken out of the canteens.

No betting or gambling was permitted, neither were games of cards or chance to be played for money. Fighting was prohibited. Any differences were always to be settled in the Service manner with your Instructor present.

Also prohibited was the lending, exchanging, or selling of any article, either personal or belonging to your kit, without your Divisional Officer's permission. You were never allowed to lend or borrow money. If you found any kit, money or personal property that was not yours, this had to be taken immediately to your Instructor. It was stressed upon us that if we were found with someone else's things in our possession we were liable to serious punishment. If we lost anything, we had to report it immediately to our Instructor.

Leave was usually given by Watches, Starboard Watch ashore and Port Watch aboard one day and changing round the next. Leave was usually given Monday, Tuesday, Thursday and Friday, 1645–2200; Saturdays and Sundays, 1315–2200. There was no leave for men under training on Wednesdays. You were only permitted on shore leave by 'Liberty Boats', the times of which were piped daily. One had to fall in outside our own Mess Deck at the time appointed, paying strict attention to all the instructions read out to us. Our Station Card had to be handed in when we proceeded on Short Leave and it was our duty to report at the Regulating Office to collect it immediately we returned on board.

All ratings were issued with a 'Station Card' at a shore Establishment or ship, given to you as a means of personal identification. Apart from your name, it stated your Rate, Ship's Book Number, Port or Starboard Watch, and Part of Watch, either First or Second. In addition, it confirmed whether you were entitled to 'G' (grog), or were 'T' (temperance) or 'U.A.' (under age). Your Station Card always had to be carried with you, and, as regulations stated, it 'should never leave your person', except in certain circumstances, when we would be told. It was suggested that the best place to carry this was in the crown of your cap. On no account was this to be lent to any other man, neither should you try and persuade another man to lend you his. If you mislaid your Station Card, this had to be reported immediately to your Instructor or to the Training Officer.

It was also a very serious offence not to return 'absolutely punctually' from your leave, and you were liable to be severely punished with stoppages of leave and pay if you failed to do so. If you were late in returning from leave through no fault of your own, for instance, because of a railway delay, you were required to bring back proof

"T'was Skegness where we did our training,
That first I quickly fell,
For this young lady prictured here,
Her name was Isobel".
(February, 1946).

from a responsible person such as the stationmaster. If you were to desert, or remain absent over leave for a long time, your pay would cease, together with any marriage, children's and dependant's allowances.

Ratings were allowed four free railway warrants a year. These warrants were in the form of a combined leave and travel warrant, and did not have to be exchanged for a ticket. Here again, these free warrants were only to be used by the rating to whom they were issued. It was an offence to sell or exchange it, or to retain the outward half on arrival at your destination.

If for any reason you wished to be absent from a muster or from some duty, you had to obtain permission from your Instructor. If you were away without leave, you were considered absent from your place of duty, a serious offence.

If you were ill you had to report to the Sick Bay, telling your Instructor first, if possible. We were reminded that you were not sick unless certified so by the Medical Department, and sickness could never be accepted as a reason for failure to carry out any duty, unless you had been excused by the Medical Department.

There were many other rules and regulations to get used to covering Pay and Identity Books, anti-gas respirators, minimising and preventing all forms of waste, participation in games, and drawing our attention to making it a habit to read the Notice Boards every day.

There was one special mention, and that was regarding promotion. We were told that the chances of promotion were the same as those of Long Service men. A large number of officers were required from 'Hostilities Only' ratings and these were selected from outstanding men. We were reminded that we were always under observation and would get on if we were worth it.

The *Royal Arthur* handbook was clear and precise, and left one in no doubt as to what was expected.

I awoke the next morning, day two of being a Naval rating, before the morning call at 0630, and together with my new colleagues who had been allocated bunks in my chalet, washed, dressed, found our way to the mess hall for breakfast, and then prepared to meet our Instructor, who told us that we would now be completing our joining procedures. We would be going for an assessment to ascertain the job we would be best suited for, and where we would be going for technical training. We would also be medically examined, have a regulation haircut, be issued with a uniform and be kitted out.

I was interviewed by a Personal Selection Officer, with whom I was required to carry out some selection tests to be considered for a job that he considered best suited to me. This would depend upon several matters, my medical grade and vision standard, the selection test results, my education and civilian occupation. Pinned to the walls in the assessment room were information sheets on all the jobs that were available, including Sick Bay Attendant, Officers' Steward, Stoker, Signalman, Artificer, Cook, Bugler, Supply Rating, Diver, Shipwright, Gunner and the like; all these had accompanying notes, prospects, length of training, place of training, and likely drafting stations. Although I read through all of them carefully, I couldn't get excited about most, and finally settled on the course of Signals. For this, the technical training included learning to operate teleprinters, on shore and aboard ship, and had the possibility also, when trained, of serving overseas. I was encouraged to read that as a Signalman I would be attached to the Communications Office, whether on shore or ship, and that at the end of the training course I would be proficient in touch typing.

The Selection Officer discussed the possibilities with me in the light of the assessment results, my background and previous office experience prior to enlistment, and considered that I would be a suitable candidate for the Communications Branch. He duly entered my name in this category on my Training Record Sheet.

With the medical examination over, and the hair cut, we passed through the Clothing Store ('Slops') where we were issued with Pusser's uniform and gear (the name given to anything supplied by the Navy), to our nearest size. At the end of it all, I had the following wardrobe:

> 1 Brown attache case, 1 soap bag, 1 waist belt, 2 pairs of boots, 1 oilskin, 1 overcoat, 1 bed, 1 blanket, 2 caps, 2 cap ribbons. 2 Blue jean collars, 1 black silk scarf, 2 pairs drawers, 2 flannels, 2 singlets, 2 towels, 2 pairs socks, 1 boot brush (hard), 1 boot brush (polishing), 1 hair brush, 1 knife, 1 knife lanyard, 1 overall suit, 1 jersey, 2 serge jumpers, 2 pairs serge trousers. Also supplied on personal loan: 1 kit bag, 2 coloured blankets, 1 pillow, 1 pillow cover, to be returned on leaving the Establishment.

In addition, the following recreational clothing was issued to all men on arrival on temporary loan, to be returned before leaving the Establishment:

> 2 pairs of drill shorts, 1 pair stockings, 2 sports jerseys and 1 pair of gym shoes.

It was made clear to us that our uniform and kit was issued free on enlistment, and that it was our responsibility to maintain every item of clothing to a high standard. Any replacements would have to be purchased from Pusser's Stores at our own expense.

Having been kitted out, we were then required to set about marking every item of clothing and equipment with our Service number and name. This had to be done clearly and precisely to laid down regulations by using stencil letters and a black marker.

A rating's uniform took a bit of getting used to. There seemed to be so many ancillary trappings in the way of blue jean collars with tapes, ribbons, silks and braid, yet in spite of all this apparent fussiness, the practicality of providing pocket space seemed to be of less significance. There never seemed to be anywhere to put anything.

Far be it for me to criticise the uniform of the Royal Navy, since I was extremely proud to wear it, and to be in the Service, but in comparison with Army and Air Force uniforms, which had an abundance of pocket space provided, the sailor suit was severely restricted. Inside the serge jumper was one pocket into which one could stuff very small personal possessions, which inevitably formed a bulge, and on bending forward, had a happy knack of falling out. There was also one vertical pocket behind the flap at the front of the trousers which was also a very confined space into which one could place only the smallest items.

Initially our Instructor demonstrated how the uniform should be worn, but it took a few days to get used to everything fitting properly. After donning the jersey, one had to start by draping the blue jean collar across the shoulders and tying the ends of the tapes together above the waist, to secure the collar in position. Next the serge jumper with the full open V front was pulled over the head and tugged down to finish around the thighs. The blue jean collar then had to be pulled out so it fell evenly over the shoulders across the back, showing the three white lines around the neck and ensuring it folded over the edge of the V-front. Then there was the black silk, said to be in mourning for Nelson, which had to be folded to a regulation width of two inches, which was tucked under the collar and draped like a halter down to the base of the V-neck jumper, and then secured by braid tapes with a reef bow, ensuring there was two fingers' length showing below. The tapes, which were to be seven inches long, were cut to form swallowtails.

After having accomplished the initial dressing up, I passed through to be officially photographed and was issued with my Official Service Number, C/JX 791680.

There were three main ports in this country, Devonport, Portsmouth and Chatham. The designation of a port prefix in one's Official Number appeared to have something to do with allocating ratings from London and the Home Counties to Chatham (HMS *Pembroke*), Scots and Irish and North Countrymen to Devonport (HMS *Drake*), and West Countrymen to Portsmouth (HMS *Victory*). In my case, my port was Chatham (C) and JX denoted Seaman's Branch.

After a couple of days the dressing process speeded up, as we all became more used to the uniform, but there was a dressing code laid down in regulations to which we were expected to comply.

Trousers: The bottoms must just touch the instep of the foot. The flap must always be buttoned up.

Jersey and Flannel: The top must be kept in a straight line across the neck, not hanging in a V.

Jumper: This must always be pulled down to the full extent. Bulky things must not be stowed in the pocket, they cause an unsightly bulge and are apt to fall out.

My first photo in uniform, as an Ordinary Seaman C/JX 791680, at H.M.S. *Royal Arthur*, Skegness, on 7 February, 1946.

Silk: The ends are sewn together. The bight is tied by the tapes, and must not be tucked inside the V of the jumper.

Tapes: The object of the tapes is to hold the bight of the silk at the bottom of the V-jumper. They must be seven inches long and tied round a two-inch-long bight of the silk in a reef bow.

Collar: The securing tapes must always be first tied round the body. When washed, the blue dye of a collar is apt to run into the white tapes if first put in hot water. To help prevent this, it is a good thing to soak the collar in cold water before washing.

Lanyard: The knot of the lanyard must be three inches above the tapes. The bight of the lanyard under the silk must not hang down too low.

Cap: This must always be worn square on the head. Chinstraps must be sewn into the required length for comfortable use. The cap must never be used as an additional pocket.

Cap Ribbon: The cap ribbon must be worn so that the H.M.S. is directly above the nose. It must be tied in a reef bow over the left ear.

Overcoat and Scarf: When wearing an overcoat, its collar must never be turned up except in very bad weather, and then it must be buttoned up in front. Scarves must be worn only for their proper purpose, and not as decoration, such as hanging down in front underneath the silk.

Boots: These must not be cross-laced. Lace ends and boot tags must be tucked away neatly.

Aye, Aye, Sir!

Having finally mastered the wearing of the uniform itself, there was one other difficulty to overcome when wearing the overcoat. One usually had to ask a colleague to put his arms under yours to hold the blue jean collar down on the shoulders to stop this being ruffled up and collecting above the collar of the overcoat. This only took a moment, but was a necessary procedure.

Two suits were issued on joining, and one of these we regarded as a special suit, kept for shore leave only. These were referred to as Number One's. Number Two suit, the other one, was used as day clothes, which together with blue overalls were used when on watch, and for scrubbing decks and polishing brass. We always took a particular pride in our Number One clothes.

The blue jean collar with white borders was always spotlessly clean, and carefully ironed. A new collar always looked new, and it was a common practice to wash the collar through and through several times to wash out some of the heavy blue dye. Regular sailors who had been in the Service a few years always showed a lighter colour blue on their collars, and we wanted to be like them. The black silk which draped around and underneath the collar needed special care too, in order to smooth out any creases.

With regard to the bell bottom trousers, here also some special attention was required. It was traditional that bell bottom trousers showed horizontal creases to each leg, representing the Seven Seas, we were told, and to achieve this one had first to turn the trousers inside out, concertina the trousers into these folds, and then press and iron them to form the creases. Then there was the ribbon around the cap, and those attaching to the bottom of the V-jumper— these also were carefully ironed.

The Royal Navy has always been commended for the personal hygiene and smartness of personnel. My personal experience of life in the Royal Navy proved this time and again; from day one, being well turned out was always a top priority.

Whatever the course selected, there were always weeks of basic training for everyone. The training course for me to become an Ordinary Signalman was not to be carried out at *Royal Arthur*, but at another Training Establishment. First I had to undergo about 10 weeks disciplinary training; for me, this wasn't going to happen at *Royal Arthur* either. I was told that I would be leaving *Royal Arthur* in

Class 151, H.M.S. *Royal Arthur*, Skegness, taken on 15 February, 1946.

just a few days to complete this at H.M.S. *Glendower*, another Butlin's holiday camp taken over by the Admiralty at Pwllheli in North Wales.

Meanwhile, during the few days I would remain at *Royal Arthur*, I was introduced to some preliminary general training, and for this I was placed with Class 151 with another 47 trainees. The working day began at 0630 and, if you were not on duty in the evening, your day ended at 1600. Those going ashore were allowed to do so three days out of four, and once ashore there was no need to report back until 0730 the next morning.

The Mess Hall, laid out with long wooden tables and benches, was housed in one of the large buildings previously used as a dance hall, and for functions in the Butlin's days. Cafeteria-style steel serving units were installed in one long line to accommodate the orderly queue of personnel. I cannot recall ever feeling hungry at *Royal Arthur*. For me, the food was adequate, though if one wished to be over-critical sometimes, the main course was inclined on occasions to be sloppy and the puddings stodgy. This was probably due to the food being prepared and cooked by new recruits who had chosen this as their job in the Royal Navy. They had neither gained sufficient knowledge nor had experience in the mass preparation and cooking of food. In any case, there was the NAAFI where one could buy various food products and numerous items of confectionery, also duty free cigarettes and tobacco.

I remained at *Royal Arthur* just nine days, and during that time I only went ashore three or four times at the most. For a new entrant to the Service, there was a lot to learn, and everyone was keen to do things right and not make mistakes. The days were full with general training procedures and instructions in one way and another, including a certain amount of marching, drill, physical training, etc., plus a certain amount of rope work with knots, splices and hitches. Because of my short stay at *Royal Arthur* I did rather regard the training there as little more than making me useful whilst I was there, but it was a very good introduction to what I could expect once I started my disciplinary training for real at *Glendower*.

The sudden change of lifestyle from being a completely free member of the public to one of regimentation, rules and regulations, came initially as a shock. I found some comfort in off-duty hours, during the first few days especially, in relaxing on my bunk, writing the odd letter home to my parents, who I knew were anxiously awaiting the first news from me, and reading. However, I enjoyed my time at *Royal Arthur*.

After the first few days settling down to a new routine, I found I could quite easily adapt and accept the conformity of Navy life, and I liked the organised way of doing things. Discipline was fundamental to the stability and reliability of Naval personnel, and this could only be achieved by everyone conforming to a strict routine at the beginning of their time in the Navy.

Battleship *Anson*, a sister ship in the "King George V" class, was built by Swan Hunter, Wallsend-on-Tyne. She was laid down in July, 1937, and completed on 22 June, 1942. *Anson* was the flagship of Rear-Admiral H. Hickling, Flag Officer Training Battleships. She returned to British waters arriving at Portsmouth Dockyard on 29 July, 1946. *Anson*, the seventh bearing the name, cost £10,000,000 to build. She was due for paying off, but then became a Training Ship at Potland. Here we see her in January, 1946.

This developed into men becoming dependable, with everyone else who was following the same code. There was a no-nonsense approach to everything concerned with Naval affairs, and after a few days trainees knew precisely what they were doing, how to do it, and when, as well as what not to do, and what was expected of them.

At the end of my nine days, I did not know whether or not I would return to *Royal Arthur*, but for now, with my brand new uniform, my kit bag and attache case containing all my personal belongings, I left for North Wales on 19th February, 1946.

> 'Recollect that you must be a seaman to be an officer, and also that you cannot be a good officer without being a gentleman."
>
> Nelson—December, 1803.

Battleship - "King George V" class.

Jane's Fighting Ships, 1946/1947, with the kind permission of Random House UK Limited.

H.M.S. *Glendower*, Pwllheli, North Wales
19 February–24 April 1946

H.M.S. *Glendower* was a Training Establishment commissioned 1st October, 1940 as an overflow for the intake of new recruits to *Royal Arthur* at Skegness.

There had not been an H.M.S. *Glendower* in the Royal Navy before this Establishment was commissioned. The name is that of the Welsh national hero, Owen Glyndwr, who was born in 1359 and in 1401 was acclaimed Prince of Wales. He took as his banner the Red Dragon of Wales on a white ground. This spelling of Glendower has existed since Elizabethan times, when he appears in one of Shakespeare's plays.

His fame lies chiefly in the patience of his strategy, his self-command, his tireless energy, and his strength of will and dogged persistence. Among the castles he took over were Criccieth and Harlech, and his activities extended to the border towns of England. For years he constituted a serious rival to King Henry IV over the Welsh country, but eventually his power waned and after a period of outlawry he disappeared in 1416.

On arrival at Pwllheli, I met up with a small group of new recruits, and together we made our way to *Glendower*. Some, like me, had travelled from *Royal Arthur*, while the others were new entrants in civilian clothes. The joining procedure for myself and the not-so-new recruits was no more than a formality, since we were only being drafted from one Establishment to another. We were, nevertheless, formally welcomed along with the others, and given various verbal orders and instructions on procedure from now on. The Divisional Officer told us that the Royal Navy, by tradition and reputation, enjoys the respect and confidence of the nation. This could only be maintained by every officer and man being loyal, obedient and efficient.

The Commanding Officer at *Glendower* was Captain A. M. Williams, R.N., and the second-in-command was known as the Commander of the Establishment. The Training was under the general direction of the Training Officer and the general organisation at *Glendower* was similar in many respects to that of *Royal Arthur*, but there were differences.

On joining *Glendower* I was attached to Top Division—there were also Forecastle and Quarter deck. Each Division was under the supervision of a Lieutenant-Commander or Lieutenant, assisted by a staff of other officers. There were also three Watches, Red, White and Blue, and I was attached to Blue Watch. My number was 1165. The Watch was approximately one third of the Division to which I belonged, and would be required for passive defence one night, stand-by duty and dog watch instruction a second night; the third night we would be allowed ashore.

Each Division was responsible for the cleanliness of a specified area in the Establishment which included lecture rooms and the huts

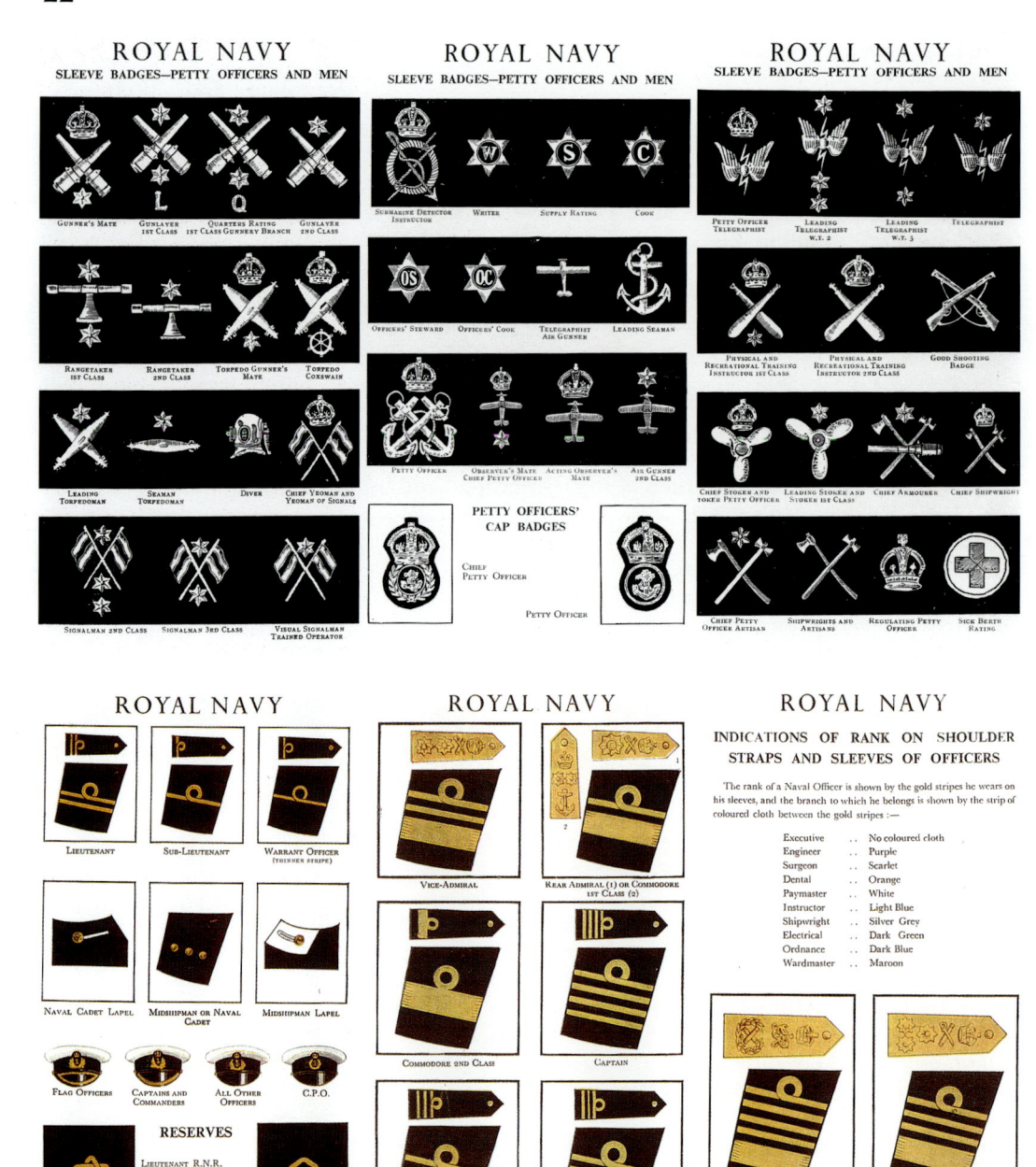

ROYAL NAVY
SLEEVE BADGES—PETTY OFFICERS AND MEN

- Gunner's Mate
- Gunlayer 1st Class
- Quarters Rating 1st Class Gunnery Branch
- Gunlayer 2nd Class
- Rangetaker 1st Class
- Rangetaker 2nd Class
- Torpedo Gunner's Mate
- Torpedo Coxswain
- Leading Torpedoman
- Seaman Torpedoman
- Diver
- Chief Yeoman and Yeoman of Signals
- Signalman 2nd Class
- Signalman 3rd Class
- Visual Signalman Trained Operator

ROYAL NAVY
SLEEVE BADGES—PETTY OFFICERS AND MEN

- Submarine Detector Instructor
- Writer
- Supply Rating
- Cook
- Officers' Steward
- Officers' Cook
- Telegraphist Air Gunner
- Leading Seaman
- Petty Officer
- Observer's Mate Chief Petty Officer
- Acting Observer's Mate
- Air Gunner 2nd Class

PETTY OFFICERS' CAP BADGES
- Chief Petty Officer
- Petty Officer

ROYAL NAVY
SLEEVE BADGES—PETTY OFFICERS AND MEN

- Petty Officer Telegraphist
- Leading Telegraphist W.T. 2
- Leading Telegraphist W.T. 3
- Telegraphist
- Physical and Recreational Training Instructor 1st Class
- Physical and Recreational Training Instructor 2nd Class
- Good Shooting Badge
- Chief Stoker and Stoker Petty Officer
- Leading Stoker and Stoker 1st Class
- Chief Armourer
- Chief Shipwright
- Chief Petty Officer Artisan
- Shipwrights and Artisans
- Regulating Petty Officer
- Sick Berth Rating

ROYAL NAVY

- Lieutenant
- Sub-Lieutenant
- Warrant Officer (Thinner Stripe)
- Naval Cadet Lapel
- Midshipman or Naval Cadet
- Midshipman Lapel
- Flag Officers
- Captains and Commanders
- All Other Officers
- C.P.O.

RESERVES
- Lieutenant R.N.R.
- Lieutenant R.N.V.R.

ROYAL NAVY

- Vice-Admiral
- Rear Admiral (1) or Commodore 1st Class (2)
- Commodore 2nd Class
- Captain
- Commander
- Lieutenant-Commander

ROYAL NAVY
INDICATIONS OF RANK ON SHOULDER STRAPS AND SLEEVES OF OFFICERS

The rank of a Naval Officer is shown by the gold stripes he wears on his sleeves, and the branch to which he belongs is shown by the strip of coloured cloth between the gold stripes :—

Branch	Colour
Executive	No coloured cloth
Engineer	Purple
Surgeon	Scarlet
Dental	Orange
Paymaster	White
Instructor	Light Blue
Shipwright	Silver Grey
Electrical	Dark Green
Ordnance	Dark Blue
Wardmaster	Maroon

- Admiral of the Fleet (G.R. indicates A.D.C. to King)
- Admiral

ROYAL MARINES

FLEET AIR ARM

where we slept. There were also separate mess decks for each Division.

One of the earliest lectures given at *Glendower* which we did not have at *Royal Arthur* was on the uniforms of officers, chief petty officers, and petty officers. The method of distinguishing the various uniforms was explained to us very early on in our training, as well as the distinguishing badges worn by ratings below that of petty officer, most of whom were dressed in the same way as we were.

Naval officers, generally speaking, were senior to officers of equivalent rank in the Army and Air Force.

ROYAL NAVY	ARMY	ROYAL AIR FORCE
Admiral of the Fleet	Field Marshal	Marshal of the Royal Air Force
Admiral	General	Air Chief Marshal
Vice-Admiral	Lieutenant-General	Air Marshal
Rear-Admiral	Major-General	Air Vice-Marshal
Commodore	Brigadier	Air Commodore
Captain	Colonel	Group Captain
Commander	Lieutenant-Colonel	Wing Commander
Lieutenant-Commander	Major	Squadron-Leader
Lieutenant	Captain	Flight-Lieutenant
Sub-Lieutenant and Commissioned Warrant Officer	Lieutenant	Flying Officer
Midshipman and Warrant Officer	Second-Lieutenant	Pilot Officer

Ranks were indicated by any of three means—by cap decoration, by shoulder straps, or by sleeve markings or badges. Duties were indicated by gorget patches ('tabs'), armlets or sleeve badges. It is quite possible that rank indications and arm badges were changed in some detail, particularly during wartime.

The rank of a naval officer is shown by the gold stripes he wears on his sleeve, and the branch to which he belongs is shown by the strip of coloured cloth between the gold stripes:

Executive	—	No coloured cloth
Engineer	—	Purple
Surgeon	—	Scarlet
Dental	—	Orange
Paymaster	—	White
Instructor	—	Light Blue
Shipwright	—	Silver Grey
Electrical	—	Dark Green
Ordnance	—	Dark Blue
Wardmaster	—	Maroon

The Fleet Air Arm, originally under the control of the Air Ministry, had since 24th May, 1939, been controlled entirely by the

Admiralty. For this reason, officers of the Fleet Air Arm wore naval uniform, but were distinguished from naval officers by the small letter "A" in the circle surmounting the sleeve stripes. Those officers who were actual pilots wore their wings on their sleeves, and not on the left breast like the R.A.F. In the early part of the war, many Fleet Air Arm pilots were R.A.F. officers who had been seconded to the Navy, but they were replaced by naval personnel as they became available.

Because the Naval Discipline Act required all naval personnel to be entered on the books of a ship, Fleet Air Arm Shore Establishments were given ship's names in the same manner that Chatham and Portsmouth barracks were known as H.M.S. *Pembroke* and H.M.S. *Victory*. Those shore stations included the names of H.M.S. *Daedalus*, H.M.S. *Peregrine*, H.M.S. *Kestrel*, H.M.S. *Merlin* and H.M.S. *Malabar*.

The Royal Marines (the 'Jollies') were originally boarding parties taken by the Navy to carry out the hand-to-hand fighting between ships which was a feature of sea battles in past centuries. During the Second World War they were primarily used as rapidly mobile sea-soldiers. Although a part of the Navy, they still retained Army rank names and indications, Royal Marine ranks being equal to their equivalent rank in the Navy, except that a major of Marines was equal to a naval Commander when afloat.

In peacetime the Royal Marines wore navy-blue uniform, and the only difference between their shoulder-strap indications and those of the Army was that the letters 'R.M.' were worn at the bottom of the strap nearest the arm. Officers' caps differed from those of N.C.O.s and rankers by having a different badge, and red piping round the crown of the hat.

The same procedure regarding the White Ensign and saluting applied at *Glendower* as it did everywhere else. The ceremony of Hoisting the Colours took place daily in ships and Shore Establishments at 0800 in the Summer and 0900 in the Winter. At *Glendower*, however, this time was altered slightly to fit in with Training Programmes.

The same disciplinary rules also applied to smoking and tobacco, except that on night leave 1 oz. of tobacco or 25 cigarettes was the limit, and on long leave of seven days or more, 8 oz. of tobacco or 200 cigarettes. This was the maximum amount of duty free tobacco that could be taken out of the Establishment. In addition, of course, similar restrictions applied to drink, betting and gambling, trafficking in any form, spitting and chewing of tobacco, fighting, playing games for money, etc., and whistling.

Only two states of health were recognised in the Royal Navy, 'fit for duty' and 'sick'. Sickness and feeling unwell was never accepted as an excuse for being absent from your place of duty or for missing a muster.

Right from day one of being a naval recruit, one quickly became aware of, and fully understood, naval rules and regulations, but at *Glendower* everything seemed much more strict, and even harsher.

The officers appeared to be more abrupt, the instructors more demanding, the words 'skulking', 'being in improper possession', 'no excuse for not knowing', 'will be severely dealt with' were used all too frequently, and one felt that even by doing the right thing one could so easily go wrong. As the rule book put it, 'there are certain standards of behaviour which, while highly desirable in all walks of life, have, in a disciplined service, to be rigorously enforced. No one here is looking for trouble, and trouble in this connection is easy to avoid if you remember these few things'.

The contentious part of all this for me, privately, had nothing to do with matters concerning the code of conduct expected, since I was fully in agreement with all of these. It was more to do with tolerance, I think. There seemed to be no tolerance for people who, perhaps for valid reasons, missed a new notice on the Notice Board or failed to fall in at a certain time due to a lecture over-running, or for minor mishaps which occur unexpectedly, like boot laces breaking just as you are hurrying to meet the deadline. Fortunately none of these things happened to me, but I knew several trainees who did fall foul of such things. Failing to observe any of the regulations was liable to get you into serious trouble, and this also applied to the ordinary offences against civil law of which we were made aware.

It was imperative that we read the Notice Board every day, and sometimes during the day, for daily orders regarding 'rig of the day'. This was either to be Number Two uniform for class training and drill, or Number Eights, blue working overalls for mess, hut and site maintenance. Failure to read the Notice Board, and not being correctly dressed, incurred serious penalties.

Whatever one's feelings about the disciplinary procedures laid down, you had to get over them. 'Absolute punctuality' was taken as a matter of course in the Navy, everyone before us had complied, we did, and all those coming after us would as well. This is what made the Navy efficient and smartly turned out.

My starting pay at *Glendower* as an Ordinary Seaman was three shillings (15p.) a day, and there was a Post Office Savings Bank on the site for depositing money if one wished. An additional advance of 3d. a day was paid to men in lieu of an issue of 'grog' if 20 years of age or over. Married men's allowance was 21s.6d. a week.

Day leave at *Glendower* given to non-duty watches was Monday to Friday 1650–2230, Saturdays 1310–2230 and Sundays 1300–2230; no overnight shore leave was permitted. We were reminded that leave was a privilege, not a right, and similar penalties applied as they did at *Royal Arthur* for breaking leave, returning late from leave, and not returning at all. It was also made clear to us at *Glendower* that there would be no home leave permitted until the complete nine weeks' training course was completed.

Having all come from various forms of civilian employment, we were regarded as being totally untrained and unfit, and as we stood at that time, we were utterly useless to His Majesty's Navy. There was a minimum standard required in the Navy. Personnel had to be fit

Sheet Bend

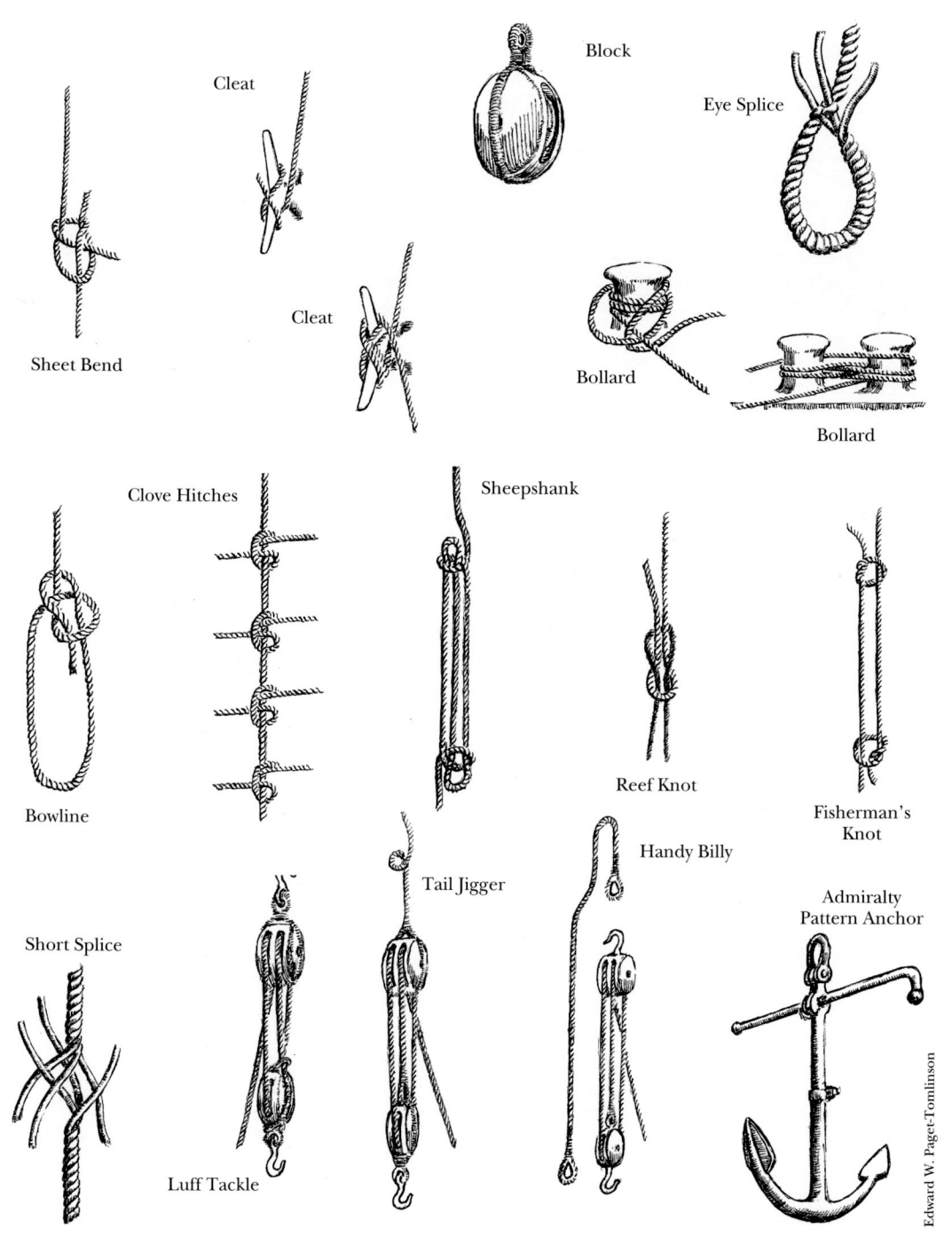

Cleat

Block

Eye Splice

Cleat

Bollard

Bollard

Bowline

Clove Hitches

Sheepshank

Reef Knot

Fisherman's Knot

Short Splice

Luff Tackle

Tail Jigger

Handy Billy

Admiralty Pattern Anchor

Edward W. Paget-Tomlinson

As an Ordinary Seaman at H.M.S. Glendower, we received instruction on knots, bends, hitches and cleats, when we were in competition with other classes to improve our speed and efficiency.

and experienced, to have ability to act and respond to orders in a recognised manner without hesitation in any situation that might arise. Naval procedure had to be fully understood, smartness and tidiness had to be learnt. There would be no tolerance for slackness or laziness, your life might be at risk and others with it. Alertness and willingness would be the norm.

All of these essential qualities seemed to me obvious and justified, and the learning curve was to be straightened from day one, from zero to the optimum and acceptable level at the end of the 9–10-week course. There was a lot to do, and a lot to learn, and

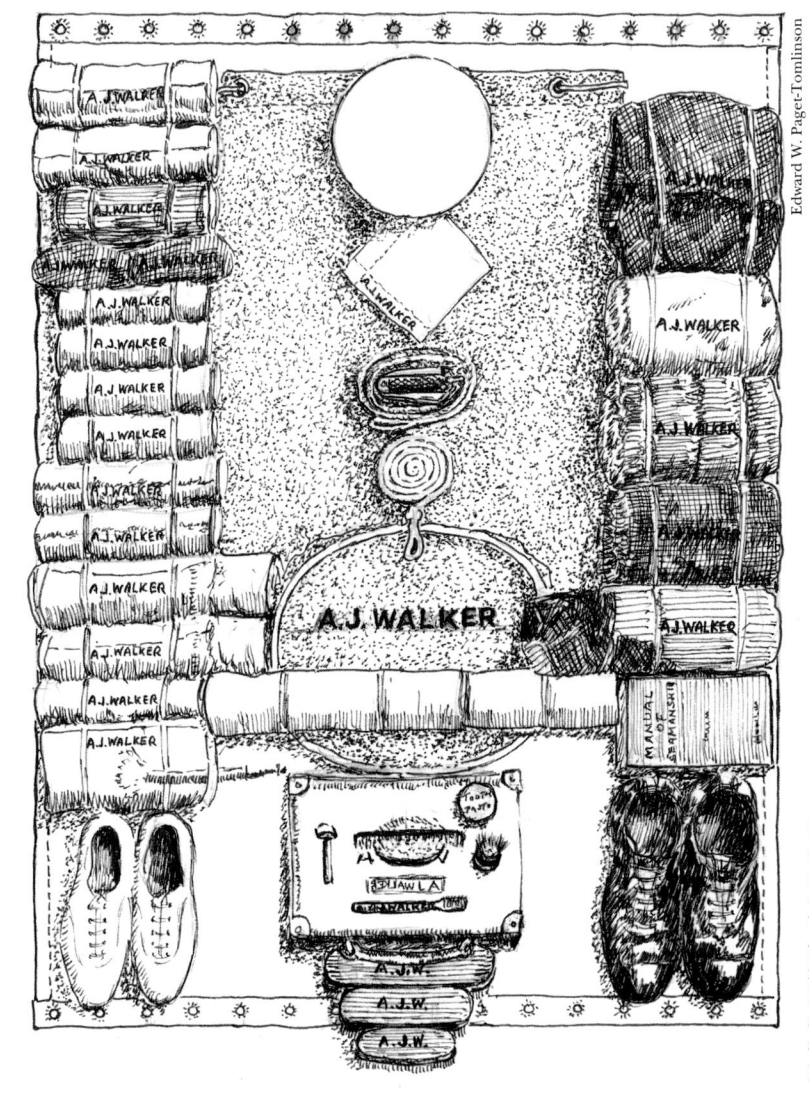

For regular kit inspection, everything had to be clearly marked and laid out carefully and precisely. Without a complete kit, you were unable to function efficiently, and to have an incomplete kit was an indication of slackness, and brought serious penalties.

it was important to be serious about the Navy's business from day one.

Day by day we worked through the syllabus, marching backwards and forwards, up and down and around and around the parade ground. Standing to attention, saluting, pack and rifle drill, target practice, assault course training, gym, physical training, and so on, it never seemed to come to an end.

As young recruits, completely unused to quite so much concentrated physical activity, we found this a little hard to bear on pretty well a daily basis. In addition to the constant marching on the parade ground, there was always the weekly 'kit inspection' where everything had to be laid out neatly on your bunk, with your name showing on every article. There was a set format for this routine and everything had to be correct.

Your kit had to be arranged on your bed at inspection time, the order was 'stand by your bed' when the Divisional Officer inspected each man's kit in turn. Inspection over, everything had to be returned and stowed carefully into your kitbag. You were solely responsible for your kit, and the weekly inspection was to ensure your kit was up to standard and everything was present and correct. Everything one possessed was either in your kitbag or in your attache case, and it goes without saying that it was your responsibility to look after it. Without a complete kit, you were unable to function efficiently, and to have an incomplete kit was an indication of slackness, and brought penalties.

One aspect of the training I did enjoy, and that was Sunday Divisions. Assembling on the parade ground for Church I found rewarding, and marching on parade with a band leading, stimulating. As our young cadet entrant to *Royal Arthur* mentioned in earlier pages, there was a certain feeling of pride on these particular occasions, which never failed to materialise Sunday after Sunday.

Before Sunday Divisions took place, there was work to put in on your uniform. Your waist belt and gaiters had to be clean and whitened, and your boots had to shine. Some trainees took great pride in their boots, continually buffing them up so the toecaps really shone like glass. With the parade over, one was usually free for the day, depending upon your Watch.

I cannot remember taking very much day leave entitlement while I was at *Glendower*. I recall going 'ashore' perhaps half a dozen times only during the nine weeks I was there. The daily routine was hard work, and it took something to get used to it; a certain amount of fatigue set in, and most of us were keen to take advantage of free time by relaxing. One of my class mates said to me 'I don't think I can take any more of this'. To encourage him, I replied 'Of course you can, if I can, you can'.

One morning when under instruction on the parade ground we were drilling with full pack and rifle. Our instructor, who was usually quite a reasonable person, bellowed out some order, and myself and a class mate standing to attention next to me saw the funny side of it, and neither of us could completely stifle a muffled chuckle. Our instructor singled us out to step forward, and ordered us both to run six times round the perimeter of two huge buildings, the Catering Block and the Drill Hall, carrying full pack and rifle at the double. The squad continued their drill while we carried out the punishment, returning absolutely breathless. The instructor ordered us to fall in, and we all continued with the drill.

For more serious breaches of discipline, trainees had to run forwards and backwards over a bridge for varying periods of time, with their arms outstretched above their heads, holding a rifle. There was one such case reported in the daily newspapers when there was an Admiralty inquiry into "Sailors Fainting Doing Drill 16". The case involved a number of young recruits undergoing No. 16 punishment, extra drill scheduled to last one hour. After 50 minutes the drill was stopped because several of the men complained of feeling ill, and the men received attention in Sick Bay, where three had to be detained. It transpired that they had been vaccinated two days previously.

Other forms of punishment included the denial of privileges, restriction or cancellation of leave entitlement, and the imposition of additional hours of scrubbing, washing down and cleaning the Mess Hall, huts and Lecture Rooms. There might also be repeated demands for a kit layout for the Instructor to scrutinize and accept or reject as he thought fit.

As already explained, it was the responsibility of your Instructor, who seemingly had almost unlimited powers, to knock young recruits into shape, but no doubt some of them became over-zealous in bringing their squad up to the required performance level.

There was one occasion, I recall, when if we had been found out we would have been in very serious trouble. One of my class mates had struck up a friendship with a Wren whose workplace was the boot and shoe department, which collected and labelled trainees' footwear and bagged them up ready for taking to a boot repair shop outside the Establishment. About 50 hessian bags of boots were ready to go on this particular day, and the previous evening my class mate and I were assigned the job, which involved loading a truck with the bags and accompanying the driver to the repair shop which was in the town of Llangefni, on Anglesey. I personally didn't know the Wren, and completely unknown to me my class mate had arranged with her to come along with us for a day out, by smuggling her into one of the spare hessian bags. I didn't like the idea at all, the whole thing being against my better judgement, and I said so, but my class mate was determined, and so was she.

Next morning we loaded all the bags, including the one with her in it, closed the tailboard, and climbed in ourselves. Apparently the truck driver knew about the escapade as well, and he too was most unhappy about it. We drove towards the entrance of the Establishment, the sentry guards gave a cursory glance over the tailboard of the truck, and waved us on. A few miles down the road, the Wren climbed out of the boot bag, and we all travelled on to Anglesey.

REMINISSING:
Away from home I'd never been
Until I reached the age eighteen
T'was then that life began to change
And everything seemed so strange.

I had to change from homely life
To days of which were one long strife,
And everything I loved did seem
To vanish into one long dream.

And now I change to Navy life
And change my ways to same,
But every now and then my thoughts
Drift back to whence I came.

At night when I climb into bed
I miss the sheets around my head
Those sheets which were so smooth and white
I fear have gone right out of sight.

I miss those carpets on the floor
That used to reach up to the door,
The warmth they gave to all our feet
Is not the same as cold concrete.

I miss the times when I did lay
In my small bed till noon of day,
My luck it didn't show to me
Until I joined the Royal Navy.

It's 'Aye, Aye, Sir' this, 'Aye, Aye, Sir' that,
'Aye, Aye, Sir' night and day,
It's never 'righto' or 'yes I will'
and certainly not 'O.K.'

About six weeks this course will last
And now already three have passed,
And soon the time will draw quite near,
When we will all be full of cheer.

Since that will be the day when I
To - Glendower I'll say goodbye,
But until that day arrives
I'll have to join in all the strives,
I'll have to be like all the rest
And to all things, just make the best.

A poem I sent home to my parents, sometime during March, 1946, while undergoing basic disciplinary training at H.M.S *Glendower*, Pwllheli, North Wales.

We arrived at the shop, unloaded, re-loaded the truck with a return load of repaired boots, and dived into a nearby restaurant for a cup of tea and a bun. I must say, it was very pleasant to be away from the Establishment for a while, and to see what we regarded as a normal way of life, which we had almost forgotten about since we joined up. I was, nevertheless, very concerned about our extra passenger and whether we would be able to get back without the sentry guards or anyone else seeing her, and indeed, whether she had been missed from her place of duty all day. I expressed my deep concern over this, so we all made a hurried start on the return journey.

Invaluable service was provided by the Woman's Royal Naval Service (WRNS) replacing manpower in whatever category, department or section and whenever called upon to do so. In this picture, Wren air mechanics receive instruction in winch operation. Two Wren trainees steady the bomb as it is wound into position by other trainees sitting on the wing of a Barracuda, which was the first torpedo-bomber monoplane, and could carry one 18" torpedo, or three 500lb bombs, depth charges or sea mines.

In general conversation on the journey I remarked to my colleague, 'I don't know why we have to keep marching all over the place all the time, do you?' My colleague replied 'It's a good job we do, wearing out all this leather, so we can have more days out like this.'

Fortunately, back at the entrance to the 'ship' the guards raised the boom and beckoned us through, and our truck drove straight round to the boot department, where we started to unload. Meanwhile, the Wren had climbed out of her bag, and at a convenient moment dropped down from the back of the truck and casually walked away. We were all exceedingly lucky that time, for had we been found out we would all (including the Wren) have faced extremely serious consequences.

Was it worth the risk? I made it clear to my colleague that I would never be a party to this kind of prank again, should he and I be singled out for the job; as it turned out, neither of us was. As for the Wren, somebody had covered for her, and luckily she wasn't missed.

The WRNS were originally formed in November, 1917, and demobilised in October, 1919, when they had reached a strength of just under 5,000. They were revived in April, 1939, under the direction of Mrs. Laughton Matthews to replace in time of war officers and men in certain Naval Shore Establishments. Their chief duties included confidential clerical work, bookkeeping, storekeeping, telephone operating, motor driving, cooking and stewarding, as well as many mechanical duties requiring a high degree of dexterity. By the end of 1944, the strength of WRNS in uniform totalled more than 70,000.

The uniform was a navy blue coat and skirt. Officers wore tricorne hats and ratings had hats similar to those worn by Sea Rangers. Ranks were indicated in the same way as for their equivalents in the Royal Navy:

Chief Officer	Lieut. Commander
First Officer	Lieutenant
Second Officer	Sub-Lieutenant
Chief Wren	Petty Officer
Leading Wren	Leading Seaman
Wren	Seaman

Apart from continually marching and drilling, we had regular sessions in the gym and physical training. We also received instruction on ropework involving the understanding of knots, splices, hitches and bends, and competitions were held between classes.

With just a few days over the nine weeks since I arrived at *Glendower*, I was informed that I would be leaving the Establishment on 24th April, 1946 . My basic training was completed, and I would be drafted to another Shore Establishment, H.M.S. *Scotia*, in Ayrshire, where I would be starting my selected technical training as a Signalman.

I cannot in all honesty say I enjoyed my stay at *Glendower*. I fully appreciated and accepted the necessity of all the training, and indeed the Navy's way of achieving it, but the nine-week-long course was quite hard going and very tiring. The time of the year may have had something to do with it as well—if the weather wasn't chilly, it was raining and dreary, and there was very little social life outside the Establishment. All the pubs were closed on Sunday—at least they would have been somewhere to spend some time—and generally shore leave became rather dull and boring, and almost a waste of time, I thought.

As the course progressed and the weeks passed there was, however, a noticeable improvement in all of us. We had grown up and were more confident than when we arrived. There is no doubt at all that the regular marching, drill and physical training did wonders for our physique, as a result of which we were transformed from Naval recruits into Naval personnel.

The officers, staff and instructors were all normal friendly people who were willing to assist and help in times of need. They did have a humorous side as well, the same as everyone else, but they had an exacting job to do, ensuring that all new entrants passed their basic training in the allotted time with flying colours. This was their responsibility, and in that they succeeded. We were all better men than when we arrived—we had passed a gruelling test over nine long weeks, we had not only matured, but had acquired the qualification the Navy was looking for, and in that *Glendower* had its reward.

"Silence! Deeds, not words!"

Lord Fisher

Token was commissioned in September, 1945, and was one of several T-class boats at Rothesay in 1946 and 1947.

H.M.S. *Scotia*, Doonfoot, Ayrshire
25 April–10 July 1946

On 25th April, 1946, I arrived at H.M.S. *Scotia*, another of the Navy's Shore Establishments, commissioned 6th January, 1942. Prior to this, *Scotia*, situated at Doonfoot in Ayrshire, had been a Butlin's holiday camp. It was springtime, the sun was shining, and I felt very confident as I approached the sentries at the entrance. I was now about to start an 11-week technical training course to become a Teleprinter Operator.

Teleprinters were used extensively at this time throughout the world. These machines closely resembled other Creed teleprinters, but numerous improvements in design and construction were introduced as well as a number of new important operating features. The latest ones were designed to meet a wider range of traffic and operating conditions in the service of administration, Press, railways and other large users of telegraph equipment, and to bring within the bounds of practicability a machine which could be introduced into commerce and industry with the assurance that it would provide an accurate and dependable service.

This model of a Creed teleprinter was used for instruction during our technical training, as well as for transmitting and receiving on board H.M.S. *Forth* and *Montclare*.

Classified now as an Ordinary Signalman, we formed Class T/P 15 for technical training on teleprinters. Photograph taken 20 June, 1946.

The Navy had adopted these teleprinters for communication between Establishments. There were two types, the transmitting and receiving teleprinter and the receiving-only teleprinter. Teleprinters, basically, were very much like an oversized typewriter, with a paper roll fixed at the back of the machine. Like a typewriter, they had a QWERTY keyboard, and depending upon model type, were capable of between 66 and 72 words per minute. Ships and Shore Establishments linked up to shore lines via the G.P.O., and messages were sent and received immediately with absolute reliability.

My training class had 15 trainee operators, and we were known as Class T/P 15. The daily routine and life generally at *Scotia* was much more pleasant, and considerably more lenient and humane, than at *Glendower*. Naval procedure, regulations and discipline were the same

Another photograph of Class T/P 15 taken later the same day.

Sketch of my chalet showing how we were billeted at H.M.S. Scotia, Doonfoot, Ayrshire.

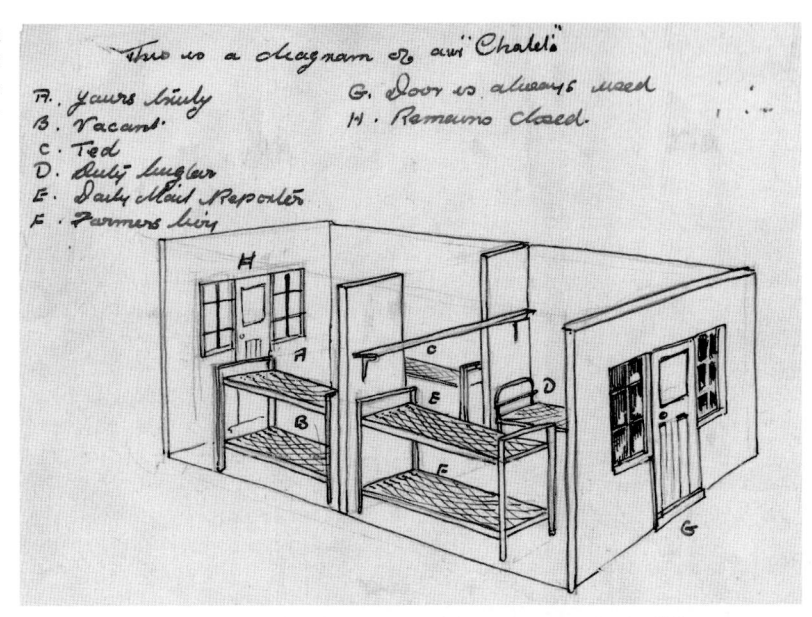

as ever, but the daily drill and marching that we had all become so used to gave way to technical training and procedures on teleprinters. Somehow, one was able to breathe more easily at *Scotia*, and one almost looked forward to being able to enjoy oneself as well.

At *Scotia* we were more individually billeted, with smaller numbers housed in chalets. The drawing of our chalet, sketched by me at the time, illustrates how we were arranged. At *Scotia* I felt we had more space, independence and individuality, which all helped us considerably to concentrate our minds on the job for which we were being trained.

The Establishment was situated very close to the beach, and only a short distance from the Heads of Ayr. My colleagues and I spent many off-duty hours during good weather swimming in the sea, relaxing on the beach, and walking the Heads.

On the beach - Joe and myself, 26 June, 1946.

Joch and myself on the beach, the same day.

Vanguard, was our very latest battleship, laid down at Clydebank 2 October, 1941, and completed in the fitting-out basin at John Brown's Clydebank shipyard on 2 May, 1946. Towed down the 14-miles channel, she parted with her tugs at Greenock and sailed under her own power into the Estuary. Her length 814 feet overall, beam 107 feet 6 inches, and cost £9,000,000 to build excluding her 15-inch. guns and mountings, of which there were eight. Her secondary armament comprised sixteen 5.25-inch. guns. She could accommodate a crew of 2,000. The first *Vanguard* helped to destroy the Spanish Armada, in 1588, and this was our most powerful battleship, the ninth to bear the honoured name. It was stated that her gunnery, damage control, and radar equipment were unexcelled. It was said also, she had the most comfortable mess deck in the Navy, electric labour-saving devices, and other amenities which combined to make her a "happy ship".

When I saw her in June, 1946, she was carrying out steaming and engine trials in the Firth of Clyde, having completed gunnery trials off the north of Ireland. This photograph was taken in September, 1950.

John and myself, 28 June, 1946.

30 June, 1946. Three scates - Joch, Bill, and Steve.

On one particular afternoon in June we were sitting above the foreshore, gazing out to sea, when one of my class mates spotted a very large warship in the distance travelling southwards. This was the first time that I had seen a warship of any kind, and my classmate identified her as the battleship *Vanguard*. I had my Baby Brownie camera with me and managed to snap her, but she was a long way off.

In addition to enjoying ourselves in various leisure activities in the Establishment and on the beach, we gradually became involved in numerous social activities in the town. We all went ashore whenever our duties permitted.

In early May, 1946, five of us arranged for a weekend pass and spent the time taking in the sights and amenities of Glasgow, staying overnight at the Sailors' Hostel in Sauchiehall Street. The first night we treated ourselves to a slap-up meal in a restaurant, which we enjoyed with relish, and followed this with a visit to the cinema.

On the second day, we were sitting in the hostel idly chatting when a mother and her daughter suddenly appeared and the mother

27 June, 1946. Cathy, Joch, Marie, Florence, and myself.

John and myself, a friend of one of my class mates who was living in the town of Ayr. 28 June, 1946.

Street photograph taken of me, 15 May, 1946, just before a YWCA dance.

Our beach, taken from the Heads of Ayr, 20 June, 1946.

A moment for quiet contemplation. Heads of Ayr 26 June, 1946.

announced that her daughter was having a 21st birthday party that evening, and they were short of men—would we like to come along? 'Sure we would—thank you very much!' The party was great fun, and in true Scottish style it was an all-night, early-morning affair. Her parents had obviously gone to great lengths to ensure their daughter had a good send off, having organised an on-going programme of party games and splendid refreshments. They opened their house to family, friends and neighbours alike, and everyone was most kind and generous to the five of us. Such an invitation as this, coming out of the blue, certainly made our weekend for us, and I believe the five of us being there did the same for them.

Obviously, most of each working day was taken up with our technical training, but as in *Royal Arthur* and *Glendower* time had to be allocated for kit maintenance and to personal hygiene in the way of washing, ironing and mending. Our uniform and working clothes had to be maintained in good order, the usual method for washing clothes being in a bucket with soap and water, then hanging out to dry.

H.M.S. *Scotia*, from the Heads of Ayr, 26 June, 1946.

The Chalets and Parade Ground, taken 20 June, 1946. Whatever the weather at *Royal Arthur*, *Glendower*, and *Scotia*, a roll call on the parade ground at 6.30 am for physical training was compulsory.

11 May, 1946. Week-end in Glasgow.

The course progressed slowly to its conclusion, and an end-of-course proficiency examination was held on 4th July, 1946. In the examination for Ordinary Signalman T/P, I qualified in all four sections, Paper, Cypher, Procedure and Switchboard with a pass mark of 378, which was the norm out of a minimum requirement of 362.

I was now qualified, all my training was complete, and I was considered fit, trained and ready to be of service to the Royal Navy. I had been away from home for five months, and I was looking forward to 11 days' statutory leave entitlement.

I said goodbye to my classmates—I had no idea whether I would ever meet them again—to others at *Scotia* with whom I had become friends, and to my Instructor. I collected all my kit together and prepared for the journey home on 11th July, 1946.

'To send ships to sea by untrained men is simple murder.'

Admiral Lord Jellicoe—31st May, 1918.

Taken from the fore-shore of our beach at *Scotia*. In the distance, Britains latest battlehip *Vanguard*. 26 June, 1946.

June, 1946. Really hard work - hand washing kit in a bucket and hanging out to dry.

Submarine Depot Ship H.M.S. *Forth* (S/m 3)   3

2 August 1946–20 May 1947

BEFORE leaving *Scotia* I was given orders that when my leave was over I was to report to H.M.S. *Pembroke*, the Shore Establishment at Royal Naval Barracks, Chatham, for posting. My 11 days' leave finished on 20th July, 1946, and I accordingly made my way there. On arrival at *Pembroke* I completed the preliminary joining procedures, which by now had become just a matter of course, and was assigned to Cookham Mess. My Watch was 2nd Port, and shortly after arrival I had an official photograph taken.

On 22nd July I passed through the drafting medical office, the X-ray department, victualling, dental, registration and pay departments. The only item of kit that I had not been issued with since enlistment was a hammock, and I collected this from the clothing department.

The dates of my leave entitlement were incorporated for Certificate of Service purposes into the period I was under orders at RNB Chatham following completion of my training at *Scotia*, that being 11th July–1st August, 1946, but effectively I was only at *Pembroke* for 11 days awaiting drafting orders. Each day I was there I waited anxiously to be told when and where I would be posted, and finally I was summoned to the drafting office where I was informed that I would be leaving *Pembroke* to join a ship based at Rothesay, Isle of Bute, in Scotland on 2nd August, 1946. Further inquiries about my posting revealed that the ship I would be joining was H.M.S. *Forth*, submarine depot ship of the 3rd Submarine Flotilla, and she was lying at anchor in Rothesay Bay.

Forth at Holy Loch during World War II as depot ship of the 3rd Submarine Flotilla. "RN Photographs".

(RNSM)

(RNSM)

Another view of *Forth* with her flotilla of submarines at Holy Loch during World War II. "RN Photographs".

Submarine depot ships were mother ships to submarines and their crews. Besides looking after the repair and refitting of submarines, they gave a home to the crews returning after each mission. Depot ships carried skilled craftsmen and their equipment included foundry and coppersmiths, plumbing and carpentry shops, heavy and light machine shops, electrical and torpedo shops and plant for charging submarines' batteries. Depot ships also carried spare parts on board and, short of submarines requiring docking, all repairs could be carried out by the ship's staff.

Submarine depot ships also had comfortable sleeping quarters for submarine crews and a spacious reception room, hot baths and a sick bay. There were also bars, a well-stocked library and even a cinema. While on board the depot ship, submariners had a complete rest, and were not required to take part in the ordinary routine of the ship. Submarines returning to the depot ship after their mission required revictualling, refuelling and rearming, and perhaps a general overhaul.

While alongside the depot ship submarines were rearmed with torpedoes. Taken from the ship's store, torpedoes were charged with compressed air (which provided the motive power) and the explosive heads were fitted. They were then swung outboard by electric crane and lowered for stowage by the submarine crew. Depot ships also had trained men on board for the replacement of any submarine crew member who might be sick or injured.

Forth, the latest depot ship, had accommodation for the crews of 12 submarines. There was a fully equipped sickbay aboard, including an operating theatre, X-ray room, and dispensaries—a complete floating hospital.

H.M.S. *Forth* was built by John Brown & Co. Ltd. at Clydebank, laid down 30th June, 1937, commissioned 12th March, 1939. She was 574 feet long overall and 75 feet beam; displacement 8,900 tons. She carried the heaviest armament yet provided for a depot ship, including eight 4.5 inch, two multiple pompons, four 3 pdr., and four smaller units. Guns were in pairs, two forward, two aft, and two sponsoned on either beam. She had a complement of 502, including 64 repair staff and 43 spare submarine crew. When operational, with as many as 12 submarines alongside, this had the potential of increasing the total number of men on board to around 1,200. Her sister ship *Maidstone*, also built at Clydebank, was launched around 10 months earlier.

I was quite excited by the news of my posting, and obviously lost no time in finding out the geographical location of the Isle of Bute, and how to get there. It seemed I needed to make for Glasgow Central station, change platforms for a train travelling westwards along the south side of the Firth of Clyde, passing through Port Glasgow and Greenock, and bypassing Gourock, and round to Wemyss Bay. From there it was necessary to catch a ferry across to Rothesay.

I left Chatham barracks very early on 2nd August, carrying my kitbag, hammock and attache case. It was going to be quite a long journey all told, and I did not want to take the risk of arriving late on board.

The journey went well, and I enjoyed it. Arriving at Wemyss Bay and standing on the landing stage awaiting the ferry, I experienced a wonderful sense of freedom. I was alone amongst a crowd of civilians who were also travelling to Rothesay, and although I began to feel nervous and apprehensive about the prospect in front of me, of joining a ship for the first time, I also had the feeling that it would be all right. We boarded the ferry, the *Duchess of Montrose*, and I stood against the rail towards the bow, looking for the first sight of my ship as we steadily approached Rothesay Bay. I remember the air was so clear and refreshing, the sun was shining, and the sea was calm and glistening in the sunshine. Excited holidaymakers on board, some returning from a day trip, others with their suitcases starting a holiday, were my companions.

It was then that the elderly gentleman spoke to me so reassuringly. 'You'll be all right, you'll enjoy yourself at Rothesay.' I could not really have known it then, but he was right.

The *Duchess of Montrose*, a turbine steamer built by Denny at Dumbarton in 1930 and used in peacetime on long-distance excursions, was getting along at a good pace, and it was not long before I could see H.M.S. *Forth*, her stern facing towards us, with a couple of submarines berthed alongside. Looking beyond *Forth*, Rothesay was coming into view.

Within minutes the *Duchess of Montrose* manoeuvred alongside the pier at Rothesay, tied up, and everyone disembarked. 'Good luck' said my new-found friend. 'By the way, the liberty boats for the ship

This photograph of *Forth* was taken 11 August, 1946, from a position almost opposite the Pavilion, and one can clearly see how close the ship was to the shore. The vessel to the left of the picture is the destroyer *Onslaught*.

After five months training and eleven days leave, I set off from RNB, Chatham, on 2 August, 1946, to join my first ship H.M.S. *Forth*, at Rothesay.

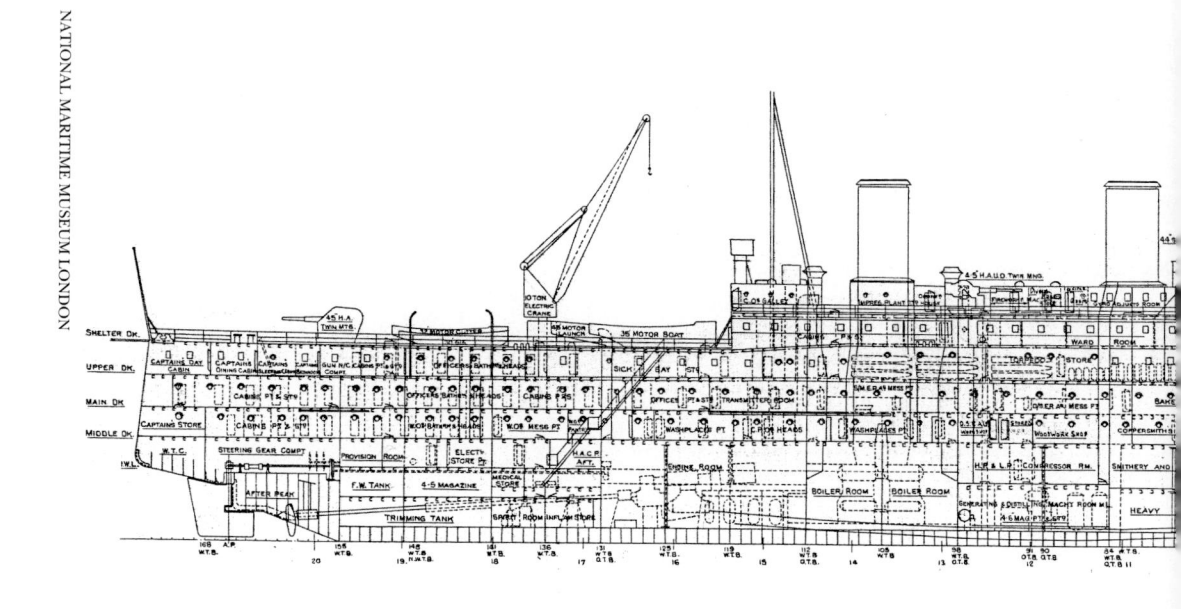

usually come alongside over there, by some wooden steps,' he said pointing to the end of the pier. 'Oh, right, thank you very much, I'll go and wait there then—goodbye.'

Liberty boats from the ship went back and forth at regular intervals during the day, conveying crew when going on and returning from shore leave, and collecting supplies for the ship. After waiting a while and taking in the local scene, I saw a liberty boat on its way, bringing crew ashore. It was soon alongside the wooden steps, and everyone clambered out. They all gave a cursory glance towards me, realising I was a new boy, standing as I was with all my kit, as I gave a friendly glance to them as they walked past me. The leading hand in the boat beckoned me to climb in, I did, and in a flash, we were on our way to the ship.

The crossing from shore to ship was only a matter of about eight minutes or so, and I was soon climbing up the gangplank on to the Quarter Deck. Arriving on board, I was met by the Divisional Officer, who pointed the way to the Regulating Office, whose staff went through the joining procedures with me. I was very nervous, completely out of my depth, and felt totally lost. I was also concerned that having now arrived, I was expected to do the job for which I had been trained. Would I be able to cope, I wondered, would I be able to do the job all right? If only there was just someone I knew who could help me right now.

I was attached to Mess 33 and reminded about Watches. My training assisted me here, for I remembered that for the day's routine the ship's company was divided into Red, White and Blue Watches. The 24 hours are also divided into Watches: **First**, 2000 to

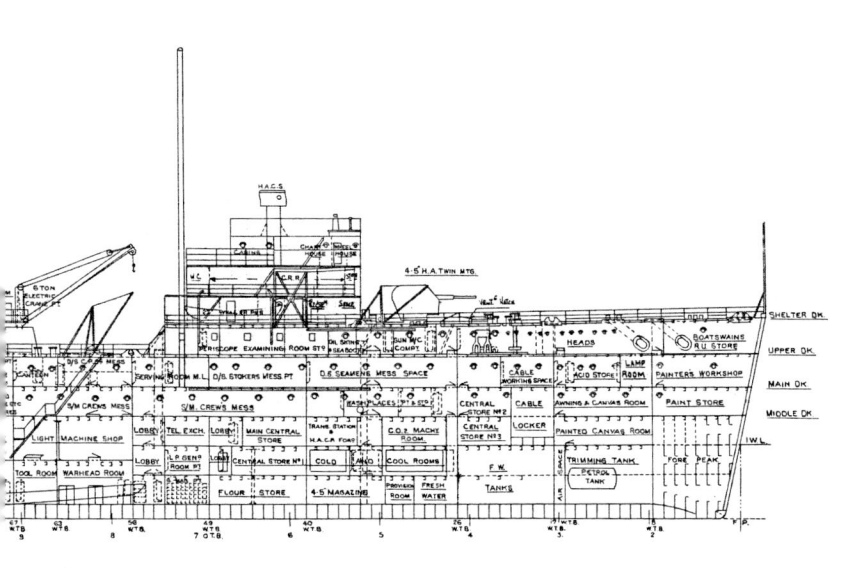

The set of Ship Plans for the building of the Submarine depot ship *Forth* were drawn to a scale of 1/16th-1 foot and are date stamped 30 November, 1938, by John Brown & Co, Ltd, Clydebank, Shipbuilding Department. Although some detail has been lost due to greatly reducing the size of this profile, the decking, layout, and superstructure, are clearly visible but unfortunately the masts, spars, and rigging, are not detailed.

Midnight; **Middle**, Midnight–0400; **Morning**, 0400–0800; **Forenoon**, 0800–1200 noon; **Afternoon**, noon–1600; **First Dog**, 1600–1800, and **Last Dog** 1800–2000. For shore leave, the ship's company was divided into Port and Starboard. It was some relief to me to note that Mess 33 was for Buntings and Sparklers, so at least I would be among Communication Branch crew.

By asking half a dozen crew on the way, I at last found my way to Mess 33. I was thoroughly bewildered by the number of solid iron ladders, bulkheads and stanchions. Huge girders were spanning everywhere, all of them bolted with countless giant bolts and nuts. Masses of cables, piping and ducting seemed to be running everywhere, horizontally, vertically, and weaving along, through, and up and down the supports and structure of the ship. There were also alleyways, companion ways, and doorways leading off in all direc-

Astute - launched 30 January, 1945, and commissioned on 21 May, was one of only two A-class boats to be completed before the end of World War II, the first of the class being *Amphion*, launched 31 August, 1944. In August, 1946, after trials and working up, *Astute* was commissioned into the 3rd Submaring Flotilla on *Forth* at Rothesay, and was one of the first submarines I saw on joining *Forth* on 2 August, 1946.

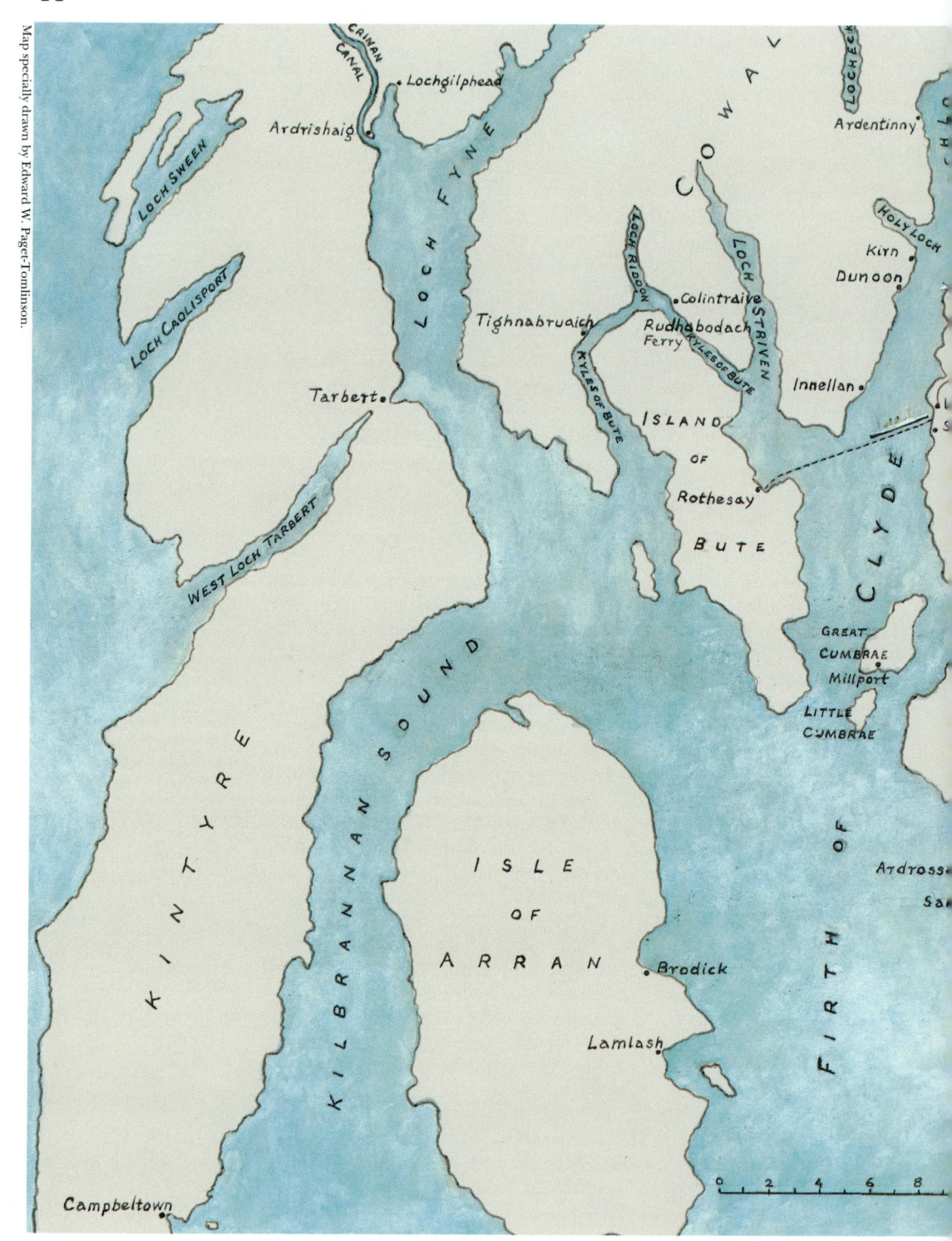

Map specially drawn by Edward W. Paget-Tomlinson.

45

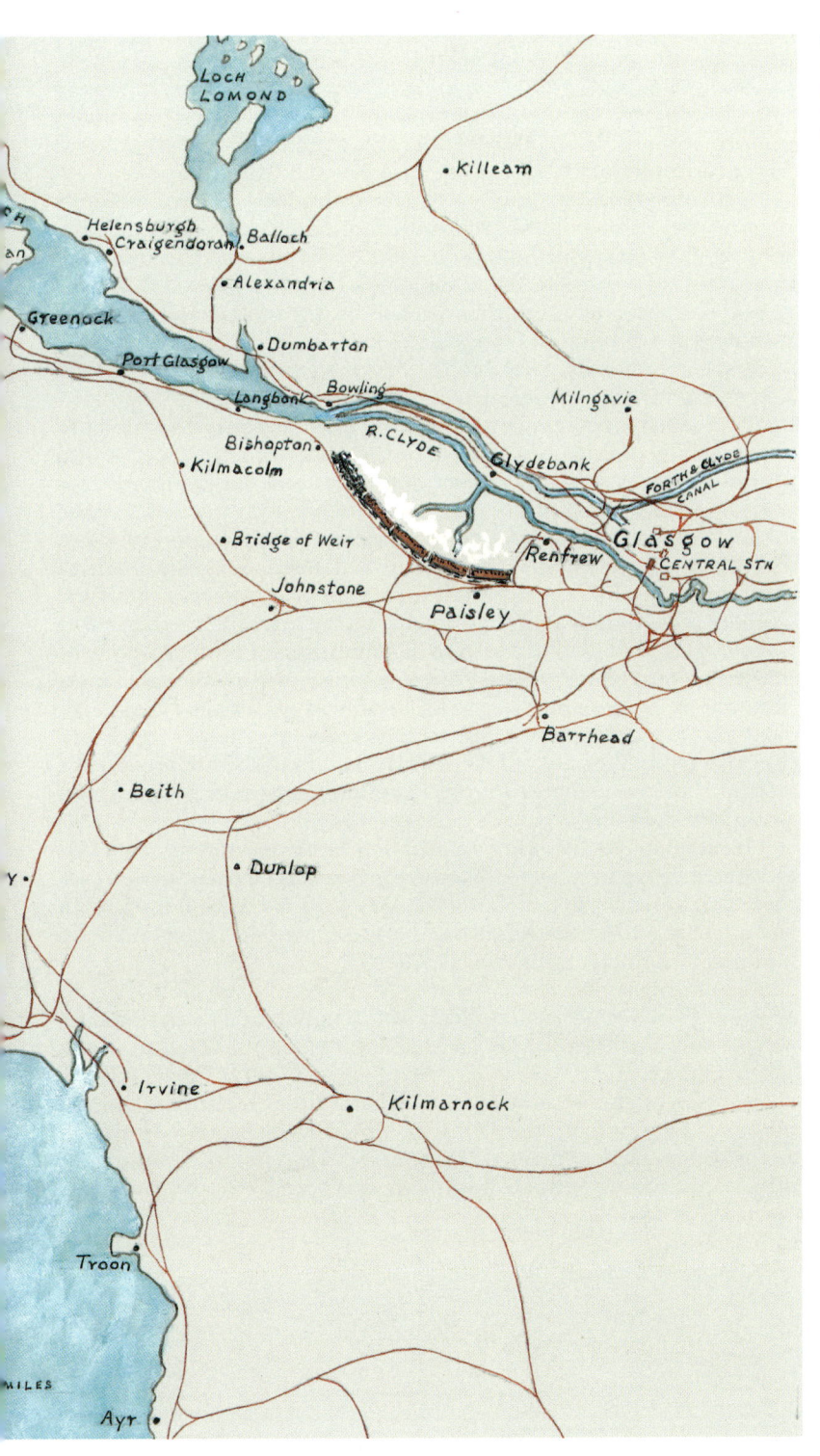

This route map from Glasgow to the island of Bute, was provided by Edward W. Paget – Tomlinson.

On the back of this snapshot, I had made the following note - "Mess 33 on *Forth*. One can clearly see the confined space for eating and sleeping. There are two messes, but we don't all eat at the same time owing to some chaps being on watch. There is usually about 10 of us at a time. The lockers are on the left, and our hammocks slung above. You can see the trouble we have finding a place to sleep sometimes. I've been ashore more times than I have slept aboard." September, 1946.

tions, and an abundance of portholes. All manner of equipment in various spaces was tidily lashed and stowed. I remember passing officers and petty officers of all ranks and dozens of ratings, some in uniform, others in overalls, all going about their duties diligently and with determination.

Arriving at Mess 33, I found two lads, obviously off duty, leisurely reading at the mess table. I introduced myself to them, and they showed me a spare locker into which I could stow my gear. Among many things I wanted to know was where I would sleep. 'Don't know mate, you'll have to wait until everyone's slung theirs,' was the reply, meaning, of course, that I would have to wait until 'pipe down' to see what space there was available to sling my hammock, and whether there were two spare hooks to hang it from.

The Mess arrangement was similar to a lay-by on a main thoroughfare—just an open area, recessed off a main gangway, with no doors into it or out. Opposite the mess area was another large open space for bringing through equipment to various parts of the ship. There were two long wooden tables, with benches on both sides. There were no portholes. Fixed to the bulkhead along the whole of one side and at the two ends were rows of metal lockers, one of which was allocated to each man for his personal possessions. The mess area was all open plan, and exposed to all and sundry whether on duty or off; everyone used the gangways and open spaces to reach their destination, it never stopped. The deckhead of both the mess area itself and the open space opposite was covered in hooks welded to the deckhead. Naturally, all the regulars had their reserved spaces for sleeping, and on no account could another take it over; certainly not a new boy like me.

I anticipated this might be a problem, as being a new arrival I had to work my way in. I was expected to sling my hammock wherever there might be a space available, as long as it did not interfere with anyone else, and I wouldn't know this until 'pipe down' when all the 'old hands' had taken up their positions.

Word got around about my arrival, and one of the crew from an adjoining mess came to me with an instruction; I didn't know who he was, nor where he stood in the pecking order, but whatever I was asked on the first day, I was pleased to do it, and wanted to get it right. 'Go down to the engine room and see the Chief Engineer, and ask him for a long weight,' the rating said. 'Right, I'll go now,' I replied, and asked him where the engine room was. I was pointed in the right direction, and told roughly how to get there, and I set off.

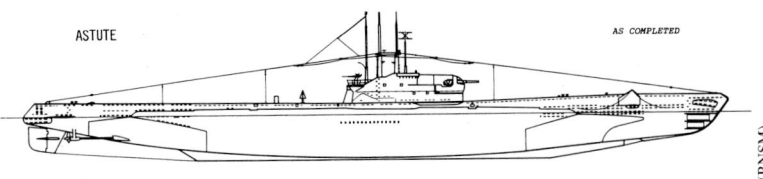

Outline profile of *Astute*.

All down these ladders again, up and along and down and across, in and out and down and down again. At last, I reached the engine room, and asked someone if I could see the Chief Engineer. After a few minutes, the Chief Engineer appeared, and I said to him 'I've been sent down to see you to ask for a long weight.' 'Right,' he said, 'sit down there.' 'Aye, Aye, Sir,' I said, and sat down on some coiled rope.

I waited a good half-hour, and when I saw him coming towards me, I said 'Oh, any chance of having that long weight?' He looked at me and a smile began to crease his face. 'You're having it,' he said.

The penny dropped, and I burst out laughing, and so did he. 'They all fall for it on the first day,' he said, putting his hand on my shoulder. 'Good luck,' he said, 'you'll be all right.' Realising I had been dropped in it, I did feel a bit of a fool; at least I felt I had broken the ice.

On my return to the mess my two new friends greeted me with smiles and laughter; they knew by the length of time I had been away that I had fallen for it. It seemed my initiation ceremony was over, and the three of us remained good friends over the following months that we lived together on *Forth*. I heard later that earlier in the day another new arrival had been sent down to the engine room to collect a bucket of steam.

My first day was a long one, taking into consideration the travelling and a certain amount of anxiety that went with my drafting orders. Hiking a full kitbag and attache case about was just about bearable, but the burden of a packed hammock as well took some carrying, but it wasn't over yet. As with hammock space, the same code applied to reserved positions at the mess table; my two messmates indicated where there was an available seat. We all had supper, chatted, and got to know one a little more, and in due course it was time to 'sling hammocks'.

Triumph, one of the "Colossus" class of Light Fleet Aircraft Carriers, was seen from time to time in the Firth of Clyde. Built by Hawthorn Leslie, Hebburn-on-Tyne, in 1942, and completed 9 April, 1946, she displaced 13,350 tons. Length 695 feet overall, and beam across flight deck 112 feet 6 ins. Bran new and showing herself off here in May, 1946.

The Fleet Aircraft Carrier *Implacable* and destroyers *Onslaught* and *Hesperus*. A view from Forth on 26 October, 1946.

As with everything else in the Navy, there was a recognised procedure set out in the *Seaman's Manual* for slinging a hammock. The 'hammock' was the canvas part, having 16 holes in each end, usually fitted with eyelets. It was slung by 'clews', a set of clews consisting of two lanyards, each spliced to its metal ring, each ring carrying eight 'nettles' (six-foot lengths of three-stranded white hemp 5/8th inch in circumference), for slinging the two ends of the hammock. The nettles are first middled, with the eye so formed secured with a racking seizing: the eye is passed through the ring and secured by passing the two ends through the eye. As each nettle has two ends, sixteen ends were thus provided, one for each eyelet hole in the end of the hammock. The 'lashing' was a length of sisal long enough to allow seven turns to be taken round the hammock and secured to its own part. The lashing had an eye-splice at one end and could be 'pointed' at the other.

SECURING THE CLEWS OF A HAMMOCK

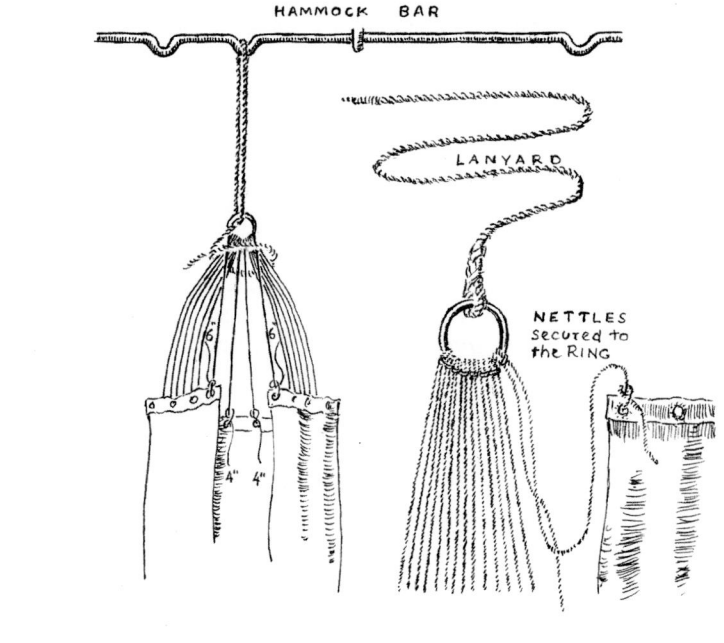

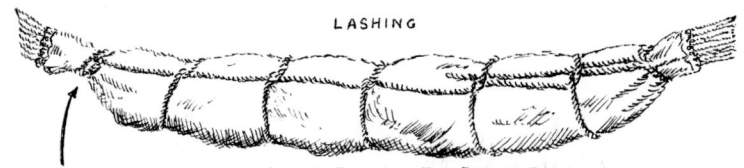

HAMMOCK BAR

LANYARD

NETTLES secured to the RING

LASHING

THE FIRST TURN IS PASSED THROUGH THE EYE OF THE LASHING
THE NEXT FIVE TURNS ARE MARLINE-HITCHED
THE LAST TURN IS HALF-HITCHED TO ITS OWN PART.

Edward W. Paget-Tomlinson

To sling the hammock one had to secure one lanyard to the hammock bar overhead (in my case we had hooks welded to the deckhead) so that the ends of the nettles hung at the level of the chest. Passing the outer nettles through the outer corner eyelet holes at one end of the hammock, one secured them by a half-hitch, leaving about six inches of the ends hanging down. Then one took the two nettles nearest the centre and secured them to their corresponding eyelet holes in the centre of the hammock-end, leaving about four inches hanging down. Next one secured the remaining nettles in a similar manner from the centre outwards, leaving increasing lengths of end hanging, and repeated this with the other end of the hammock and the other clews. Then one had to plait the ends of the nettles up in threes, leaving them inside the hammock.

One slung the hammock between two hammock hooks by passing the lanyard over the hook, back up through its own ring, and then forming a sheet bend over the nettles. All that remained was to distribute the bedding evenly over the length of the hammock and tauten up the slack nettles if necessary.

To keep the head of the hammock apart, a 'stretcher' could be used, but this was optional. This consisted of a length of wood about two feet in length with a V cut out at both ends, these Vs taking over the top two nettles on each side.

There were also regulation instructions as regards lashing up a hammock, and with this one had first to distribute the bedding evenly over the length of the hammock, leaving about six inches clear at each end to prevent bunches of bedding and blankets oozing out of the ends when it was lashed.

The hammock then had to be lowered until it was breast high, and you would stand on the left side facing the head. The lashing was passed over the hammock and the end rove through the eye and drawn taut; this was the first turn. The succeeding turns were as follows: The lashing had to be coiled up and passed up and over the hammock with the right hand and brought under the hammock into the left hand, then over its own standing part and hauled taut by swinging on it. This hitch was called a marline hitch. The final turn was taken around the neck of the hammock at the foot and was secured on its own part by a half-hitch. The end was then passed neatly along the hammock under each turn.

The clews were stowed by twisting the nettles round right-handed and tucking under the turns of lashing along the hammock.

At first all this seemed terribly complicated, but in practice, after doing it a few times, it was very easy and both the slinging and lashing up could be done within a few minutes.

Every morning after lashing up the hammocks had to be stowed in a 'pen' just a short distance down the gangway from our mess. In our mess there were ten of us, with another ten in the adjoining mess. Each mess had different meal times, but at night in this confined environment, everyone was in the same place, doing the same things at the same time. While some were undressing, others were unlashing their hammocks at the same time as a few were climbing into theirs, rocking from side to side as they did so. Others were opening the folds of their blanket and flopping one end over the hammock, prior to climbing in. While all this was happening there was a continuous flow of crew passing through to the gangways, albeit in smaller numbers. There seemed to be no streamlining of all these practices, nor any arrangement for all this to be done in shifts.

Neither was there any system as regards squaring up hammocks to form orderly lines. I read somewhere that there was a regulation distance of 24 inches between hammocks, but this did not work in practice. Hammocks were slung haphazardly at different angles, some with their head pointed at another's waist, some feet first near another's head, and everyone facing in different directions. Spaces varied considerably from about 12 inches away from another at the feet end to perhaps 36 inches away at the head. Looking up from the deck, it was like seeing a mass of canvas cocoons.

The practice of slinging a hammock was pretty simple after having a few goes at it. In the slung position, one usually draped the blanket over the hammock so it hung down on both sides, ready to lever yourself on to the blanket, and once in you wrapped the overhanging ends over you. One's weight inside the hammock tended to draw the strings tight and stretched the edges of the canvas at the head and foot towards a closed position. A stretcher was used at the head position to stretch the strings apart and kept the canvas edges away from your face.

It was usual to sleep in one's underclothes, and to keep your socks on, just in case there was an emergency when one would be at least partially dressed. It was also quite usual to place one's boots at the head with rolled up clothes on top to form a pillow. When in your hammock in the period before 'pipe down' this was more often than not the time for reading a newspaper or magazine, and also an ideal

A very fine view of *Affray* with her name plate clearly visible, making headway. After commissioning on 12 November, 1945, she joined the 5th Submarine Flotilla at H.M.S. *Dolphin*, and in May, 1946, was accepted by the Royal Navy. By October, 1946, she was with the 3rd Submarine Flotilla at Rothesay, when I saw her on a number of occasions.

Wright & Logan

Outline profile of *Affray*.

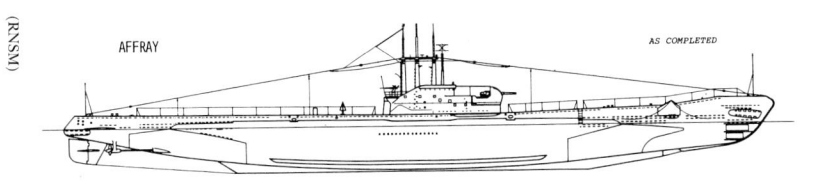

time for writing a letter. However people occupied themselves before lights out, their unfinished books, magazines, papers and letters were left until the morning, and lashed up inside your hammock to finish the next night.

Even after lights out, it was some while before you could get to sleep. You had to wait until everyone stopped walking about on your deck, since quite frequently, by not stooping or bending low enough when making their way through your section, people would give your hammock the occasional knock.

That first night I became a little desperate, since it seemed there was not a vacant space anywhere to sling my hammock. No-one seemed particularly helpful, and I was reticent about pushing myself forward on my first night aboard. I considered there was nothing else for it but to find a quiet corner somewhere and make the best of it. I settled for what I thought was a suitable place in a sheltered corner between bulkheads, outside on deck. It was summer time, a fine night, and in the circumstances, I thought that that was the best thing I could do. This will suffice for my first night, I thought, but tomorrow I would get this sorted out once and for all.

On my first day on board, I made the following note in my diary.

> 2 August 1946. Came aboard *Forth*, allotted a mess and got a rough idea of goings on. Nothing happening until 0830 tomorrow morning, report to Regulating Officer. Two subs and destroyer in. Subs—Ventura (P68) Aeneas (P427) Destroyer 103.

Next morning, I raised the matter of sleeping accommodation with my mess mates, and none of them realised I hadn't found a pitch. By one of them moving his hammock one hook to his left, and another adjoining hammock using a spare hook to his right, sufficient space was provided for me. As it turned out, this position suited me fine, since immediately above me was a giant girder, the flanges of which were particularly useful for levering myself both into and out of my hammock.

On the second day, everything was falling into place. I now had a locker, a place at the mess table, and somewhere to sleep. I had made friends and had been accepted as a messmate, and as one of the crew. I had also spent some time in the Communications Office familiarising myself with the layout and equipment, and I was able to catch up on some news about *Forth*, the first being that the Captain's name was W. S. Woods and another that *Forth* had fairly recently replaced the submarine depot ship *Cyclops* in Rothesay Bay.

Aeneas surfaced in Rothesay Bay, 12 August, 1946.

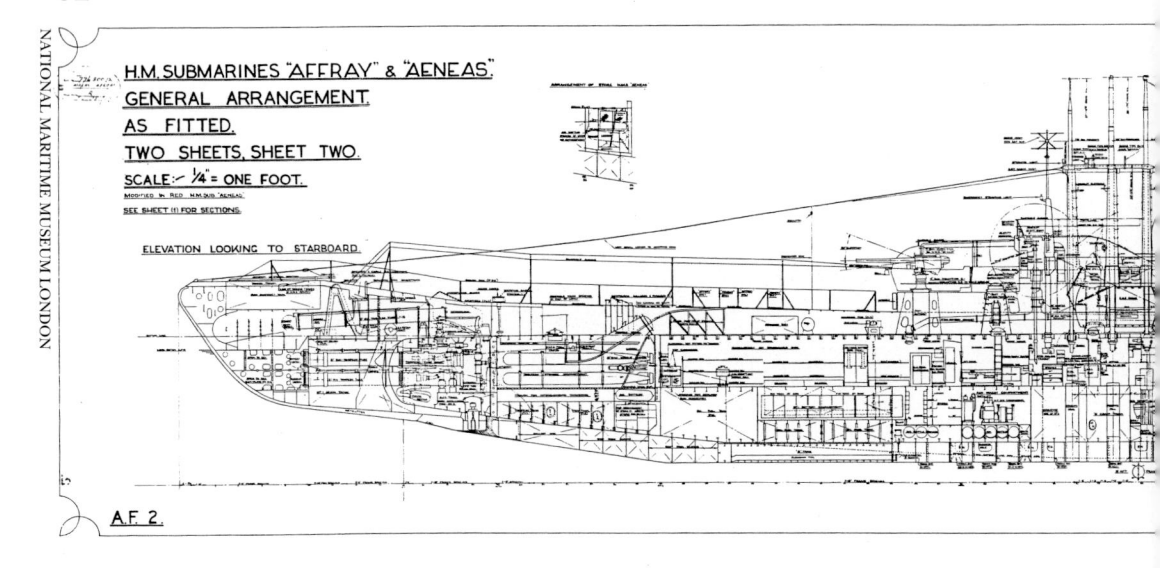

The *Cyclops* had for most of the war been stationed in Rothesay. She was a rather dirty coal-burning vessel built in 1905 as the merchant ship *Indrabarah*. She was commissioned as a repair/depot ship 5th November, 1907, and was with the Home Fleet at Scapa Flow

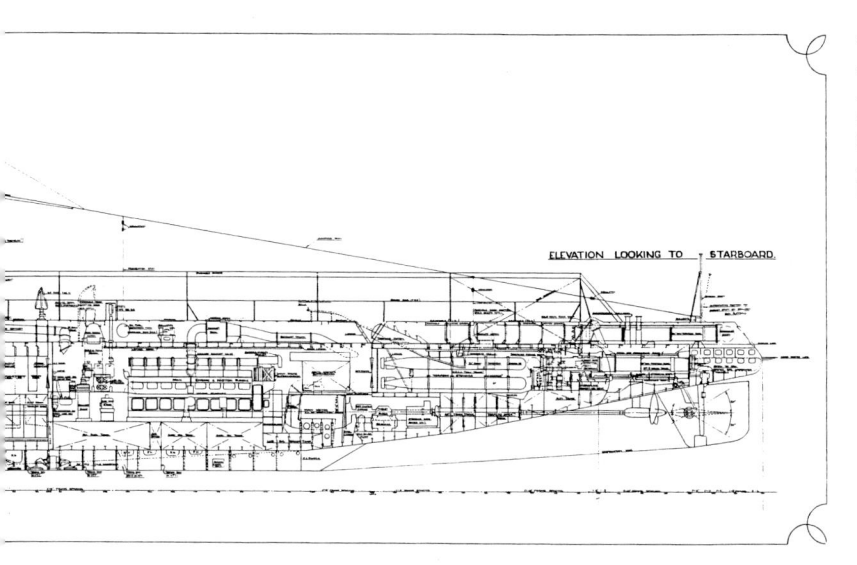

The profiles of A-class submarine *Affray* and *Aeneas* reduced from original drawings of 1/4 - 1 foot. Modifications for *Aeneas* were shown in Red but no date was given.

in the First World War. Between 1920 and 1922 she was converted to a submarine depot ship, and in June, 1940, came to Rothesay as depot ship of the 7th Submarine Flotilla. She was paid off in 1945. *Cyclops* had a displacement of 11,300 tons and was 477 feet long overall and 55 feet beam. She had a coal capacity of 1595 tons, and a complement of 266.

As a depot ship she was inadequate and uncomfortable. She had been due to be scrapped earlier, but owing to the shortage of shipping because of the war she was temporarily saved. Submariners used to refer to her as 'Cycle Box'. In spite of *Cyclops* being old and rather smoky, she and her crew were well regarded by everyone in Rothesay.

The Buteman, Friday 1st February, 1946

H.M.S. 'Cyclops' Farewell

An outstanding feature of Rothesay Bay since 1940, H.M.S. *Cyclops*, submarine depot ship, is expected to sail soon for a southern port, and will probably be decommissioned thereafter. She has been out of the Bay all this week and up-river in preparation for her departure from the Clyde, but it was expected that she would be back this weekend. The officers had arranged an 'At Home' for local guests for tomorrow (Saturday) evening, but the date of this function has been postponed until it is definitely known when the ship will return from the upper reaches of the Firth. A 'Farewell Dance' will be held in the Pavilion on Wednesday evening.

As depot ship of the 7th Submarine Flotilla, *Cyclops* played an important part in the war, and a great many officers and men attached

The A-class submarine *Aeneas* was the very first submarine I saw when I joined my ship *Forth* at Rothesay in August, 1946. Built by Cammell Laird, Birkenhead, she was launched 25 October, 1945, and photographed here soon after commissioning on 24 May, 1946. Source unknown.

to her won distinction for outstanding gallantry in face of the enemy. A number of them had their wives and families resident in the Burgh and island, and Rothesay, having the honour of being their Post Office address, appeared frequently in lists of decorations and awards. It is estimated that about 95 per cent. of the crews of British, as well as a number of Allied submarines, spent part of their training and rest periods here.

Cyclops is one of the oldest ships in the Navy. Very few of her original crew are now with her, many of them having been reservists and now demobbed, but the citizens of the Burgh and island will bid farewell to her with much regret. Officers and men of the ship's company have throughout the war years played an active and beneficial part in local affairs and have contributed greatly in work, cash, and charitable causes. Happy associations have been formed which will endure for many years after *Cyclops* has cast loose from her moorings in Rothesay Bay for the last time.

The Buteman, Friday 8th February, 1946

H.M.S. 'Cyclops'—Farewell Functions

H.M.S. *Cyclops*, the submarine depot ship which has since the summer of 1940 been a conspicuous feature of Rothesay Bay, is scheduled to leave at 2 p.m. today. Officers and crew of the ship, and of the submarines attached to her, constituting the 7th Submarine Flotilla, have for so long formed a part of the Burgh's life that the departure of the ship, even

Cyclops photographed here in June, 1935, was the first of the depot ships to arrive at Rothesay in 1939, when she became depot ship of the 7th Submarine Flotilla. *Forth* replaced her at Rothesay in 1946, as depot ship of the 3rd Submarine Flotilla, when *Cyclops* was towed away to be scrapped.

though as seems probable, it will be followed by the arrival of another depot ship, is felt to be an occasion to be commemorated. Through the vicissitudes of war, *Cyclops* and her attendant submarines were objects of much interest to both residents and visitors. Submarines sailed from Rothesay from time to time on operational and training duties. Several did not return, and although, with the veil of secrecy necessarily drawn over war operations, these could not be mentioned, the community sorrowed with the bereaved wives and relatives. Members of others were decorated for brave deeds done during their tours of duty, and though again the censor drew the veil over the locations, Rothesay shared in the congratulations to these gallant men.

It was therefore fitting that the occasion of the ship's leave-taking this week should be commemorated. *Cyclops* is one of the oldest ships in the Navy, and it is likely that after being decommissioned this spring, on her return south, she will not figure for long on the Navy list.

'H.M.S. Pavilion' Dance

Early on Wednesday evening Captain Ingram and the Ward Room Officers entertained Provost Muir, the Magistrates, and a number of friends to an 'At Home' on the ship, and later in the evening the Burgh repaid the compliment by entertaining over 350 of the officers and crew, together with friends, at a Farewell Dance in the Pavilion.

Council Chambers Ceremony

Yesterday forenoon Capt. Ingram and senior officers of *Cyclops* visited the Council Chambers, and were entertained by the Provost and Magistrates to light refreshments. Provost Muir, in welcoming them, said we had come to regard *Cyclops* as part of our town. She had been here over five years. Personnel had come and gone, and the job they came to do had been completed. They had contributed to our sense of security during the war. He was sure the Commanders had many anxious moments as their ships went into enemy waters, and for the citizens, it made for a feeling that they were playing a part in the war. The Burgh had been very happy to have *Cyclops* and the 7th Submarine Flotilla, but the time had now come to say good-bye. Officers and men of the ship would be welcome back any time they wished to re-visit our town. He wished them God speed, a good journey, and blessings where ever they were.

Enjoyed Their Stay

Captain Ingram, replying, thanked Provost Muir for his very kind sentiments. He would like to repeat what he had said several times before, that they had inflicted themselves on the Burgh, requisitioned houses, and generally broken things up—(laughter)—but the citizens had taken it in good part, and they left here with very genuine regret. Speaking for all the ship's company, they had enjoyed themselves

Woodbridge Haven and the "Intrepid' class destroyer *Icarus*, which was broken up at Troon in 1947. 26 October, 1946.

because they had been made so welcome, and would remember Rothesay all their days. They wished the Councillors and the Burgh the very best of luck.

Commander Morgan, speaking as 'almost the oldest inhabitant', said he thought how lucky it had been for the 7th Submarine Flotilla to have been stationed at Rothesay, with its magnificent Pavilion, three cinemas, their Church of Scotland canteen, where the maximum of sleepers for one night had been 500, and other facilities. It was very nice for sailors to get away from their ships, even if only for a few pints of beer. They had been very happy here. On behalf of the lower deck he would like to say how much they appreciated all the kindness and facilities given them.

A Memento

Captain Ingram said the ship's company wanted to leave a memento with Rothesay, so they were having the ship's crest cast in brass, and would send it to the Provost when completed.

Provost Muir said the people of Rothesay would appreciate this very much indeed. It would be a valuable addition to the crests already on the chamber walls.

The Pavilion Management had spared no pains to make the dance a red letter night. As the guests entered the lobby, they saw the representation of a ship's bridge and a scenic view of Rothesay Bay. Both walls of the lobby carried imitation portholes, and the rooms entering from it were marked as 'Admiral's Quarters', 'Captain's Quarters', 'Cabin', etc. On the first flight of stairs was 'the Quarter-Deck', above it still further up 'Spirit Room', 'Mess Room' and so on. The ballroom was brilliant with flags and

The S-class submarine *Safari*, built by Cammell Laird, Birkenhead, was commissioned 14 March, 1942. In November, 1943, *Safari* joined Submarine Depot Ship *Forth* and the 3rd Submarine Flotilla at Holy Loch, and in 1944, joined Submarine Depot Ship *Cyclops* and the 7th Submarine Flotilla at Rothesay. *Safari* had an outstanding service record and was the 7th highest scoring British submarine of World War II damaging and sinking a total of 51,839 tons of shipping. Subsequent commanders in late December, 1943 and 1944, were Lt Cdr. DAB Abdy and Lt. JRG Harvey. *Safari* was photographed here in September, 1943. "RN Photographs".

(RNSM)

coloured lights, and having a place of honour on the stage was the *Cyclops* bell. *The Buteman* reported on the celebrations and entertainment, which included a sprightly exhibition of sword dancing and other contributions. Apart from *Cyclops* officers and crew, and the friends who came with them, there was a large attendance of the public generally, and the total was not far short of a thousand.

In January, 1946, one of the submarines attached to the 7th Submarine Flotilla based on *Cyclops* all through the war sank in the English Channel on her way to the breakers. This was reported in *The Buteman* on 11th January, 1946.

'Down for the Last Time'—End of Submarine Safari

The British submarine *Safari* which, during the war, did brilliant work in the Mediterranean, sank in the English Channel on Monday night while on her way to the shipbreakers. The Admiralty stated that no one was on board and no lives were lost.

Towed by a tug, she left Portsmouth Dockyard on Monday night for Newport, Mon, to be broken up. Off St. Albans Head, Dorset, the tug crew suddenly felt a jar. The navigation lights in *Safari* flickered, and she tilted and dived for the last time.

Her war service was chiefly in the Mediterranean, under the command successively of Commander Ben Bryant and Lieut.-Commander R. B. Lakin, and she and her crew were well-known in Rothesay, to whose waters she returned from her trips of derring do.

Under the former, *Safari* sank or damaged 34 enemy vessels, and under the latter, 45 vessels including a U-boat.

About six weeks before I joined *Forth*, I was told, the ship had been on summer exercises, and this was reported in *The Buteman*.

The Buteman–28th June, 1946

Admiral of Submarines—In Rothesay on Sunday

A very notable visitor to Rothesay on Sunday will be Rear-Admiral G. E. Creasy, C.B., C.B.E., D.S.O., M.V.O., R.N., Admiral (Submarines), after the summer war exercises which he has been conducting during the past week in the Irish Sea and North Western Approaches. He will arrive on H.M.S. *Woodbridge Haven* which will be flying his flag. Taking part in these exercises were sixteen submarines of the 3rd, 5th and 7th Submarine Flotillas, H.M.S. *Woodbridge Haven*, H.M.S. *Forth*, and destroyers and escort vessels. The *Forth* was back at her usual stance on Wednesday, and the rest of the Force will steam into the Bay on Tuesday, leaving here either on the 4th or the 5th, with the exception of the 3rd Submarine Flotilla. Visitors will not be able to inspect any of the ships in the Bay on Sunday in view of the fact that the programme entails an amount of preparation and organisation.

"DOWN FOR THE LAST TIME"
S-class submarine *Safari* at Portsmouth on her return from the Mediterranean in September, 1943. *Safari*, which during the war, did brilliant work in the Mediterranean, sank in the English Channel in the early days of January, 1946, while on her way to the shipbreakers. The Admiralty stated that no one was on board and no lives were lost. Towed by a tug, she left Portsmouth Dockyard for Newport, to be broken up. Off St Albans Head, Dorset, the tug crew suddenly felt a jar. The navigation lights in the *Safari* flickered, and she tilted and dived for the last time.

Her war service was chiefly in the Mediterranean, under the command successively of Commander Ben Bryant, and Lieut-Commander R.B. Lakin, and she and her crew were well-known in Rothesay to whose waters she returned form her trips of derring do.

Under the former, *Safari* sank or damaged 34 enemy vessels, and under the latter, 45 vessels including a U-boat.

"The Buteman, 11 January, 1946".

Woodbridge Haven was a Depot and Repair ship for Coastal craft, built by Swan Hunter, between 1944-1945. She frequently visited Rothesay in 1946 and 1947. Displacement 1,652 tons, length 307 feet 4 inches, and beam 38 feet 6 inches. This picture was taken in July, 1947.

Taken from *Forth* on 26 October, 1946, the Light Fleet Aircraft Carrier *Theseus*, and destroyers *Onslaught* and *Hesperus* at Rothesay.

The teleprinters on board *Forth* seemed identical to those on which I had been trained, and I felt quite happy about my position in the Communications Office. Finding my way around the ship, though, was going to take a few days; there were going to be parts of it where I would probably never need to go at all.

Meanwhile, there were many things to learn, not the least of which was the location of the NAAFI stores. Crew could buy almost unlimited supplies of cigarettes from the NAAFI at duty free prices, around ninepence (4p) for a packet of 20. On 'stand easy' there was always a rush to form a queue for cigarettes ('coffin nails'), tobacco ('tickler'), and confectionery ('nutty'). One learnt quickly that lavatories were 'heads' and 'grog' was rum issue, only made to men over 20 years of age, and that the call that woke you in the morning was 'Heavo, Heavo, Lash up and Stow' (your hammocks), though in practice there were numerous alternatives to this, some of which were very choice. As in Training Establishments, the boat that took you ashore was the 'liberty boat'. 'Dhobi' was washing and 'Rabbits' were presents.

At Shore Establishments, all notices of the day were displayed on a Notice Board, and you were expected to read these every day. On board all orders were 'piped' through the tannoy system all over the ship, and everyone heard them at the same time. Mess tidyness was arranged amicably between ourselves, when tables and benches were scrubbed floors swept and washed, and utensils cleaned and tidied. All these chores had to be done in spick and span fashion in readiness for regular inspections.

The day began at 0630 with either physical training or cleaning ship for an hour or so before breakfast, which included such dishes as sausages in gravy, bacon and tomato, fried egg, etc. For dinner at around 1230 we had lamb stew and dumplings with a choice of potatoes, cabbage and beans, spotted dick, brown Windsor soup and the like. There was teabreak at around 1600, and supper at 1900. Cold suppers included corned beef, beetroot/lettuce, while hot ones were perhaps rissoles/fish cakes and mashed potatoes. Sundays were always a little more special, with meat, such as roast pork/roast beef/ chicken and roast potatoes, followed by fruit cake and puddings.

At meal times 'cooks to the galley' was piped. Each mess had a rota of two at a time for collecting and preparing the food from the galley, serving it, washing up afterwards and clearing away all the leftovers. Food scraps and remains, cigarette ends and the like were collected in a bucket, known as the 'gash bucket', and this had to be carried up on deck and tipped into a 'gash chute', a steel trunking fixed over the side. One had to take the precaution of averting one's face in times of strong wind. I was introduced to this chore very quickly, being a new messmate; I had no difficulty in locating the gash chute, since there was always a flock of seagulls in attendance hovering and squawking around the chute vent on deck and pecking over the discarded spoils at sea level.

A great deal has been written and spoken about Forces food, and I would not want to be too ungracious about the food, nor the cooks when it comes to the meals we had prepared on board. Neither would I wish to be at variance with those of my colleagues in the various complaints broadcast from time to time. It is customary, and traditional perhaps, to ridicule the food dished up at meal times, whether or not the criticism is justified, and whether the preparation, cooking and presentation deserved it.

Normally there was very little to complain about with regards to the ingredients themselves. Presumably on *Forth* the produce arrived by liberty boat from local suppliers in the town of Rothesay. While there might be some truth in unfavourable comments on the cooking side, in the main I found the meals acceptable. Some of the dishes arrived half cooked, sometimes the eggs were runny, on occasions the dumplings were inclined to be leaden and the vegetables soggy. To be fair, accepting the scale of the preparation process, the cooking times and readiness, I found the dishes were

A German destroyer before being towed away and blown up. Rothesay, October, 1946.

Writing home.

The A-class submarine *Auriga* seen here, was for a time attached to the 3rd Submarine Flotilla based on *Forth* during the summer of 1946, at Rothesay. *Auriga* was built by Vickers-Armstrong, Barrow, and was launched 29 March, 1945, and commissioned 24 September, the same year.

Alaric was another of the A-class boats which spent some time at Rothesay during 1946 and 1947. She was built by Cammell Laird, Birkenhead, launched 18 February, 1946, and commissioned the same year. Source unknown.

Night watch working on Teleprinters in the Communications Office on *Forth*. The blue jean collar was dispensed with in night duty attire. September, 1946.

agreeable. One had to discount the time it took for 'mess cooks' to bring the meals from the galley to the mess and serve it, when sometimes the food was not as hot as one would have wished. Without hesitation, I cannot remember a time when there was a case for rejecting any meal, and consigning it to the 'gash bucket'. It was no good having a fad, if you didn't eat what was prepared, you went hungry.

Normally, there was about a quarter of an hour 'stand easy' around 0945 when there was a rush to the NAAFI to buy confectionery and biscuits, and a mug of tea or hot chocolate.

On board also was the 'Pusser's Stores' which sold everything of Naval issue, needles and thread, underclothes and replacements for maintenance of uniforms and kit. I recall I purchased a Christmas card from the Pusser's Stores which had a small photograph of *Forth* for posting home.

My duties as teleprinter operator in the Communications Office worked out well. The work was interesting, and I was able to put into practice everything I had been taught. In addition to communicating with various Naval bases, the Admiralty, other ships, submarines and Shore Establishments, we were in direct communication with the Bridge, and frequently my duties included manning it. The Training Establishment at *Scotia* had done a good job in training me to play my part in the Communications Branch of *Forth*. The Communications Office was rather basic in appearance, and the equipment, tubular chairs and dangling wiring was untidy, but this was my office, and I felt comfortable working in it.

Dress during the working day was either No 2 uniform when on watch or off duty and blue working overalls for washing down, scrubbing and cleaning decks. After 1600 when on watch 'night attire' was No 2 uniform but the blue jean collar was dispensed with. When off duty, one usually relaxed, wearing the jersey only and dispensing with the serge jumper.

I cannot recall with complete accuracy how much the pay was for an Ordinary Signalman at this time; it was about £1. 3s. (£1.15) a week, and was paid every two weeks. To collect this, full uniform had to be worn, and one had to line up with the others before the Paymaster with officers in attendance. As your turn came, it was usually the job of a Chief Petty Officer to order 'Salute, off Cap, Name and Number!'

On my first day ashore, I decided to take out a rowing boat to see if I could get closer to the ship to take some photographs. I only had my Baby Brownie camera, and in the few photographs I managed to take, *Forth* still looks a long way off, although she was lying comparatively close to the shore. I did wonder whether the effort of rowing all that way, further than I envisaged, was worth it, since the sea could have been calmer, and it was very strenuous, but at least I had my first picture of my ship to send home.

In September, 1946, I was called as a witness over an incident that happened ashore. It wasn't a particularly serious affair, but never-the-less the matter had to be investigated, and an enquiry was held on board. Present at the hearing was the Captain, the Lieut.-Commander, the Officer of the Watch, the Regulating Officer and a small escort.

I found the experience of being present at such an enquiry tense and somewhat nerve-racking, but it gave me an insight into procedural matters and how the Navy dealt with breaches of behaviour. I was called to 'the table' on two occasions, and the hearing lasted ten days.

First thing in the morning, and after 1600 until around 2130, Mess decks were supplied with music piped through by sound reproduction equipment. This was usually a pleasant mixture of stirring marches played by brass bands and popular modern and dance music. I enjoyed this immensely, and so did everyone since most sang, whistled or hummed the melodies as one followed another, whilst everyone got on with their letter writing or reading. Although the mess had an open environment, situated as it was off a main gangway, a feeling of relaxation was present. One got used to all and sundry walking through the gangway past our mess, and it was quite possible to sink into a state of oblivion and not be aware of them at all. Most of us smoked cigarettes or tobacco, some more than others, but there was plenty of fresh air coming into the mess area from vents in the ducting, so the atmosphere was not unbearable.

Off duty, some read papers, magazines and books, others wrote letters, caught up on their sewing and mending, washing and ironing, and the odd one or two used to slump over the table with their heads on crossed arms, snoozing, perhaps after a late night ashore.

On the same day, I hired a rowing boat to get nearer to *Forth* to take some photographs, and soon realised that she was further away than she looked from the shore.

A good view of *Affray* taken at sea January, 1946. Only commissioned two months earlier, this photograph could have been taken when she was at Birkenhead for acceptance trials, or enroute to Rothesay for alterations. Source unknown.

(RNSM)

The submarine *Venturer* is pictured here at Holy Loch on 28 August, 1942. Proudly bearing Norwegian place names, three former British submarines left Rothesay Bay for Norway in the latter part of September, 1946. Transfer of these vessels to the Royal Norwegian Navy was effected at a ceremony aboard H.M.S. *Forth* on Thursday 5th September, 1946, when Commodore J.E.Jakobsen, O.B.E. accepted on behalf of his Service. Present at the ceremony was Rear Admiral G.E. Creasy, C.B. C.B.E. D.S.O., Flag Officer Submarines and Captain W.S.Woods, of H.M.S *Forth* and the Third Submarine Flotilla. A Marines band played British and Norwegian National Anthems as *Venturer* became *Utstein*, *Votary* changed to *Utvaer*. Norwegian flags were broken on each craft as they passed into Allied hands.

Already closely linked with the Norwegian Navy, *Viking* and *Venturer* both built by Vickers-Armstrong at Barrrow-in-Furnace, and completed in 1943, operated off the coast of Norway with Norwegian submarines based at Dundee during the war. Then manned by British crews *Venturer* sank two U-boats in Norwegian waters and four ships: while *Viking* was credited with one vessel sunk and another badly damaged, besides working with the Coastal Command on training exercises of an operational nature. *Votary*, built by Vickers-Armstrong at Newcastle and commissioned in November, 1944 had operated with Western Approaches Training Command.

Both *Viking* and *Venturer* were put into reserve early in 1946. Norwegians took them over shortly before coming to Rothesay in July, 1946, for refit, repairs and trials. Their personnel normally consisted of 36 men with four officers. Quick-diving boats, they were very manoeuvrable. En-route to a Norwegian submarine base, they were due to touch at five ports, including Bergen and Trondheim.

Serving with Lieut, Commander Valvatne, D.S.O. D.S.C. of the *Votary*, on his earlier commands, the *Ula* and *Utsira*, were Lieuts. Hatlam-Olsen, and S.Strouslan, now in charge of *Viking* and *Venturer*. *Ula* is claimed to have been the first submarine to start the attack on German shipping off the Norwegian Coast.

"The Buteman 6 September, 1946".

Around this time, in September, 1946, I was all spruced up and dressed in my Number Ones, in haste to catch the first liberty boat ashore shortly after 1600. I was on my way to fall in for permission to leave the ship when I discovered I had forgotten my duty free cigarettes. Short of time, I dashed down below, making my way to the mess, cut a corner of the gangway short and banged my head on a flange jointing of a main vertical cast iron pipe, which stunned me momentarily. I stood there holding my head with a handkerchief, and I could see it was bleeding. An officer walking towards me stopped and asked me if I was all right. 'I think so, Sir, I've banged my head on this flange'. He looked at my head and said 'better go to sick bay and get it attended to'. 'Aye, Aye, Sir,' I said, and 'thank you'.

I never knew whether the sick bay I attended was for submarine crews or was the sick bay for the rest of the ship's company. By 1946, the two may have been amalgamated, but whichever it was, the sick bay was scrupulously clean and tidy, and very well equipped. It was also very quiet and peaceful, and indeed seemed so remote from all the activity just the other side of the door. The doctor decided that I should have three stitches, and after a few moments respite, I felt much better.

I told the doctor I was planning to go ashore for the evening, and he suggested I should take it easy for the rest of the day. 'Aye, Aye, Sir' I replied. I thanked him for his help, returned to the mess, and abandoned any further attempt to proceed ashore. The following morning I was fully recuperated and resumed my normal duties.

It was now September, and I had been on *Forth* for a month. I have mentioned earlier that on the day I joined *Forth* I had made a note in my diary of the vessels that were alongside, the submarine H.M.S. *Venturer* being one of them. At a ceremony on board *Forth* on Thursday, 5th September, three British submarines were handed over to the Royal Norwegian Navy, when *Venturer* became the *Utstein*. I have a picture of her taken during the latter years of the war, and a later one when she was in the hands of the Royal Norwegian Navy.

On the reverse of this photograph taken on 26 October, 1946, I made the following note - "Taken from *Forth* at Rothesay. The P421 is the submarine *Affray*. The destroyer is *Opportune*. The part of the ship where the submarines are alongside is called the "Well Deck". The submarine right alongside is *Aeneas* and the P338 is *Teredo*.

A rather shabby looking *Montclare*. This picture was taken in March, 1946, before docking at Portsmouth to be re-converted as a 21,000 ton Submarine Depot Ship. Although I had no idea at the time, she was due to take over the role of the *Forth* in May, 1947, as depot ship of the 3rd Submarine Flotilla at Rothesay.

A later picture of *Utstein* (ex Venturer) taken in 1951, looking very smart and seaworthy in the ownership of The Royal Norwegian Navy.

Myself on the Flag Deck of *Forth* at Rothesay, September, 1946.

I have already referred to the pleasure most of us derived from Sunday Divisions at Training Establishments, where we marched round the parade ground with a brass band playing. Every Sunday morning on *Forth*, as on every other ship in the Royal Navy, the ship's company assembled for Divisions and saluted the flag. I always enjoyed the ceremony of running up the White Ensign. It may have something to do with tradition; whatever it was that triggered deep inside of us a certain sense of pride in our country and respect for all that we stood for, it was stimulating and thought provoking.

Disciplinary procedure existed on board as it did at Training Establishments, and anyone found not properly dressed for duties that he was on at any particular time was subjected to a kit inspection; every article of clothing had to be meticulously laid out in order, each one labelled or marked with your name, and the kit layout had to be precise and complete.

The daily routine duties, when not on watch, included the seemingly endless scrubbing and hosing down decks. Summary punishment for minor offences often resulted in additional deck scrubbing on hands and knees, at the discretion of the Divisional Officer. An alternative or additional punishment could also include cancellation of shore leave.

As during our training, one continually had to allocate some free time to making and mending, washing and ironing and general kit maintenance to keep everything up to standard. On some ships and Establishments, Wednesday was usually allocated for this, but on *Forth* there was no specific time allocated and it was left to each man to see to his personal hygiene and to ensure that his kit was always at the required standard.

There was always one thing that you could never get away from, and that was from each other. We were all living and working in a close community, where on many occasions we all did the same things at the same time. The ablutions or 'heads' were usually crammed with fellow crew members, all jostling for the taps, basins and toilets, particularly at certain times in the mornings and evenings. At times, the commotion and hurly burly was indescribable. As part of our training, our Instructor impressed upon us the need to get on with one another, and in such confined and overcrowded situations as this there was no

Tribune was built by Scotts' Shipbuilding and Engineering, Co, Ltd, Greenock, and commissioned 17 October, 1939. *Tribune* had an active and successful service career during the war, patrolling the Atlantic, Bay of Biscay, and escorting convoys to Halifax and North Russia. She had a long refit in the latter part of 1941, and for a while was transferred to the 3rd Submarine Flotilla at Holy Loch, in late 1942. From June, 1943, *Tribune* was used as a training vessel until scrapped in July, 1947. "RN Photographs".

alternative. One soon learned, however, that opportunities did present themselves when there were less crowded moments in the washing areas, and it was often possible to take advantage of this.

It was refreshing, therefore, to go ashore, taking the full shore leave entitlement and staying overnight to regain independence and individuality, and I refer to this in more detail in a later chapter.

Meanwhile there was always plenty of daily activity on *Forth*, since it was normal to have a number of submarines alongside at any given time. Some were departing on sea trials and training exercises, others were returning from sea, manoeuvring, cleaning ship or carrying out maintenance work. These submarines were largely the A-class boats which had been built for action in the Pacific, though the war had ended before any of them entered service, but we also had T-class boats alongside from time to time and sometimes an S-class boat. Towards the end of September, 1946, Rothesay Bay became quite busy not only with submarines but also with other vessels arriving, including aircraft carriers, repair ships and destroyers. We even had a German destroyer brought in before being towed away to be blown up.

As already explained, the role of submarine depot ships was to maintain their submarines and provide comfort for their crews on returning from missions. Depot ships were either built as such or adapted from existing vessels, and played a particularly important role during wartime. No doubt crews of submarine depot ships were encouraged, from time to time, to join the Submarine Service, and this was probably a useful source of recruitment. In late September, 1946, an afternoon was set aside for any crew member of *Forth* to have an opportunity of being shown over one of the submarines alongside. There was no commitment or obligation, and it was intended only to stimulate interest.

Barry on the reflector on *Forth* in September, 1946.

About a dozen of us, from various branches of the ship, assembled on the Well Deck, from where we were escorted on to the deck of one of the submarines, and we climbed inside. I did not make a note of the name of the submarine at the time, and cannot now recall which one it was, but without a doubt it would have been an A-class. To me, it seemed like one long tube crammed full with pipes, wheels, instruments, cables, gauges and valves. Everything throughout was neat and tidily compacted and stowed.

Tribune at Blyth in 1941. Internal view in Control Room of Hydroplanes positions. Lieutenant G.M. Knoll (standing), with C.P.O. F. Miles on After Planes, and P.O. Cass on Fore Planes. Noll was lost in submarine *Untamed*. Source unknown.

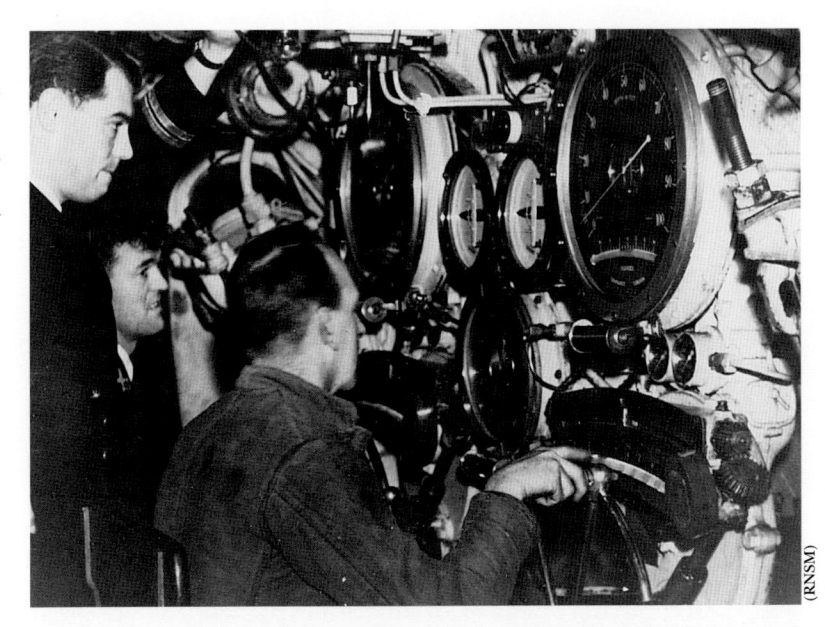

It all seemed terribly confined and enclosed, and I wondered how on earth a crew of anything up to 60 or so were able to spend days and nights at a stretch in such restricted conditions. It was obvious one had to be of the right temperament to be in the Submarine Service, and to be able to adapt to such demanding conditions. I had nothing but admiration for the designers and builders of such an intricate and complex assembly of engineering, and nothing but praise for the bravery of those who served in them.

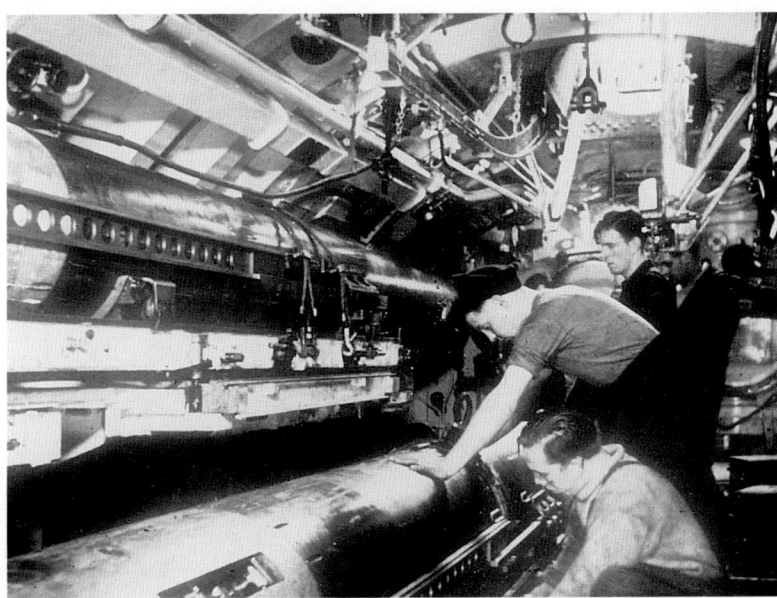

Working on torpedoes in *Tribune*. Internal view of Torpedo Stowage in Fore End. Source unknown.

(RNSM)

Submarine *Tribune*.
Internal view of Tube space looking forward Port side. Source unknown.

The T-boat *Tribune* was for a time attached to the 3rd Submarine Flotilla based on *Forth* at Holy Loch during the war. These internal views give just some idea of the confined living and working conditions in these submarines.

In October, 1946, one of the running blocks on the spar of the foremast on *Forth* became fouled up, preventing the running through of lines, and the Divisional Officer asked for two volunteers from the combined mess of buntings and sparklers to go up the pole and free this off. Three of my mess mates and I raised our hands, and on this occasion McMillan and Wooden went aloft to fix it on 26th October, 1946. My other mess mate and myself were placed in reserve in case the same thing should happen again, which it did. On the reverse of the photograph I took of McMillan and Wooden I made the following note—'I went aloft 21 February, 1947. Height approximately 145–150 feet'.

On board *Forth* - McMillan and Wooden 'up the pole'. Height approximately 145-150 feet. 26 October, 1946.

Internal view of *Tribune* working on torpedoes. The rating in the centre is Able Seaman Frank Askew on loan to *Tribune* for making the film 'Close Quarters'. Note pins out of 'gates' to allow torpedo to be lowered off the loading rails, and also the alteration to the water-tight door clips carried out in Swan's Yard in 1941. Source unknown.

(RNSM)

We were now in the last few weeks of 1946, those dark short days of winter to which our geographical location brought its fair share of rain and wind, though I do not recall it ever snowing. Leisure-time on board was spent in watching films and more frequent letter-writing to family and friends, as well as reading, relaxing and listening to the piped music. Ashore, everything was different too; it was the 'closed' season for holidays, and the crowds had vanished. Many of the holiday amenities and facilities were closed as well for annual maintenance and refurbishing in preparation for next season, when everything would become alive again.

In considering my own position at this time, life generally for me over the previous months of being in the 'Andrew' (slang for Royal Navy) had been both exciting and satisfying, and I was enjoying every minute of it. I liked the life on board, and mixed well with my messmates, both on board and whenever we met up at venues ashore, where I enjoyed a continuous and lively social life. I began to wonder, though, just how much longer all this would last.

Out on the town - Rothesay, November, 1946.

> The going on in the routine of a station, if interrupted, is like stopping a watch—the whole machine gets wrong.
>
> Nelson to Sir Alexander Ball,
> 7th June, 1804.

Home Fleet Autumn Manoeuvres   4

H.M.S. *Forth*
29 October–6 November 1946

BY THE END of September, 1946, I was due for a long leave, since I had only taken 10 days since enlistment. I didn't ask for it, but it was offered me, and I decided to take it. I was enjoying life no end in Scotland, but it would be nice, I thought, to see my parents, my brother and friends at home, and to catch up with all the news.

It could have been only a day or so after I arrived home that I received a Post Office telegram dated 25th September 1946 from C/O *Forth*.

> Your leave now expires 13.00 Tuesday 29th October. Ship under sailing orders.

This came as a complete surprise, since I had no idea what this meant, neither had I any intimation at all before setting off on leave that *Forth* might be leaving Rothesay. Where were we going, I wondered. Would we be moving to another home base, or perhaps somewhere abroad?

My leave ended well before the departure date, and back on board my colleagues in Communications had learnt that we would be joining a major autumn exercise with the Home Fleet, and that we would first be heading for the Irish Sea.

Flagship of the Home Fleet, Admiral Sir Neville Syfret's battleship *King George V* puts to sea from Invergordon with the cruiser *Diadem* on 29 October.

Associated Press

The "Dido" class cruisers *Dido* and *Cleopatra*, joined the 2nd Cruiser Squadron from Portland. I was able to photograph them here at Red Bay, Northern Ireland, from the fo'c'sle of *Forth*. 30 October.

Ships of the Home Fleet leaving Red Bay, Northern Ireland, from the fo'c'sle of *Forth*, 31 October.

The "Dido" class cruiser *Cleopatra* on her way to join the 2nd Cruiser Squadron, 30 October.

Associated Press

This was my first experience of being on a ship in what to me were extreme weather conditions during many of the days we were at sea. One of the worst moments was encountering a storm of great strength with beating rain and gale force winds whipping up gigantic seas. The noise was incredible. The ship was lurching and heaving, its bow completely submerging as it ploughed its way onward before rising out of the sea like a tormented whale, bringing with it mountains of water washing over the fo'c'sle. With hardly time for this to drain away, the ship pitched and plunged into the waves again in relentless pursuit of its objective. The rain was heavy and hard, with a screeching wind, and it was cold, very cold and treacherous; this, I thought, was the unholiest place on earth.

I do not know which was worse, the pitching and rolling or the noise, the rain, and the bitterly cold wind which cut right through you. All of this made many of us, not used to such foul weather, sick as dogs, but there was nothing we could do about it. The incessant ongoing of the ship under such horrendous weather conditions as those, in any other situation would for many of us have been intolerable.

Most of the time I was on the Flag deck, and like many of the crew on duty, exposed to those atrocious elements, was clothed in duffel coat, oilskins and rubber boots. Being on deck was bad enough, I dreaded to think what it must have been like for those of the crew who were closed up below in sections of the ship such as the galley or engine room. Perhaps the lucky ones were those off duty, lying in their hammocks and able to maintain relative perpendicular stability while most things around them were tossing and churning.

The strange part about my experience was that I never gave a thought as to whether the structure of the ship could withstand such battering by the sea, nor whether such perilous conditions might even capsize us. I was far more concerned with how I was feeling, and keeping my balance.

During these exercises I quickly became aware of the fact that I was a far better dry land sailor than a sailor at sea. It had nothing to do with being at all worried or scared, but was all to do with the state of my stomach. I really did believe that if I could have overcome the constant sickly feeling, I would thoroughly enjoy every minute of it. There I was, an absolute novice at coping with being on a ship in such rough seas, and in some of the worst weather I considered imaginable, and I did wonder whether I would ever get used to it. Regardless of the weather, however, we all had our job to do, and that had to be done however we all felt.

There was one comfort that all of us enjoyed on board, whether at sea or when moored in Rothesay Bay. During the autumn and winter months, mess mates supplied those on night duty with a continual supply of steamy mugs of thick blocks of cocoa mixed with hot water and Nestlés milk. This was indeed an acceptable beverage, and sustained us all during the night and the early hours of the morning.

Mercifully there were periods when the sea was calmer and when the weather generally improved, and I was able to take photographs of some of the ships that were taking part in the exercises.

Our first destination turned out to be Northern Ireland. We anchored at Red Bay, Bangor, while waiting for the main fleet to assemble. We knew nothing about this at the time, and only read in the National Press some days later that we were about to take part in a major battle as part of the Home Fleet Manoeuvres, and various ships and submarines were joining from their various anchorages.

Whilst anchored at Bangor, Watches of the ship's company were allowed a few hours ashore, and I chose to spend my free time in making the short train journey to Belfast. It was raining, dull and dreary, and I did no more than buy some Irish linen from a shop in the city which I intended to post home to my mother as a present, since I would not have any leave entitlement that Christmas. With that, I returned to the ship. I heard the next day that around 24 of the ship's company had been detained by the Royal Ulster Constabulary overnight, due to over-enjoying themselves at a local dance hall.

With shore leave over *Forth* got under way with her escort vessels. Since the Signals Branch formed part of the Communications Department on the ship, it would normally be reasonable to assume we would have had an advantage ahead of the ship's company in most matters concerning the ship and its movements, but on this occasion we knew nothing as to where we were going, what we would be doing, and for how long. We were told, however, that from now on we would be assuming wartime procedures, and part of the exercise would be in a blackout.

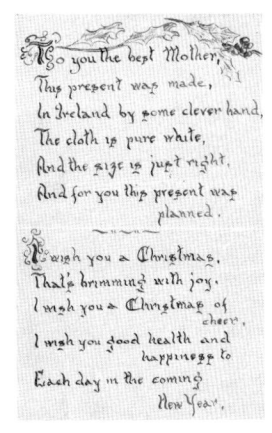

Poem from me to my mother, October, 1946.

"Battle" class destroyer *St Kitts*, 5th Destroyer Flotilla, making headway to Portland from Invergordon on 29 October.

I made a note on the reverse of this photograph taken 31 October, 1946, *Duke of York*, but as it turned out, she was not on the exercises, and this must be *King George V*.

Taken from the Flag deck of *Forth*, battleship *King George V*, 2nd Battle Squadron, 1 November.

A shot of the cruiser *Dido* from *Forth*, somewhere at sea on 2 November.

Taken the same day, 2 November, the cruiser *Diadem* returning to her position after fuelling from *Forth*.

When one is at sea, one could be anywhere, and this is how it was with us. I only learnt more about the exercises and what part we were all playing after we had returned to Rothesay. My father posted to me a newspaper cutting which appeared in one of the National dailies; the report was dated 28th October 1946.

Home Fleet Going To War—Northern Exercises

Young bluejackets, some only a few months in the Navy, will have their first taste of 'battle' during exercises for which the Home Fleet will put to sea this week. The battleship *King George V* and the aircraft carrier *Implacable* will take part, with cruisers and destroyers, all equipped with radar and other scientific devices.

The exercises will take the Fleet round the North of Scotland and through the Irish Sea to Portland. In the early stages, the ships will be split up to take part in exercises individually, and as squadrons and flotillas.

As the Fleet nears its destination on Saturday, there will be another mock battle.

On one of the nights at sea we were under blackout conditions, which was a little scary, since there were numerous vessels operating at various distances around us, but everywhere was pitch black, and we appeared to be totally isolated.

Eventually a little more information filtered through to us, and we were told that *Forth* would, with others, form part of a 'Fleet Train' representing oilers and stores ships to replenish fuel and supplies to the main fleet, which was assumed to be returning from an operation in the North Sea, and that we would have a protective screen of destroyers and frigates against an expected submarine and air attack.

All this sounded very exciting, and I wondered whether we would actually see anything of the action. I was able to take a few photographs, for example of the cruiser *Dido* off the starboard bow, and one of the cruiser *Diadem* returning to her position after refuelling from *Forth*, as well as one or two others from time to time. I hoped we would see some of the submarines as well, but this was not likely, of course, since their role was to penetrate the protective screen and attack the stores ships, so I did not hold out any hope for this. I also wanted to know which submarines they were and whether any were from the 3rd Submarine Flotilla based on *Forth* at Rothesay.

We needed little to remind us of the time of the year; it was dark and gloomy everywhere, the sea was rough and it was raining hard. Apart from this, although we had a protective screen around us, *Forth* was rigged for action in readiness for expected torpedo attacks. Although we knew this to be only a mock battle, there was a great sense of realism about it all, and from time to time, only momentarily perhaps, it was very easy to believe that this was the real thing. I can remember the ship being on alert, and the mood of the crew tense.

Associated Press

The "Dido" class cruiser *Diadem*, 2nd Cruiser Squadron, leaving Invergordon 29 October.

In these assumed battle conditions, all the training we had undergone was now put to the test where a high degree of professionalism and ability was expected. One became acutely aware of the importance of the training we had received, and of the rigid procedures adopted during peacetime exercises, which is a reflection only of the importance of them in wartime when lives depend upon them.

I recall reading an article by Hamilton Fyfe which appeared in an issue of *The War Illustrated* in August 1943 which firmly places the atmosphere of war into context. Having had the opportunity of a tour in a submarine earlier in the year, I was able to appreciate just a little what living and working in a submarine was like in peacetime. One can only imagine what this is really like in wartime, being closed up in combat conditions, perhaps lying submerged for several hours with the threat of the enemy lurking above, and with the fear of dying at any moment.

HIS MAJESTY'S SUBMARINES

I take a family interest in submarines. My brother, Herbert C. Fyfe, wrote the first book about them. That was just before the end of last century, when most people either guessed little of their possibilities or dismissed the idea of under-water boats as 'ridiculous Jules Verne stuff'. Even now, says the writer of a Stationery Office booklet prepared by the Ministry of Information for the Board of Admiralty and called *His Majesty's Submarines*, 'to the layman even now the submarine is still a novelty, strange and little understood'; this branch of the Navy is still 'cloaked in mystery'. Well, if that is so, this account of its doings in the European war will go far to dissipate the fog of ignorance. It will also spread more widely the admiration and gratitude felt by those who have been able to follow those doings closely, for the men who have shown such pluck and

10" Reflector

Aldis lamp

dogged endurance and, as the booklet puts is, 'high-hearted determination', and contributed so mightily to the defeat of the German enemy.

What the crews of a submarine endure can be fully realised only by those who have served in one under war conditions. To begin with, there is very little room to move about or even to sit or lie still. The ship is 'closely packed with a bewildering mass of pipes, valves, gauges, instruments, electric cables'. The air becomes thick and sleepifying while you are submerged during the daylight hours. It is an immense relief when in the dark the vessel rises to the surface and the engines are started.

Instead of the silence there are engine noises and the sound of the sea. The boat lurches into a roll, and men can move and breathe freely. A draught of fresh night air is sucked through. There comes the welcome order: Carry on smoking. Somebody begins a song. Breakfast will soon be ready. 'Midday' dinner is at midnight, and supper just before dawn.

Soon after that the crew settle down with a sigh to another period of tedium, doing nothing for the most part, relieving their dry throats with boiled sweets, which are served out to them as a regular ration, and longing for the dark hours again.

Complicated and Deadly Instrument

But most of those who serve in submarines will agree that life in them has its compensations.

In that small dim world below the sea there is a unique companionship. A submarine is a self-supporting unit and the members of her company must have confidence in each other. There is discipline, but with it a democratic spirit which compensates for much of the hardship. It is a rare comradeship shared by all, from the commanding officer to the youngest member of the crew.

Above all it is necessary that the captain should be trusted by his crew. He looks through the periscope, he alone knows what is happening above in sea and sky, he must decide swiftly what is to be done and he must decide correctly, for the slightest error, an inaccurate estimate of distance, or a few seconds' delay may cause not only the failure of an attack, but the destruction of the ship and the whole company.

'The most complicated and deadly instrument of war', the submarine is styled. The description is exact so far as it goes. We might add that it is among the most expensive. Not in itself only, but in the ammunition with which it does its deadly work. Each torpedo discharged costs £2,500, and is for its size as complicated a piece of mechanism as the submarine. Small submarines carry four, large ones eleven, ready to be fired; also some spares. The 'human torpedo' is for use against ships in harbour or at anchor which cannot be drawn into the open for a battle at sea. Two men wearing diving-suits sit astride it. They drive it slowly by its electric batteries towards the target, under which they dive. A charge like that of a torpedo is then detached and fixed to the hull of the enemy ship. A fuse is set and the 'human torpedo' gets away as quickly as possible so as to be out of range when the explosion occurs.

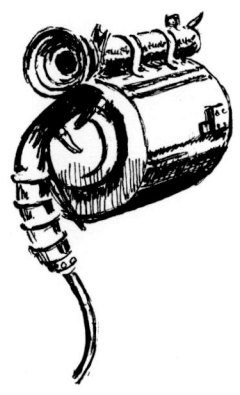

75

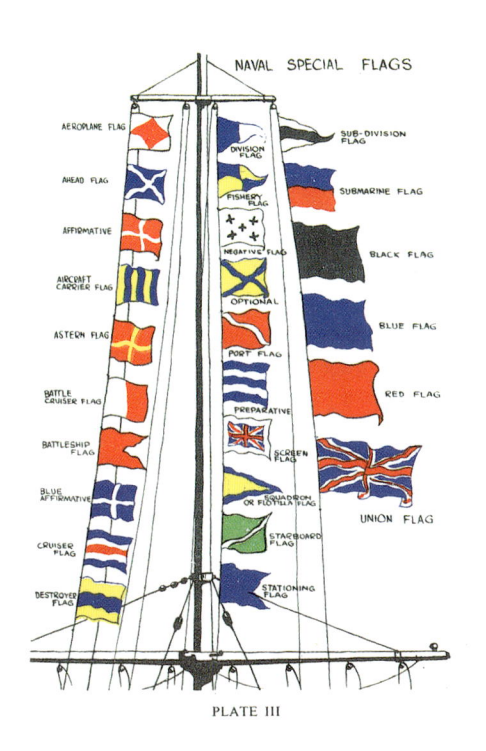

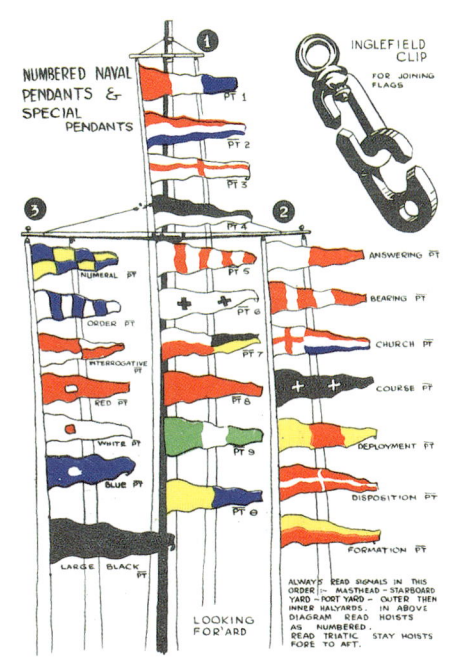

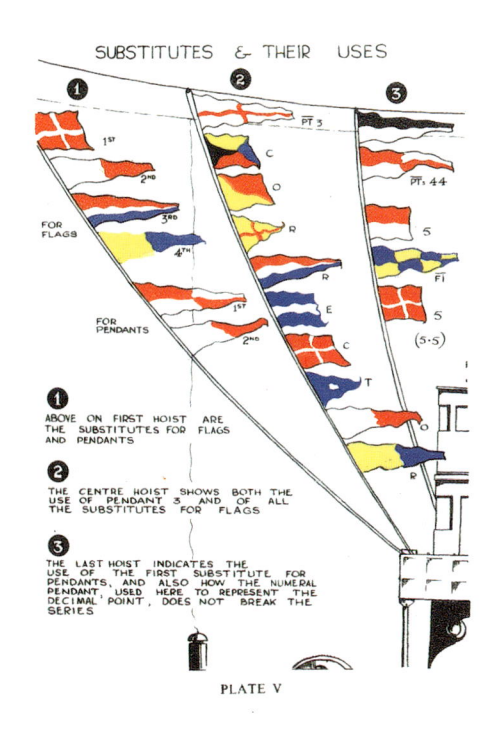

20 M/M Twin Oerlikon Gun Mark X1A, Mounting and Support, fitted forward on submarine *Aeneas*. Note the safety rail fitted on *Affray* only. Reproduced from the original building plans, with kind permission from the National Maritime Museum London.

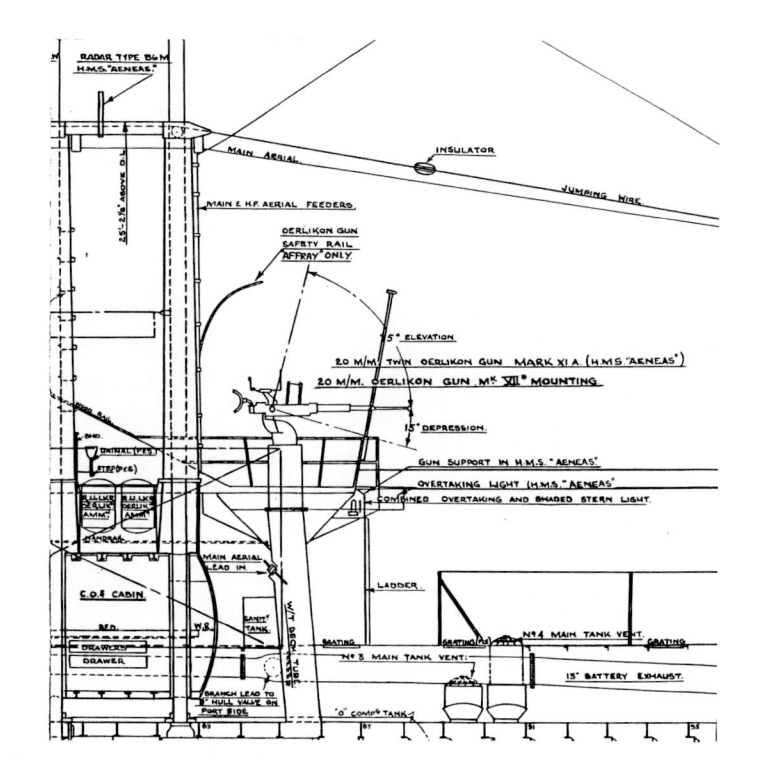

4" Gun Mark XX111, Mounting and Support fitted aft on submarine *Aeneas*. Clearly visible also is the hinged ladder to the hatch openings of the Gun access trunk. Reproduced from the original building plans, with kind permission from National Maritime Museum London.

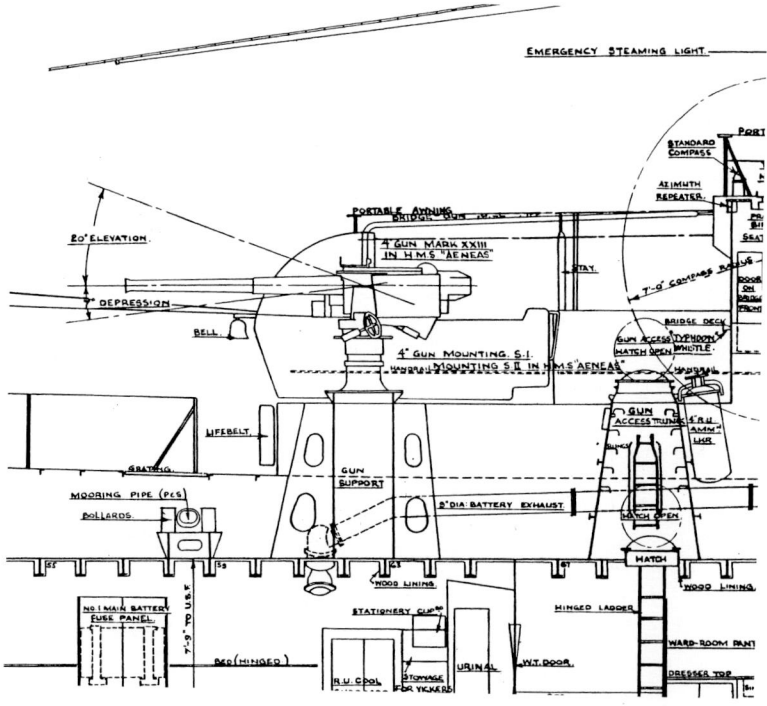

There are also midget submarines for use in much the same conditions. They did a fine job when they entered the Norwegian fjord where the German battleship *Tirpitz* lay and damaged her badly. Of this exploit, the full story has not yet been released, but what they did was to navigate first of all a thousand miles of rough sea, then to pass through the enemy minefield and go up the long, narrow fjord where 'every conceivable device which could ensure their destruction' was known to be in use. They slid past listening posts, nets, gun defences. They actually reached the nets, only two hundred yards from the *Tirpitz*, designed to protect it against such attacks as theirs. From there they launched their missiles. These caused an immense explosion. The battleship was lifted several feet into the air. One submarine was seen from the *Tirpitz's* deck and fired at with rifles. Guns were trained on their supposed positions, depth-charges were dropped. They could not make their way back out of the nets. Two were scuttled by their crews, who were then taken prisoner. The third was never heard of again.

This operation 'for daring and endurance is unique even in the annals of the Royal Navy'.

The effect of depth charges bursting round a submarine is a severe test for the nerves.

You hear faintly at first and then louder the 'chuffle-chuffle' of a destroyer's screws. Then it comes—a great metallic clang, the 'tonk' they call it. The boat shudders; the corking, a special form of paint used to prevent metal surfaces from sweating, falls in a white shower; depth gauges are put out of action; glass is broken. It comes again, a second terrible crash, followed by another, and the boat lurches and shudders. There is a pause and you wait for the next blow.

This might go on for as long as the best part of an hour. One captain, recording an attack which lasted forty minutes, said he was much impressed by the bearing of all hands during this unpleasant time, 'But particularly so with that of J. V. Crosby, Acting Leading Telegraphist, who, knowing full well when an attack was developing, calmly continued giving the information for the records as though it was merely a peacetime exercise that was in progress.' The sea-pressure on a submerged submarine is an added anxiety to its commander when a depth-charge attack is on. Its weight is some 130 pounds to the square inch, and it has been known to bend a steel pillar four inches thick.

Foul air is another worry. This is sometimes so bad that it makes the engines difficult to start. Its effect on human beings can be imagined. In one engagement the *Tetrarch* was under water for 42 hours and 40 minutes. When she came to the surface and fresh air could be breathed again, most of the crew were dizzy, many violently sick. The harder you work, the more you exhaust the wholesome atmosphere, because you breathe more quickly. So the men in submarines have to spend as much time as possible, while they are submerged, lying still or at any rate doing as little as possible. This is the time when boiled sweets come in useful—may even be life-savers. A bag of peppermint bullseyes has been known to revive a working party when they were literally gasping for air.

Another T-class boat built by Cammell Laird, Birkenhead, was *Thrasher*, launched in November, 1940, and commissioned 13 April, 1941. *Thrasher* was highly active throughout the war serving in the Atlantic, Mediterranean and then in the Far East. She was machine gunned, depth charged and hit by bombs. In August, 1943, *Thrasher* joined the 12th Submarine Flotilla at H.M.S. *Varbel*, Port Bannatyne, on the Isle of Bute, and in December, 1945, she was officially paid off and stricken from the Active List. In March, 1947, she was towed to Briton Ferry yard near Swansea and broken up for scrap.

Thrasher was photographed here in December, 1945.

Bomb Disposal Under Difficulties

This was during the long ordeal undergone by the *Spearfish* when she was trapped in shallow water off Norway. Depth-charges exploded round her about every two minutes. Were the crew rattled? Listen!

A sixpenny sweepstake was started among them on the time of the next explosion, the stake to be settled on the next pay day. No words were spoken. A seaman moved softly through the boat, booking the bets, which were agreed to by signs.

Depth-charges were bad enough. Bombs from the air were worse. They could be avoided by submerging, but this was, to say the least of it, inconvenient. Highly dangerous was the situation of the *Thrasher* when it was discovered that two unexploded aircraft bombs lay on the forward casing. The discovery was made at night. The submarine lay on the surface, but the enemy patrols were not far off; at any moment she might have to submerge. Two of the crew, Lieut. Roberts and Petty-Officer Gould, volunteered to remove the bombs. They were exposed to two risks. The bombs might explode, the ship might have to go under suddenly, in which case they would almost certainly be dragged down and drowned.

They went about the operation with quiet confidence. It took fifty minutes, and they had only faint torchlight to work by. They had to lie on their stomachs, one pushing, one pulling, till they manoeuvred the bombs overboard. Their task was not made easier by the second of the two missiles giving off a loud twanging sound every time it was moved, 'which added nothing to their peace of mind', as the official report put it. They both received the award of the Victoria Cross, and well they deserved it.

Hamilton Fyfe/The War Illustrated
© IPC Magazines Ltd

The S-class submarines, built in large numbers between 1932 and 1945, generally had a surface displacement of 715 tons, and 990 tons submerged, and were powered by diesel engines and electric motors producing 1,900 hp and 1,300 hp respectively, with a maximum surface speed of 14.75 knots. There were numerous variants within the groups of boats built: some boats such as *Seneschal* and *Selene* (commissioned June 1944) carried six 21-inch bow torpedo tubes, one 4-inch deck gun and a 20 mm Oerlikon gun, while others such as *Spiteful* (commissioned October 1943) and *Sturdy* (November 1943) had six 21-inch bow torpedo tubes and one 21-inch stern tube, with one 3-inch deck gun and one 20 mm Oerlikon. S-boats were 217 feet in length, 23 feet 9 inches beam, and normally carried 12/13 torpedoes and a crew of 44/48.

The T-class operated in home waters, the Mediterranean and the Far East, and together with the S-boats were among the most successful of the Second World War. Though similar to the S-class, the T's were larger, having a length overall of 273 feet 6 inches/275 feet and a beam of 26 feet 6 inches. They were also built in large quantities, 22 in the first group and 30 in the second. Of those possibly taking part in the Home Fleet Autumn Exercises, *Tradewind* was commissioned in July 1943 and *Teredo*, one of the latest, in October 1945; the class had a displacement of 1,319 tons surfaced and 1,571 tons submerged. The T's were propelled by diesel engines and electric motors developing 2,500 hp and 1,450 hp respectively, and had a maximum surface speed of 14/15 knots. Again, various modifications of design were introduced with a view to increasing their capability, but generally these boats carried eight 21-inch bow torpedo tubes, of which two were external, two 21-inch external tubes mounted amidships and firing astern, and one 21-inch external stern torpedo tube. Twelve mines could be carried in lieu of 17 torpedoes. Other armament included one 4-inch deck gun, one 20 mm Oerlikon gun and three 0.303-inch Vickers machine-guns. They also carried 26 mines and a crew of 61.

The S-class submarine *Spiteful*, built by Scotts' Shipbuilding, Greenock. She was launched 5 June, 1943, and commissioned the same year. *Spiteful* was one of the S-boats supporting the Opposition Force under orders on N.O.I.C. Londonderry. This is a later photograph of her taken in November, 1958.

Possibly taking part in the exercises was the T-class submarine *Teredo*. Built by Vickers-Armstrong, Barrow, she was launched 27 April, 1945, commissioned 22 October, the same year, and completed 5 April, 1946. *Teredo* was the last of the T-boats to be built by Vickers-Armstrong at Barrow. In May, 1946, she joined the 3rd Submarine Flotilla based on *Forth* at Rothesay, and took part in exercises involving a simulated attack with three other boats from the 7th Submarine Flotilla on the battleship *King George V*. Four cruisers, nineteen destroyers and escort vessels participated. Three of the submarines scored twelve torpedo hits on *King George V*, but it was not clear if *Teredo* was one of them. This photograph was taken in 1945. Source unknown.

(RNSM)

The two A-class submarines taking part in the exercises, *Aeneas* and *Alcide*, both of the 3rd Submarine Flotilla based on *Forth* at Rothesay, were the very latest in submarine design, incorporating all-welded construction. They had been designed for action in the Pacific, but hostilities ended before these boats entered service, and many others on the drawing board were cancelled. *Aeneas* was commissioned in May 1946 and *Alcide* three months later. Class displacement was 1,120 tons surfaced and 1,620 tons submerged, and they carried a crew of 61. Propulsion was by diesel engines and electric motors, and they had a maximum speed of 18.5 knots; length overall was 281 feet 9 inches and beam 22 feet 3 inches. Armament included six 21-inch bow torpedo tubes and four 21-inch stern tubes. They also carried one 4-inch deck gun, one 20 mm anti-aircraft gun, three machine-guns, 26 mines and 20 torpedoes.

With the exercises over, we arrived back at Rothesay in the early hours of the morning of 6th November. It was such a relief when *Forth* finally came to a standstill, and her engines stopped. We had

Aeneas was one of the A-class boats making up the Opposition Force under orders of N.O.I.C. Londonderry. Here we see her in December, 1946.

Wright & Logan

been on the move for some eight days. None of us were much the wiser with regard to our involvement, the ships and submarines taking part, and indeed whether we won the battle or not. These matters did not become clearer until I obtained a copy of the *Daily Telegraph* on Monday 4th November 1946, wherein I found some good coverage of the exercises as well as the names of a few of the vessels taking part.

The Daily Telegraph
Sunday 3rd November 1946

R.A.F. FOUND BLIND SPOT IN NAVY'S RADAR

Attack at 50ft in Exercise

I flew from here in a Beaufighter which took part in the 'attack' on the Home Fleet, including the battleship *King George V*, 35,000 tons, as the warships were on their way back to Portland yesterday.

For four days the Fleet had been on autumn manoeuvres, in which there had been a series of surface actions and attacks by submarines. This air strike was the culminating effort.

Today R.A.F. officers and naval observers were co-ordinating their reports. First impressions indicate that by eluding the naval radar successful attacks were made on the ships.

My pilot had been briefed to achieve surprise by flying low in the radar 'blind spot'. We were to intercept and attack the ships south of Start Point, Devon. Visibility was stated to be 'bad but clearing'.

Coastal Command provided aircraft to both sides in the F.E.X.9 Exercises, which included Beaufighters and Mosquitos. For illustration purposes, four Bristol Beaufighters Mark X. are seen here in loose port formation sometime during the last war.

Photograph, courtesy of the Imperial War Museum, London. CH.17873.

Opposite: The projected programme for the exercises included the battleship *Duke of York*, but in subsequent changes to the ship list, she was replaced by *King George V*. This splendid view of the *Duke of York* and the carrier *Implacable* following at a distance, was taken at a different time, and is included here for illustration purposes only.

Tight Formation

Mosquitos took off first and the Beaufighters followed a few seconds later. Over the sea at Portland Bill we kept in tight formation, flying at 50 feet.

Ahead were the dark shapes of the destroyers and a moment later we were over them. We saw the *King George V*, with her cover of four cruisers of the Dido class and eight destroyers in V formation.

The Mosquitos went in first shooting their rockets at the splash targets towed by the battleship and cruisers. Lights began to twinkle in the ships, representing naval anti-aircraft fire.

Then it was our turn. We shot over the *King George V* at mast height, catching a glimpse for a brief moment of the searchlights flashing at us. Climbing to 1,000 ft. we looked back to see the long curving wake the battleship had made by her evasive action.

Diving into cloud for 'protection' my pilot said he would attack again. This time he intended to cross the centre of the ship. The next moment we were in a steep dive. Our wingtips seemed to touch the mast, and then we were up aloft again.

The squadrons re-formed over Alderney and flew along the French coast as far as Brest. The Mosquitos were to make yet another attack with torpedoes represented by smoke bombs. We set our course for Portland, flying at 1500 feet and seeing our target from approximately 10 miles.

The 'enemy' became clearer and grew in number. Again the lights began to twinkle. The Home Fleet had spotted us. The destroyers surrounding the *King George V* closed in and steamed at full speed. The Mosquitos swept on, laying their smoke bombs while the Beaufighters made independent attacks.

Again re-forming over Portland Bill lighthouse, we flew back to base.

Playing their part was the Mosquito. This photograph (issued in 1944) shows three Mosquito Fighter Bombers fitted with bombs under the wings, flying to attack targets in France.

Photograph, courtesy of the Imperial War Museum, London. CH.12411.

Associated Press

Associated Press

The "Swiftsure" class cruiser *Superb* (C.S.2) 2nd Cruiser Squadron, with *Diadem*, left Invergordon for Portland 29 October, and was joined by the cruisers *Cleopatra* and *Dido*. This photograph of *Superb* shows her off well, but was taken at a different time.

"Battle" class destroyer *Solebay* (C.D.5) 5th Destroyer Flotilla.

MORE STRENUOUS THAN WAR

Convoy Manoeuvre

Among ships taking part in the exercises was Britain's newest cruiser, the Tyne-built *Superb*, 8000 tons.

As Capt. W. G. A. Robson climbed from her bridge at Portland, he said: 'In some ways peace-time exercises are more strenuous than wartime actions. We have three days' work before us preparing an analysis of the exercises.'

The main force came from Pentland Firth and, rounding the North of Scotland, they were joined by units from Portland and Londonderry.

South of the Hebrides four supply vessels, forming a 'fleet train', were used to embark imaginary supplies and fuel to every ship in face of a combined underwater and air attack.

Officers bent over radar screens and six submarines were plotted before any harm could have been done.

Object Achieved

Later there was a convoy exercise. The *King George V* lurked in St. George's Channel while the *Dido*, 5,540 tons, and *Cleopatra*, 5,450 tons, moved as a convoy under the protection of the *Superb* and *Diadem*, 5,450 tons, and a destroyer screen.

Again the attacking force was discovered by radar. From the flagship a signal went out, and in a few minutes the escort laid a smoke screen. The primary object—the safety of the convoy—was achieved.

During the night *King George V* was shadowed by cruisers. Destroyers were directed to attack and dashed in.

One loomed less than 10 yards from the bows of a cruiser. Engines were put astern and a turn by the cruiser averted any possible danger.

© The Daily Telegraph 1946

By this time I had served on *Forth* for nearly three months, and whether it was due to my performance in Communications during the exercises or to my general attention to duties on board I do not know, but the following Thursday, 7th November, 1946, I was promoted to Signalman, and my mess mates thought that this called for a small celebration.

In Tudor times, sailors were entitled to a ration of one gallon of beer, but great difficulty was found in keeping beer from going sour at sea. For this reason wine was issued to ships in the Mediterranean in the 17th Century, while on other stations, and especially the West Indies, rum became the official beverage. Before 1740, the ration of rum was served neat, but in that year Admiral Vernon ordered it to be diluted with water, and it became known as 'Grog'—'Old Grogram' being the Admiral's nickname, from the grogram cloak he wore. Until 1946 or thereabouts the proportion was three parts of water to one of rum, but from that time onwards it was two to one. Men were allowed to take a cash allowance in lieu of rum if they so desired at the rate of 3d. a day.

Rum was issued daily at about a quarter to twelve, and Chiefs and Petty Officers drew their half-gill lots neat—commonly known as 'neaters'. Rum was issued from a round wooden tub, broader at the base than at the top, and emblazoned on the outside 'THE KING GOD BLESS HIM' in large brass letters.

Fame (S.O.) 3rd Escort Flotilla, joined in the final stages of the exercises on arrival at Portland on 2 November. She was built by Vickers-Armstrong, Barrow, under the 1932 Programme. Begun in July, 1933, launched June, 1934, and completed April, 1935. Displacement and dimensions were very similar to *Hotspur*, and she is seen here in February, 1947.

Wright & Logan

The importance of the daily issue of rum was never underestimated.

I was under age for 'grog' entitlement, since one had to be 20 years of age or more, but on the day of my promotion my mess mates who did qualify each gave up a nip to provide me with 'sippers', a voluntary concession on their part to celebrate my promotion. I had been at sea for the first time, an experience of a lifetime I thought, and with a mock battle involving some of our prestigious ships it was the nearest one could have come to the real thing.

The immediate excitement of having been included in such an important event obviously waned over the coming weeks, but it was succeeded by others as the months passed. Indeed, following my release from the Navy in January, 1948, I never spared any time to research this more fully, until now.

Hotspur, a destroyer and the sole survivor of her class, was built under 1934 Programme by Scotts' Shipbuilding & Engineering Co. Ltd, Greenock. Displacement 1,340 tons, 323 feet overall in length, and a complement of 145. Building began in February, 1935, launched in March, 1936, and completed the same year. *Hotspur* formed part of the screen for the "Fleet Train" with the 4th Escort Flotilla. She was photographed here in May, 1947.

Wright & Logan

Obviously it has been necessary to research the Autumn Exercises of 1946, since it forms an integral part of my story, but I was having little success in finding additional information until I received a reply to my cry for help in *Warship World* seeking information on the Clyde Naval Review in 1947. Having assisted me so much with that chapter, Mike Cox undertook research for me on the Home Fleet Autumn Manoeuvres of 1946, and I have so much pleasure in thanking him for his thoroughness in providing me with such comprehensive reports and schedules, and for his close attention generally in researching the Resources of Naval Historical Branch, MOD, Gt. Scotland Yard.

HOME FLEET AUTUMN MANOEUVRES—F.E.X.9

Left Invergordon for Portland—0130 hrs 29.10.46
2nd Battle Squadron — *King George V* (C. in C. Home Fleet).
Advance Training Carrier — *Implacable*.
4th Destroyer Flotilla — *Myngs* (D.4), *Zephyr, Zenith, Zest, Zealous*.
2nd Cruiser Squadron — *Superb* (C.S.2), *Diadem*.

Joined 2nd Cruiser Squadron from Portland 30.10.46—*Cleopatra, Dido*.
5th Destroyer Flotilla — *Solebay* (D.5), *St. James, St. Kitts*.

Joined at dawn 30.10.46 by 'Fleet Train'
Submarine Depot Ship (S.M.3) — *Forth* ⎫
Fleet Oiler — *Black Ranger* ⎬ representing Fleet Oilers
Destroyer ex Rothesay, Rosyth Command — *Onslaught* ⎭
Fleet Tug — *Freebooter*   representing Stores Ship

Screen for 'Fleet Train' from Londonderry
4th Escort Flotilla
Destroyers — *Crispin* (S.O. 4th E.F.), *Hotspur*..
Frigates — *Loch Arkaig, Loch Fada, Loch Veyatie, Loch Dunvegan*.

Opposition Force under orders of N.O.I.C. Londonderry
Six submarines formed part of the Opposing Force, and it is fairly certain the following took part—
Aeneas ⎫ — 3rd Submarine Flotilla, Rothesay, joined the same time
Alcide ⎭   as *Forth*.
Seneschal — from Invergordon.
Springer — from Portland to Londonderry.
Spiteful — In reserve at Londonderry.
Sanguine ⎫ — At Londonderry 21.10.46–4.11.46.
Sea Devil ⎭

The above lists seven submarines in all. *Seneschal, Springer* and *Spiteful* are definitely shown as taking part, and from the movement card it is thought that *Sanguine* and *Sea Devil* did so as well. *Alcide's* movement

Sanguine is another of the S-boats likely to have taken part from Londonderry. She was built by Cammell Laird, Birkenhead, and commissioned in April, 1945. In August, 1945, she left Holy Loch for passage to the Far East, reaching Malta by the time the war ended, she then returned to the UK. Her motto was "We strike to kill". *Sanguine* was photographed here in September, 1947.

card also shows that she was definitely involved, in which case it might be that *Aeneas* did not take part. *Scorcher* was in reserve at Londonderry at the time and could possibly have made up the number; if so, perhaps *Aeneas* and *Alcide* were not part of the Opposition Force.

Final stages of Exercises on arrival at Portland

Joined at 0915 hrs, 2.11.46—11 Destroyers and Escorts of 3rd Escort Flotilla from Portland. From records obtained, it is not possible to provide a complete list with accuracy, since the 3rd Escort Flotilla was made up of only eight ships—*Fame* (S.O. 3rd E.F.), *Easton*, *Hedingham Castle*, *Kenilworth Castle*, *Leeds Castle*, *Oakham Castle*, *Tintagel Castle* (*Flint Castle* was not available). The remaining four could have been, with some certainty—*Offa* (S/m Target Vessel, Portland, attached to 7th Submarine Flotilla), *Helmsdale* (Underwater Weapons Establishment, Portland), *Rotherham* (Experimental Duties/Trials, Portland), and either *Opportune* or *Paladin* (Submarine Target Vessels, Portsmouth).

The Opposition Force under Orders of N.O.I.C. Londonderry, included five S-class submarines, and it is thought likely that *Sea Devil* was one of them. She was built by Scotts' Shipbuilding & Engineering Co. Ltd, Greenock, and was commissioned in March, 1945. Her motto was "Me timete" (Fear Me). Here we see her in August, 1949.

Possibly *Leeds Castle*, a corvette in the "Castle" class was one to have joined in the final stage of the exercises at Portland, under Senior Officer Commanding 3rd Escort Flotilla, in *Fame*. *Leeds Castle* was one of many in her class, built by W.Pickersgill & Sons, Ltd, Sunderland, and launched in October, 1943. Displacement generally 1.060 to 1,100 tons, 252 feet overall in length, and beam 36 feet 8 ins. Here we see her in June, 1947.

Of the likely T-boats taking part in the final stage of the exercises from Start Point to Portland, almost certainly one of them was *Tradewind*. The number could have been made up from Londonderry, otherwise *Thermoplae* may have been another drawn from the 5th Submarine Flotilla at Portsmouth. *Thermoplae* was built at Chatham Dockyard and commissioned in September, 1945. She was photographed here on 27 August, 1946.

Seven submarines from the 7th Submarine Flotilla took part in F.E.X.9, from Start Point to Portland Bill on 2.11.46. Almost certainly five of the seven were—*Saga, Sceptre, Seneschal, Statesman* and *Tradewind*. The remaining two could have been *Sanguine, Sea Devil* or *Springer*, which were located at Londonderry on 4.11.46. One wonders whether they could have been in the Portland area on 2.11.46 and back in Londonderry by 4.11.46. If not, then possibly the other two were drawn from the 5th Submarine Flotilla at Portsmouth, and could have been *Sentinel, Sirdar, Tabard, Teredo, Telemachus, Thermoplae* or *Thule*.

It would appear from the Exercise Reports that the surface ships and Coastal Command aircraft formed the Blue (friendly) Force and the submarines the Red Force for the first part of the Exercise on Thursday, 31st October, together with attacking aircraft from Coastal Command. Coastal Command provided aircraft to both sides.

On Friday, 1st November, *King George V*, acting as three (notional) 8-inch cruisers was Red Force (hostile) attacking a convoy represented by *Cleopatra* and *Dido* escorted by *Superb, Diadem* and destroyers (Blue Force).

In the final phase on 2nd November, the Home Fleet joined by the 3rd Escort Flotilla from Portland formed the Blue Force and the Red Force was made up of seven submarines disposed between Start Point and Portland Bill.

The thinking that lay behind the exercises and the course of events is revealed by the Monthly Intelligence Report, September–December 1946, which was made available to me by the Naval Historical Branch, Ministry of Defence.

NAVAL HISTORICAL BRANCH, MOD.
Monthly Intelligence Report. September–December 1946

The commander-in-Chief, Home Fleet, flying his flag in H.M.S. *King George V*, with H.M. Ships *Implacable* and *Zephyr*, *Superb* (C.S.2), *Diadem*, *Solebay* (D.5), *St. James*, *St. Kitts*, *Myngs* (D.4), *Zest*, *Zealous* and *Zenith*, left Invergordon for Portland northabout on 29th October. The Fleet was joined in due course by H.M. Ships *Cleopatra*, *Dido*, *Crispin*, *Onslaught*, *Forth* (Captain S.M.3), *Aeneas* and *Alcide* and on the way engaged in exercises in which methods of defence learned from the experience gained by convoys to North Russia were to be tested.

HOME FLEET EXERCISES—November 1946

With the return of peacetime conditions the activities of the Home Fleet have begun to resemble more closely their pre-war pattern—a spring cruise to Gibraltar, summer and autumn cruises, and three leave periods a year at Home ports.

Portland is at present the principal fleet base, and on each occasion that the fleet sallies forth on a cruise or returns from its travels, a programme of fleet exercises is arranged, or as the short title would have it 'F.E.X.' F.E.X.1 was born when H.M. ships *Rodney* and *Birmingham* and the Second Destroyer Flotilla left Rosyth in November, 1945.

The march in time is indicated by the fact that F.E.X.9 was planned and carried out by the Home Fleet on passage from Invergordon to Portland at the end of October, 1946. A feature of these programmes has always been the co-operation of Coastal Command with whom practices have been arranged whenever possible, and more recently mutual benefit has been derived from exercises planned in conjunction with the Joint A/S School at Londonderry.

Offa (S/m Target Vessel, Portland, attached to the 7th S/m Flotilla) was an "Onslow" class destroyer, and could have been one of the vessels involved in the final stage of the exercises on arrival at Portland. Built by Fairfield Shipbuilding and Engineering Co. Ltd, Govan, she was launched in March, 1941.

Zenith, pictured here, together with *Zephyr, Zest, Zealous*, and *Myngs* (D.4) 4th Destroyer Flotilla, joined the fleet bound for Portland northabout on 29 October, under the Commander-in-Chief Home Fleet, flying his flag in *King George V*. *Zenith*, a destroyer in the "Zambesi" class, was built by Wm Denny & Bros, Dumbarton, and was launched in June, 1944. Displacement 1,710 tons, length 362 feet 9 ins, beam 35 feet 8 ins, with a complement around 186. *Zenith* was photographed here in June, 1946.

On the occasion of sailing from Invergordon it was decided to make an all-day exercise with Londonderry the principal feature of the programme. F.E.X.9 was therefore built up around this event.

Geography and peacetime speed restrictions dictated that the fleet should leave Invergordon at the distasteful hour of 0130 on Tuesday, 29th October, 1946. By this time, a large assortment of photographers and pressmen, ranging from Reuters to the *Calcutta Morning News*, had been embarked, and the fleet consisting of H.M. Ships *King George V* (Commander-in-Chief, Home Fleet), *Superb* (Rear-Admiral Commanding Second Cruiser Squadron), *Diadem* and *Implacable*, and the Fourth and Fifth Destroyer Flotillas, sailed.

A further cameraman from Gaumont British, posting north with all dispatch, arrived to photograph the departure of the fleet, but as this occurred at dead of night, he was disappointed.

Independent exercises, A.A. firings and manoeuvres were carried out during daylight on Wednesday the 30th while off the north coast of Scotland, followed by a night passage through the Minches.

The protective screen for the "Fleet Train" comprised two destroyers and four frigates of the 4th Escort Flotilla, and one of these was the frigate *Loch Veyatie* photographed here in August, 1946. There were quite a number of "Loch" class frigates, *Loch Veyatie* being built by Ailsa Ship Building Co, Ltd, Troon, in 1945. Displacement 1,435 tons, length 307 feet, and beam 38 feet 6 ins. She had a complement of 103.

REPLENISHING AT SEA

For the purpose of the following day's exercise, the fleet was assumed to be returning from an operation in the North Sea to replenish with fuel and stores from its train, with which a rendezvous had been arranged for dawn on 30th October: the replenishment would take place in waters where there was risk of submarine and air attack.

Similar problems confronted us, of course, during the war, particularly during North Russian convoys and in the Pacific, and the rapid fuelling and storing of a fleet at sea will certainly play a major part in operations of the future. The exercise was designed to provide an opportunity to study this problem more deeply. The objects of the exercise were defined as:

(1) To exercise submarines in attacking a well-protected force.
(2) To investigate the problems of replenishing a fleet at sea from the Fleet Train in waters where submarines and air attack might be expected.

Joining the fleet at dawn on 30 October, Submarine Depot Ship *Forth* (S.M.3) formed part of a "Fleet Train", together with fleet oiler *Black Ranger*, and the destroyer *Onslaught* all representing Fleet Oilers. Also part of the train was the fleet tug *Freebooter* representing a Stores Ship.

Wright & Logan

Freebooter, a Fleet Tug, represented a Stores Ship in the "Fleet Train". She was one of four in the "Brigand" class, built in November, 1940, by Fleming & Ferguson, Paisley, under 1936, 1937 and 1938 Estimates. Displacement 840 tons, 174 feet overall in length, beam 32 feet, with a complement of 43. This class of tug were fitted for salvage work and had towing winches for work with battle practice targets. She was photographed here on 8 May, 1947.

(3) To exercise ships in the transfer of stores and in oiling at sea.

At dawn a rendezvous was made with the Fleet Train consisting of H.M.S. *Forth*, R.F.A. *Black Ranger* and H.M.S. *Onslaught*, representing Fleet Oilers, and H.M.S. *Freebooter* representing a store ship. The train was screened by six ships of the Fourth Escort Flotilla. H.M. Ships *Cleopatra* and *Dido*, which had sailed from Portland, also joined the Commander-in-Chief at this time.

At the rendezvous all available destroyers and escort vessels were stationed on a circular screen round the Fleet Train. The air defence of the fleet and control of air strikes was vested in H.M.S. *Implacable*, which operated inside the screen astern of the train. Provision was made for the release of destroyers from the screen if it was found necessary for H.M.S. *Implacable* to break out in the course of flying operations.

Control of the fuelling and storing programme together with the direction of surface forces was exercised by the Commander-in-Chief. Air forces in support of this operation were aircraft from H.M.S. *Implacable* and V.L.R.* aircraft of Coastal Command. Forces opposing the operation were six submarines acting under the orders of the Naval Officer-in-Charge, Londonderry, Naval aircraft from R.N.A.S. Eglington and one V.L.R. aircraft of Coastal Command.

In order to give all ships an opportunity to fuel and store during the time available and in order to test fully the administrative and communication arrangements, individual ships were ordered to remain alongside oilers or store ships for 20 to 30 minutes only. Replenishment took place continuously from 0800 until the exercise ceased at 1400—battleships and cruisers fuelled astern of the oilers while destroyers and escort vessels fuelled alongside.

SUBMARINES FOILED

Shortly after the exercise started air patrols sighted and reported submarines ahead of the fleet. This is not the place to go into a detailed analysis of individual attacks, but it appears that no submarine was able to penetrate the screen undetected and deliver an effective attack. It was brought out, however, that submarines of the future with a high submerged speed may approach from astern where inevitably the screen is at its thinnest.

*Very Long Range.

The British Fleet Oiler *Black Ranger* formed part of the "Fleet Train" joining the fleet at dawn on 30 October. Built by Harland & Wolff, Govan in 1940, she was one of a number in the "Ranger" class. Displacement varied between 3,313 to 3,417 tons gross, and she was photographed here in March, 1948.

Wright & Logan

In the "Implacable" class of Fleet Aircraft Carriers, was *Implacable* (pictured here) and *Indefatigable*. The order to build her was given to Fairfield Shipbuilding, Govan, in February, 1939, and she was completed 28 August, 1944. Displacement 23,000 tons (32,000 tons full load), overall length 766 feet 2 ins, beam 95 feet 9 ins. She carried over 60 aircraft, and a complement of around 2,000. *Implacable* was a familiar site at Rothesay. This is a later picture of her in May, 1949.

An enemy air formation was detected during its approach to the fleet during the forenoon. Unfortunately bad weather and low visibility prevented H.M.S. *Implacable* from flying off fighters to intercept this strike.

Before the exercise was completed H.M.S. *Crispin* (Commander (D), Fourth Escort Flotilla) closed H.M.S. *King George V* to transfer 'medical' stores. These were handled with great care, particularly when the heads of several prime Irish turkeys were seen to be protruding from the net suspended from a jackstay between the two ships.

No exercises were arranged for Thursday night, which was a welcome respite after a very strenuous day. H.M.S. *King George V* proceeded independently so as to be in a position 20 miles from the Second Cruiser Squadron and the Fourth and Fifth Destroyer Flotillas at 0900 on Friday, 1st November, 1946.

The Advance Training Carrier *Implacable* left Invergordon for Portland on 29 October. The air defence and control of air strikes was vested in *Implacable* which operated inside the screen astern of the "Fleet Train". Shortly after the exercises started, bad weather and low visibility prevented *Implacable* from flying off fighters to intercept an enemy air attack.

ATTACK ON CONVOY

At this time H.M.S. *King George V* assumed the guise of three 8-inch cruisers (Red Force) attacking a convoy represented by H.M. Ships *Cleopatra* and *Dido* screened by destroyers and supported by H.M. Ships *Superb* and *Diadem* (Blue Force). The hazards of the previous day—air and submarine attack—were now deemed to be non-existent. The intention of the Senior Officer Red Force was to close the convoy to within effective gun range as rapidly as possible, altering course only to avoid torpedo attack from the opposing destroyers. In pursuing this course, he was influenced by the recollection of the ineffectiveness of the German sorties against Russian convoys when more circumspect measures were attempted.

Onslaught, photographed here in July, 1946, formed part of the "Fleet Train" when she represented a Fleet Oiler. She was built by Fairfield Shipbuilding & Engineering Co. Ltd, Govan, in 1941. *Onslaught* (ex *Pathfinder*) was one of several in the "Onslow" class destroyers, and was one of the first to be built under War Construction Programme.

The "C" class destroyer *Crispin* (S.O.4th Escort Force) provided a screen for the "Fleet Train" from Londonderry. Others forming the protective force, included the destroyer *Hotspur*, and the frigates *Loch Arkaig, Loch Fada, Loch Veyatie* and *Loch Dunvegan*. *Crispin* is seen here making headway on 30 October.

Four battleships were built in the "King George V" class, *King George V, Duke of York, Anson* and *Howe*. Pictured here is *King George V* as she sets sail from Invergordon to join the fleet, on 29 October. Built by Vickers-Armstrong (Tyne), she was laid down in January, 1937, and took four years to build up to completion on 11 December, 1940. Fully loaded, her displacement was about 44,650 tons, length overall 745 feet, beam 103 feet, and carried a wartime complement of around 1900. She was protected from enemy gunfire by very thick armour belts, and she had a speed of 30 knots. Armament included ten 14-inch guns, each gun capable of hurling a shell, weighing nearly a ton, for a distance of about 25 miles. At this range the shell travelled nearly as high as Mount Everest.

Destroyer attacks developed as expected and although analysis showed that not all torpedoes were successfully avoided, the convoy which had retired under smoke was brought under fire. In situations such as this, the Senior Officer of the Force covering the convoy has a difficult decision to make. The safe and timely arrival of the convoy is his primary concern, and therefore unnecessary retirement or diversion of the convoy, coupled with the release of destroyers, must be avoided until it is clear that the raider is committed to an action as opposed to a feint attack. Undue delay, however, may give him little time and sea room in which to dispose his forces to beat off the attack when it develops.

The remainder of Friday was fully employed with a fighter direction exercise with aircraft from the Naval Air Station at Dale, manoeuvres, depth-charge firings by destroyers, the running of paravanes by H.M.S. *King George V* and a night encounter exercise followed by night shadowing by the cruisers. The fleet rounded Lands End at 0130 on Saturday, 2nd November, and at 0830 were off Start when R.A.F. Mosquitos and Beaufighters from Thorney Island attacked splash targets towed by H.M.S. *King George V* and H.M.S. *Superb* with rocket projectiles. At 0915 the fleet was met by 11 destroyers and escort vessels of the Third Escort Flotilla from Portland.

Fifteen vessels were now available to screen the heavy ships and control of the screen was vested in the Captain (D), Fifth Destroyer Flotilla, acting as Rear-Admiral (D). It was found that the volume of traffic on T.B.S.* made the handling of this large screen and its redisposition to cover gaps caused by destroyers dropping back, a difficult matter.

Disposed between Start Point and Portland Bill were seven submarines of the Seventh Submarine Flotilla. Individual attacks were delivered as the fleet proceeded eastwards, of which analysis shows that three were successful.

At 1300 the fleet was formed into two columns and manoeuvred as a whole into Weymouth Bay. The programmed time of arrival was 1400, and with a view to encouraging the press to draw a favourable comparison between the Royal Navy and the Southern Railway timetables, H.M. Ships *King George V* and *Superb* leading the two columns passed simultaneously through the eastern and northern entrances to Portland Harbour at 1400 exactly.

It might be helpful to the reader to understand the reasoning why certain vessels assumed the roles of others, and this is not unusual in times of limited budgets.
(1) As no 8-inch cruisers were available, *King George V* pretended to be 3 × 8-inch cruisers rather than herself. It would have to be in 8-inch gun range to 'fire' rather than firing from its normal range. (Red Force—nominally therefore 3 × 8-inch cruisers.)
(2) *Cleopatra* and *Dido* took on the role of a merchant convoy rather than themselves as 6-inch/5.25-inch cruisers.
(3) *Superb* and *Diadem* acted as themselves as 6-inch/5.25-inch cruisers acting as support for notional convoy made up of *Cleopatra* and *Dido*.

Ships of the 5th Destroyer Flotilla taking part included *Solebay* (C.D.5) pictured here, *St James* and *St Kitts*. For the purpose of illustration, the photograph shown here in May, 1950, shows the 5th Destroyer Flotilla on a later exercise, and was taken from *Solebay* with *St James* leading *Sluys*, *Gabbard* and *St Kitts* coming into line.

*Talk Between Ships/Talkback System.

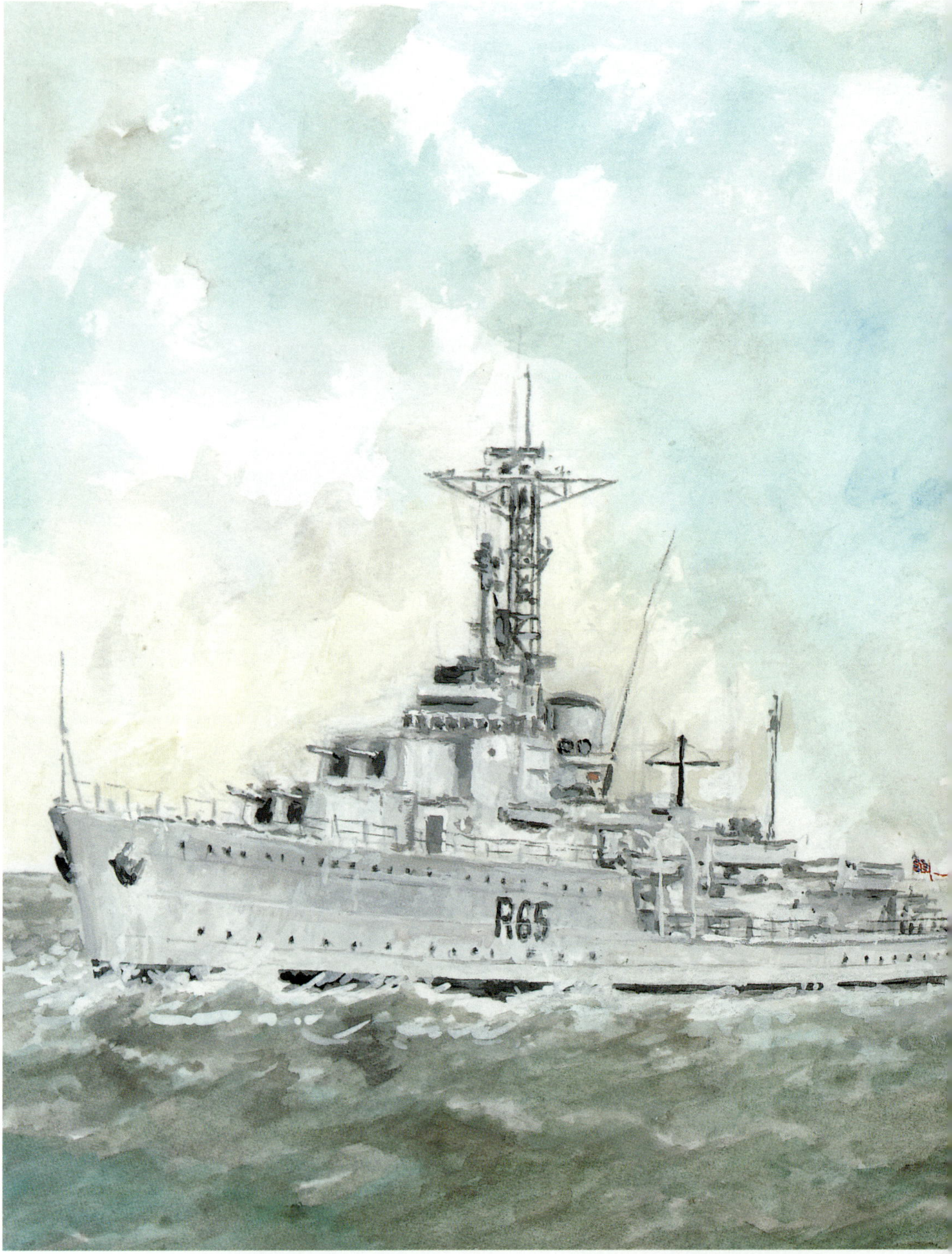
R65

101

Ships of the Royal Navy arriving at Portland at the end of the Home Fleet autumn manoeuvres in November, 1946. The "Battle" class destroyers *St.James* ahead of *St.Kitts*, 5th Destroyer Flotilla, with the battleship *King George V* following behind. (painting by Edward W. Paget-Tomlinson from a picture published in the Daily Telegraph, 4 November, 1946. Source unknown).

A nice view from *Solebay* with the flotilla full steam ahead.

This was similar to *Forth* assuming the role of a Fleet Oiler along with *Onslaught* and one 'genuine' oiler—*Black Ranger*—earlier in the exercise.

I do not think that the importance of submarines has been fully recognised, neither do I think that it has been realised how completely their advent has revolutionised naval warfare. In my opinion, as the motor vehicle has driven the horse from the road, so has the submarine driven the battleship from the sea.

Admiral Sir Percy Scott—1st June 1914.

Another view of *Superb* taken from a different angle, and a few years later.

Submarine Depot Ship
H.M.S. *Montclare* (S/m 3)

5

21 May–3 November 1947

TOWARDS the end of 1946 there was going to be a big change for me, the crew and the ship. *Forth*, we were told, was due for a refit, and we would be leaving Rothesay within the next 24 hours or so and heading for Devonport Dockyard. In a few weeks' time most of us would be transferred to *Montclare*, another submarine depot ship which would be taking the place of *Forth* at Rothesay as depot ship of the 3rd Submarine Flotilla.

Apart from the excitement of transferring to another ship, I was thrilled to learn that we would be returning to Rothesay. This really was good news, even though it would mean saying goodbye to *Forth*. From being a new recruit, *Forth* had changed me into a responsible Navy man, and taught me everything I needed to know. Obviously now I would be much better equipped, more proficient and more confident from the word go on joining another ship, and I hoped that *Montclare* would turn out to be as friendly and happy a ship as *Forth* had been.

We arrived at Devonport Dockyard during the first few days of January, 1947, and berthed alongside the quay. The transfer on to *Montclare* was not due to take place until 21 May, and over the following days and weeks I frequently took opportunities of standing on the fo'c'sle of *Forth* to view the changing scene in the dockyard. I was inspired by the sight of all these magnificent ships, many of which had been in action in various parts of the world during the war, while others were new, only recently completed.

Here at Devonport, one of our chief Naval bases in this country (the others being Chatham and Portsmouth), one could not help but be aware of a sense of greatness; a dignified humility seemed to fill the atmosphere, a quite deference for all that had gone on before. By the quayside lay some of our splendid warships, seemingly lying motionless in solitude and reverence for all their sister ships and lives lost in fierce battles at sea.

At Devonport, for me, the sight of such an assembly of different class ships and submarines was indeed inspiring. Although I had previously seen some of them at a distance when at sea during the Home Fleet Autumn Manoeuvres in November, 1946, this was the first time I had seen them close up.

The 35,000 ton battleship *King George V*, a splendid sight if ever there was one, hardly rippling the water as she was gracefully manoeuvred by tugs. This ship, which took about four years to complete, had an extremely powerful armament including ten 14-

A view from the boat deck of *Forth* in Devonport dockyard. Immediately to the right is the battleship *King George V* and to the far left, the Training Establishment ships *Defiance* and *Imperieuse II*, February, 1947.

Immediately ahead of *Forth*, the 45,000 ton, battleship *King George V* barely breaking water while being carefully towed by tugs at Devonport in March, 1947.

The Fleet Aircraft Carrier *Illustrious* being manoeuvred by tugs at Devonport, March, 1947.

Battleship *King George V* at Devonport, March, 1947.

From the fo'c'sle of Forth *at Devonport. On the left is the Fleet Aircraft Carrier* Victorious *and behind the destroyer is the Submarine Depot Ship* Montclare. *2 February, 1947.*

Commissioned only days before this photograph was taken, Alliance, *one of our very latest A-class submarines arrives alongside* Forth, *in March, 1947.*

inch guns, each capable of hurling a shell weighing nearly a ton for a distance of about 25 miles. Lying there also was the aircraft carrier *Illustrious* with her sister ship *Victorious* and the latest carrier *Implacable*. Further ahead lay our newest cruiser, *Superb*, and two sister ships to *King George V*, the battleships *Anson* and *Howe*. Berthed almost opposite to us was the Stokers' Training Establishment ship *Imperieuse*, and close to her was *Defiance*, the Torpedo Training Ship. There were also several other vessels at their moorings in the distance, but these could not be identified with any certainty.

I also had an excellent opportunity of taking a particularly good shot of the A-class submarine *Alliance* as she was coming alongside *Forth*. She was one of our latest submarines, only commissioned 11th March, 1947, and I was looking at her brand new.

As a youth during the war years I used to buy copies of the *War Illustrated* and *Sea Cadet*, and in them I read about some of the major sea battles involving many of our finest ships. Reporting was restricted in the early years of the war, for obvious reasons, with regard to the identification and movements of warships, but towards the end of the war many stories were told of sea battles and fleet involvements. It all took quite a while for this to sink in when one considered that many of the ships we saw in the dockyard had been in the front line defending our country. I did not overlook the fact, either, that *Forth* had served throughout the war, providing a base and a home for servicing and repairing her submarines and caring for her crews. Submarine depot ships have been described by some as hulks, but they played an extremely important role. They were very costly to equip and maintain with their workshops, machinery and repair shops, in addition to providing comforts and hospital facilities for submariners. The function of a depot ship was to move from base to base, rather than patrolling the high seas, since the loss of these ships in battle was a severe loss to the submarines and their crews who were maintained by them.

When at Devonport awaiting transfer onto Montclare *I saw many of our fine ships. These great ships were indeed a magnificent sight. This photograph shows the Fleet Aircraft Carrier* Victorious *in a striking pose. A sister ship to* Illustrious, *she began building at Vickers-Armstrong, Tyne, in May, 1937, and was completed 15 May, 1941.*

Associated Press

Although *Forth* was due for a refit, I believe an early departure for Devonport was brought about by a coal crisis which threatened to bring the dockyard to a standstill. It was vital to the yard that electricity supplies were maintained, and *Forth's* submarines were employed to generate power for the various wharves. *Forth* had the task of maintaining the 11 submarines taking part in what was known as 'Operation Blackcurrent', which lasted from 10th January to 9th May, 1947.

"Operation Blackcurrent"

In February, 1947, there was a critical coal crisis in the country, and *Forth* was in Devonport to maintain her submarines in working order to enable them to generate power to the dockyard. Submarines working singularly produced enough power to equal 140 tons of coal per week, but found that when the submarines were worked in "series" the total amount of power produced, was equivalent to 400 tons of coal per week.

Submarines were employed at various wharves in the dockyard, and in the event of any one submarine breaking down, they were to be replaced by any one of two submarines which were being kept unoccupied.

Submarines taking part in "OPERATION BLACKCURRENT" included, in the A-class - *Alderney* and *Alaric*, T-class - *Tradewind*, *Token* and *Taciturn*, and S-class - *Seneschal*, *Selene*, *Spur*, *Spiteful*, *Sturdy*, and *Scythian*.

Whilst at Devonport on 21st February, 1947, another line was fouled up in a running block on the foremast spar on *Forth*, and as I had volunteered to go aloft previously, the Divisional Officer approached me with an instruction to get it fixed without delay. Barry, a mess mate of mine who had also volunteered with me the first time, said he would go up if I did.

I really cannot describe adequately what this was like. I had no problem climbing up the vertical steel ladder strapped to the mast, I just kept going, but I never seemed to reach the top. I refrained from looking down until I had climbed into the crow's nest. Barry was not

Scythian was built by Scotts' Shipbuilding and Engineering Co Ltd, Greenock. She was launched on 14 April, 1944, and commissioned 11 July, the same year. *Scythian* was used for the making of the feature film "The Man Who Never Was", when she played the part of His Majesty's submarine *Seraph* and had *Seraph's* pennant number 'P219' painted on her conning-tower for that purpose. *Scythian* was one of three Group 2 S-boats, *Sea Devil* and *Scotsman* were the others.

T-class submarine *Taciturn* was completed 7 October, 1944, and after her first working up patrol in home waters she was in the West Java Sea, and South China Sea when she was narrowly missed by a torpedo fired by a Japanese submarine. *Taciturn* was one of three T-class boats generating electricity under "Operation Blackcurrent". We see her here in the Far East in 1945. Source unknown.

far behind, and soon he was standing beside me. Looking down I saw my mess mates and other members of the crew who had gathered round, all minuscule in stature and seemingly like motionless flies with their faces tilted upwards to watch the action.

It was a clear day, cold, and the sea a little choppy, but fortunately, no real wind. Even so the movement of the ship at that height was obviously very noticeable, as the incline from the perpendicular became greatly accentuated as the whole ship swayed from port to starboard. To put it plainly, I was scared stiff, if only for a moment. I took in the whole length and size of the ship, which appeared far more like a toy boat on a pond than a 9,000-ton warship on the sea.

Barry and I stood for a few moments acclimatising ourselves to the height and movement, weighing up and considering the best approach to the faulty block, and establishing the nearest ropes in the rigging in the vicinity to hang on to. There was nothing else for it but to get on with it. Barry and I had arranged between ourselves that I would lead and attend to the block, and in the event of any difficulty, he would follow me out on to the spar.

A familiar sight in Rothesay was the T-class submarine *Taciturn*. She was built by Vickers-Armstrong at Barrow, launched in June, 1944, and commissioned on 3 September, that year. Her motto was "Deeds Not Words".

Selene was also built by Cammell Laird, Birkenhead, launched 24 April, 1944, and commissioned 10 June, the same year. These S-class boats were reputed to be able to "crash-dive" in 30 seconds. *Selene* was one of the seventeen Group 3 S-boats of the 1942/43 building programme.

Leaving the relative safety of the rostrum and making a first move outwards, I became paralysed with terror. Sitting with the cross-bar between my legs, I was absolutely petrified to go any further, but I knew my mess mates would be encouraging from below, and if I turned back, then Barry would have to do the job instead of me, and he was terror-stricken as well. Inch by inch, and clinging on to every available rope for dear life, I painstakingly edged my way forward, and ultimately reached the block. It was a simple enough task: the running line had become knotted and had jammed between the spigot and the inside of the block. It was only necessary, therefore, to free the knot from inside the block and undo it.

Needless to say, it was a tremendous relief to climb back into the rostrum; even being there was bad enough. I never wanted to volunteer for anything such as this ever again. It was necessary to free the line, but the way of doing it involved tremendous risk. The height and sway alone were enough to send cold shivers down one's spine, but the completely unprotected exposure of being out on a spar, with no real safeguards, only rigging to cling on to, was blood curdling and horrifying.

Another view of the A-class submarine *Alliance* making her way to Rothesay in 1947, to join the 3rd Submarine Flotilla. After being with us for a few months, *Alliance* was on trial exercises in the English Channel. This photograph was taken sometime in June, 1947. Source unknown.

The flotilla of submarines at Devonport in the early part of 1947 generating electricity to the dockyard, included *Alderney*, one of the latest A-class boats. She was built by Vickers-Armstrong, Barrow, and launched 25 June, 1945. Her first commission began on 2 November, 1946, when CO, Lt.I.S.McIntosh, D.S.O. M.B.E. D.S.C. R.N. formally accepted her for service in the Royal Navy. Source unkown.

(RNSM)

After a few moments in the rostrum to regain my composure, I considered I had done enough for King and Country that day, and set about climbing down as quickly as I could. The crew gave me a cheer as we reached the deck, the Divisional Officer just said 'Well done Walker, run along now', to which I replied 'Aye, Aye, Sir', and we all resumed our duties. Wooden, one of my mess mates who went up the pole on the first occasion, had been drafted to another posting, but McMillan confessed he was frozen stiff with fear, and would never volunteer for anything like that again.

Spur, an S-boat built by Cammell Laird, Birkenhead, launched 17 November, 1944, and commissioned 6 January, 1945. In December, 1945, she was at Rothesay, and remained in the immediate post-war period attached to the 7th Submarine Flotilla for training and exercises. In November, 1946, she was taken in hand for refit at Devonport, during which time she became one of the eleven submarines under "Operation Blackcurrent".

Wright & Logan

This great carrier *Indefatigable* was in the Devonport area during the few months I was there in early 1947. *Indefatigable*, a sister ship to *Implacable*, was built at Clydebank, begun in November, 1939, and completed 3 May, 1944.

Shore leave at Devonport continued as normal, and I took my leave entitlement along with the others. Having worked in London for several months before enlistment, I was able to see for myself some of the war damage around St. Paul's and the London Docks, which I considered bad enough, but I was absolutely shocked to see what had happened to the City of Plymouth. The whole city was devastated, rubble everywhere, and hardly a building standing which was not damaged in one way or another as the result of five bombing raids on Plymouth in April, 1941. The city was attacked by 640 German bombers, leaving 750 people dead and 30,000 homeless. Few public buildings and houses escaped damage.

The T-class submarine *Tradewind*, seen here in May, 1948, was built at Chatham Dockyard. She was launched 11 December, 1942, and commissioned 24 July, 1943. She looked a little different during "Operation Blackcurrent" from when she was built, since in August, 1946, she arrived at Portsmouth to be converted for acoustic experimental work. Her external bow tubes were removed and her bow fined. Four of her bow torpedo orifices were blanked off. Her superstructure and Bridge plating was faired and a 'Niebelung' unit was faired into the fore-end of her Bridge. Her low-power periscope was removed and an ANF Radar mast fitted in its place. All gun armament and upper deck torpedo tubes were also removed. Her Type 129 asdic/Sonar Unit was removed from the fore-end of the ballast keel and replaced with a German 'Balkon' Unit. A type 120 retractable asdic/Sonar Unit was also fitted.

THE WESTERN WALL OF LONDON
"A general view of the devastated Cripplegate area of London, photographed on Tuesday 22 July, 1947, from a building in Jewin Crescent looking over the area guarded by the Roman Wall, where new excavations are to be carried out. On the left is the Church of St. Giles, Cripplegate, and to the right of the Church is the bastion at the corner where the Wall turns sharply east and south. To the right, but not easily identifiable, are the remains of two other bastions and parts of the wall".

I recall the NAAFI in Plymouth, which was operating fairly normally, standing in a sea of rubble. Part of a church was standing, and a cinema. We frequently visited the NAAFI, and the cinema, possibly the only one left standing; every time there were long queues. It certainly was an eye-opener to see such large devastated areas, and to realise how many of our towns and cities must have suffered in this way.

Not far from the dockyard was a row of shattered shops, a few of which were functioning fairly normally, and one of these was a tailor. Having very recently been promoted to Signalman, and since I was still wearing the uniform I had been issued with on joining, I decided to buy a smarter made-to-measure 'Tiddley' suit in a smoother cloth than the rather rough standard-issue serge. Clothing coupons were still somewhat of a problem, since rationing was still in force, but the tailor was keen to do business and prepared to accept additional cash in lieu of coupons, so I was able to do a deal with him.

I was thrilled when I collected my new uniform from him about a couple of weeks later, and I decided to keep this as my special suit for shore leave only. The tailor, whilst conforming to regulation requirements, had given a little more depth to the V-neck of the jumper, and the bell-bottom trousers were about an inch wider. The cloth was superb, and the suit had shape and style, and wearing it felt altogether different from the Pusser issue.

Shore leave at Devonport and Plymouth was generally dull, and there was simply no comparison with Rothesay. This was, however, the real world, where the legacy of war was apparent all around for everyone to see. There was little to do in the way of entertainment, or

Tugs being employed to bring *Montclare* alongside *Forth* in readiness for the transfer of personnel - February, 1947.

places to go, and one could not help but gaze in absolute amazement at all the devastation everywhere one looked; one began to appreciate the terrible loss of life and suffering the city and its people had been through.

The weeks gradually passed, and one day I saw my next ship berthed across the dock from where *Forth* was lying. As I stood on the fo'c'sle I watched as she was being brought alongside by tugs. I marvelled at the careful handling by the tugs, as they slowly pulled

Captain J.E.Slaughter, Captain of the Submarine Depot Ship *Montclare*.

A really splendid picture showing the two Submarine depot ships alongside one another for the transfer from *Forth* onto *Montclare* on 21 May, 1947. *Montclare* is secured along the port side of *Forth* which has the gangplank in position for access to both ships. This photograph was taken sometime in March, 1947, at Devonport.

Bottom left: This picture of bombed and shattered buildings in Queen Street, Devonport, could have been taken during the few months I was there in 1947. Yet, in May, 1951, the date of this photograph, twisted metal, broken masonry and rubble spilling out onto the pavement and road, still remains. Photograph kindly supplied by City of Plymouth Museums and Art Gallery.

Bottom left middle: Another photograph of Queen Street, Devonport, taken in May, 1951. Buildings that were not demolished in the blitz, stood shattered, stark and empty. There was so much devastation everywhere one looked. City of Plymouth Museums and Art Gallery.

Bottom right middle: The remains of some of the flats in Monice Square, Devonport. Any which escaped being flattened were left gutted and ruined. This photograph was taken in July, 1951, and kindly suppplied by City of Plymouth Museums and Art Gallery.

Bottom right: The *Prudential* building in Bedford Street, Plymouth, taken in May, 1951, suffered heavy damage. The roof has collapsed, and rubble from adjoining buildings lay strewn around the frontage. Whole streets of houses were bomb blasted leaving many thousands of people homeless. City of Plymouth Museums and Art Gallery.

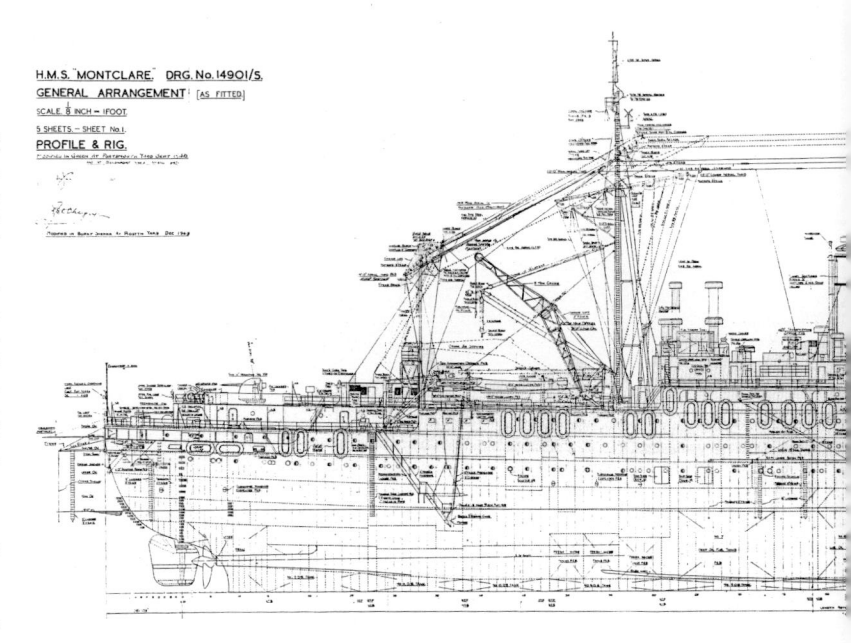

her away from the quay before swinging her round and positioning her to line up bow to stern with *Forth*. As the tugs pushed gently on her port side she finally came to rest directly alongside *Forth*, where she was secured. My time on *Forth* was coming to an end.

The transfer to *Montclare* went smoothly, the date of my transfer being officially recorded in my Service record as 21st May, 1947. A number of my colleagues transferred with me, whilst others bid their farewells, with some going on leave, others leaving the Service or being drafted to new postings.

Transferring from one ship to another was rather like moving home without taking any of the furniture with you. My colleagues and I, as buntings and sparklers, only had to deal with ourselves and our personal kit; we were not expected to be involved with any general work in preparing the ship and the equipment that went with it.

NATIONAL MARITIME MUSEUM LONDON

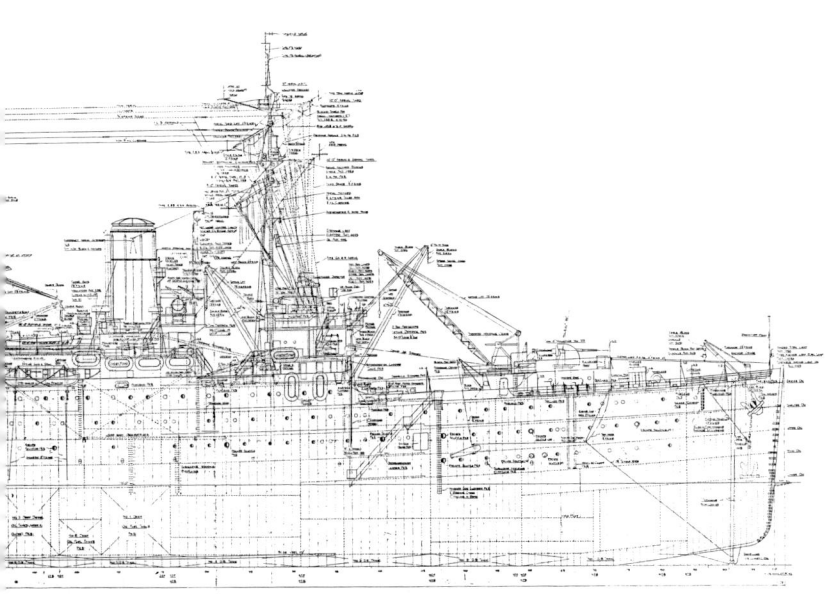

The drawings for the modifications to Submarine depot ship *Montclare* were drawn to a scale of 1/8th - 1 foot. Those carried out at Portsmouth Yard in September, 1946, and at Devonport Yard in April, 1947, in readiness for our transfer from *Forth* in May 1947, are shown in green on the original drawings. Those shown in Burnt Sienna were modifications carried out at Rosyth Yard in December, 1949. Some detail has been lost in reproducing these drawings but the ship structure and layout show up well in this profile.

Indeed, this had been the case on board *Forth*, where our seamanship ship duties ended with rotas on deck scrubbing and cleaning, and never were we involved at all in general ropework, casting off or tying up. No anchor work, lifeboat maintenance, crane or derrick work, nor anything else concerned with the preparedness or running of the ship, formed part of our duties, neither did we have anything to do with the ship's provisions and supplies. We were quite ignorant regarding all these essentials.

Montclare was built by John Brown in 1921 as a 16,314-ton Canadian Pacific Railway liner, and plied between Southampton and the East. In March, 1931, she ran aground in dense fog on the rocks of the island of Little Cumbrae in the Firth of Clyde. Three hundred passengers were on board, some of whom clambered to safety over the rocks after being landed by the ship's boats. Later she was pulled off by tugs.

Below: Bomb blast and fire ruined many buildings, such as these flats in Monice Square, Devonport, and left countless others unsafe and desolate. This photograph was taken in July, 1951, and kindly supplied by City of Plymouth Museums and Art Gallery.

Transfer of personnel from *Forth* to *Montclare* was completed on 21 May, 1947. Quite a number of us transferred from *Forth* including one or two from Communications, and others were drafted to new postings.

Opposite: *Montclare* making smoke, and about to set sail for Rothesay. 21 May, 1947.

These interesting notes on the background of *Montclare* came up on my teleprinter one day whilst on duty in the Communications Office. The message went on to say that *Montclare* was taken over by the Admiralty early in the war and began service as an armed merchant cruiser. In March, 1942, she was docked at Southampton to be adapted as a Submarine Depot Ship, though she was not used for this purpose as it was decided to re-convert her as a Destroyer Depot Ship. In March, 1945, she steamed for the Far East to become Flagship of the famous British Fleet Train as a Destroyer Depot Ship. Early in 1946 she was docked at Portsmouth to be re-converted as a 21,000-ton Submarine Depot Ship. Additional officers' cabins and messing space for junior ratings were constructed. In addition to her complement of 500, plus repair staff ratings, she had to accommodate about 70 submarine crew.

Another view of the A-class submarine *Auriga* attached to the 3rd Submarine Flotilla at Rothesay. This photograph was taken as she was leaving Portsmouth Harbour. Source unknown.

(RNSM)

"RN Photographs"

"RN photographs"

A magnificent view of *Montclare*, now as depot ship of the 3rd Submarine Flotilla, with four of her submarines in Rothesay Bay, in June, 1947.

Profile of the Submarine Depot Ship *Montclare*.

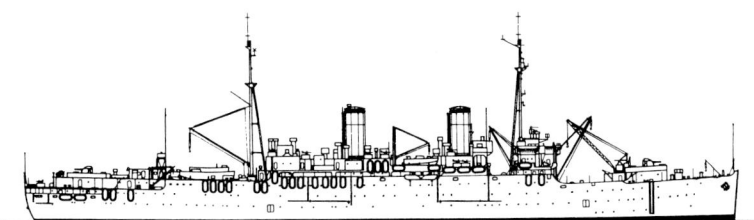

'*Montclare* is 550 feet long, beam 70 feet, and is now under the command of Captain J. E. Slaughter, D.S.O., R.N.', the message ended.

We arrived back at Rothesay on 30th May, 1947, dropped anchor and tied up to the permanent mooring buoy in Rothesay Bay. Life on board had quickly resumed normal routine. Buntings and sparklers were now in Mess 61, lockers had been allocated, mess places arranged, and new faces had become friends. The sleeping arrangements were roughly the same as on *Forth*, and we as transferees had taken up similar positions for slinging our hammocks as we had had on *Forth*.

There was, however, one big difference, I wasn't a new boy any more, and I had my say along with everyone else whenever the occasion required it. The mess seemed a little more spacious on *Montclare*, as did the area for sleeping, though not by much, since these areas still seemed overcrowded. Generally the whole ship had more of a feeling of spaciousness about it. *Montclare* certainly had a greater displacement than *Forth* but was around 25 feet shorter and around 5 feet less in beam. The agreeable feeling one gathered about the ship undoubtedly had something to do with the fact that *Forth* had been built as a Depot Ship, whereas *Montclare*, although being older, had originally been built as a liner. My office, too, was very similar in size to the one on *Forth*, and the teleprinters and equipment were also similar. In contrast to *Forth* the areas of deck appeared larger, and this didn't lessen the scrubbing and hosing down.

T-class boat *Token* was built by Portsmouth Dockyard, launched 19 March, 1943, and commissioned 3 September, 1945. In March, 1946, she was with the 3rd Submarine Flotilla based on *Forth* at Rothesay, when she took part in "Operation Exodus", a full-scale exercise to give (COQC) Commanding Officers Qualifying Course, experience in attacking a large target, this being *Forth*. In May, 1946, she took part with submarines *Auriga*, *Thermoplae*, *Affray* and *Tantalus* in "Exercise On Guard", a simulated attacking exercise in the Irish Sea on the new battleship *Vanguard*. *Token* with Snort is seen here entering Portsmouth harbour in May, 1948. (copyright - Wright & Logan).

A-class submarine *Aurochs* making her way to Rothesay in June, 1947, to join the 3rd Submarine Flotilla based on *Montclare*. *Aurochs* was one of a number of A-class boats designed for action in the Pacific. Built by Vickers-Armstrong, Barrow, launched 28 July, 1945, and commissioned 29 December, 1946.

Wright & Logan

Lending a hand hosing down and scrubbing decks on *Montclare*. June, 1947.

Due to the haphazard and cramped sleeping arrangements on *Montclare*, it was very refreshing to spend the night ashore whenever possible.

A typical scene in Rothesay Bay. This photograph taken in August, 1947, shows *Mull of Kintyre*, on the left, and *Woodbridge Haven* to the right. On the starboard side of *Montclare* are the submarines *Alliance* (P417), *Aurochs* (P426), and another A-class.

It was a great feeling to be back at Rothesay. We had been away about four months, and there was a lot to catch up on. It was Springtime, the ferries were busy, and dozens of visitors were coming to Rothesay at the start of the holiday season. The daily routine on board settled down as ever, with the everlasting cleaning of decks, kit maintenance, washing, ironing and mending clothes, and writing home to family and friends. About twice a week films were shown on board in the evenings in a large area set aside for the purpose, and these shows were usually well attended. The air very quickly became thick with cigarette and tobacco smoke, and a dash for the gangway was commonplace as soon as the film ended.

After a few weeks of being back at Rothesay, quite a number of vessels started arriving in the bay. They were gathering, we were told, for a Review which was to take place in the latter part of July off Greenock/Gourock on the Firth of Clyde. It was to be a major event, and *Montclare* would be taking part.

In June, 1947, I was reading *The Rothesay Express* when I noticed a reference to the former submarine depot ship *Cyclops*. The paper stated that *Cyclops* had been taken in tow in that month from the Clyde to the Bristol Channel, where she was to be broken up. Three months previously she had been brought back to the Clyde after breaking away from tugs in the Irish Sea.

Ted Fisher securing submarine lines on *Montclare* at Rothesay in August, 1947. Submarines alongside are *Alliance* and *Aurochs*.

During the summer months the crew of *Montclare* were from time to time allowed to go swimming off the side. The normal procedure was that swimmers descended the Accommodation Ladder from the Bridge Deck on the starboard side and entered the water from the lower rungs. I only went swimming once, and on this singular occasion about a dozen of us assembled on the Bridge Deck at the point of descent, when someone said 'how about diving off from here?' This was followed by much banter and jibing as to who would dare do it, and who would go first. Looking over the rail, the water did seem an awful long way down, but after further hesitation, dithering and deliberation, I decided to follow through with the challenge. I volunteered to do it if two others would follow, and in the end, there were three of us. I summoned up my courage, and dived off.

This drawing is meant to be me reading a book a few days before leaving for Rothesay. The artist, one of my mess mates, called himself "Zach".

Submarines alongside *Montclare* at Rothesay, taken sometime in August, 1947. *Alliance, Taciturn, Ambush, Alderney,* and *Alaric*.

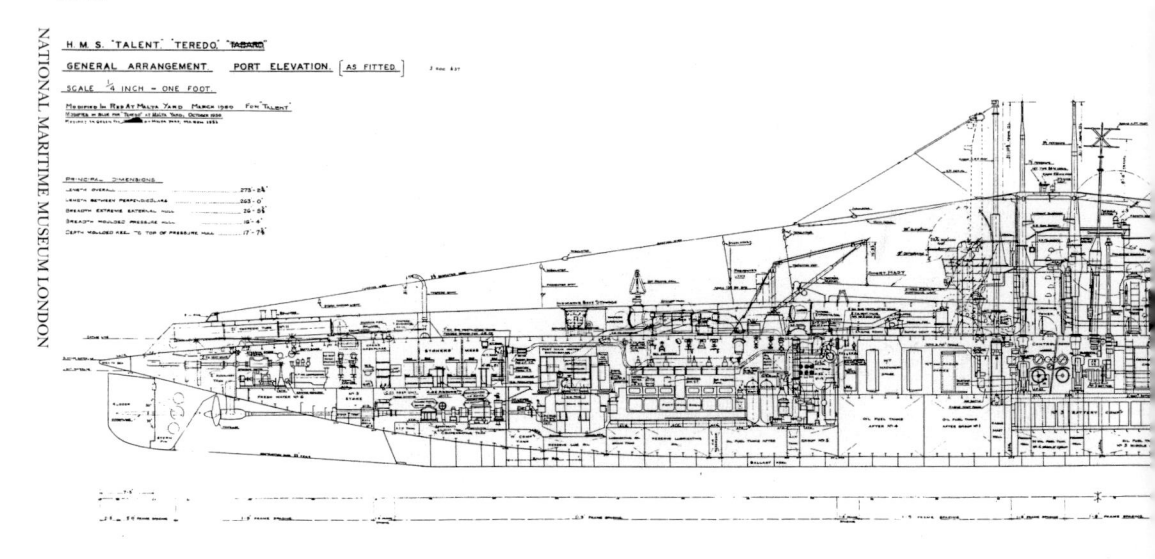

An impressive view of the T-class boat *Teredo* getting underway. *Teredo* was attached to the 3rd Submarine Flotilla based on *Forth* during 1946, and for a time on *Montclare* in 1947. This photograph was taken in May, 1947.

The Bridge Deck was 28 feet above the water line. On the way down, I was in free fall, twisting and tilting, completely unable to keep a level plane, and gathering speed as I fell past the portholes of the Shelter Deck and Upper Deck and past the Main Deck. Suddenly I hit the surface of the water, plunging down and down and down. I do not remember how cold the water was, but I do recall being in a state of sheer panic whilst submerged. I realised all too quickly that I must have gone deep. I could feel my ankles and legs mingling with the reeds or some other vegetation, which told me I was near the bottom of the Clyde waters in Rothesay Bay.

Whatever it was down there stimulated my arms and legs into paddling as fast as they would go, to propel me as speedily as possible to the surface. I was gasping, choking and breathless when I surfaced, and my head was throbbing like anything.

Original drawings for the T-class submarines *Teredo* and *Talent* drawn to a scale of 1/4" - 1 foot. Modifications for *Teredo*, carried out at Malta Yard in October, 1950, were shown in blue. There were also modifications shown in green at Malta Yard carried out in March, 1953, but it is not clear which submarine this applied to.

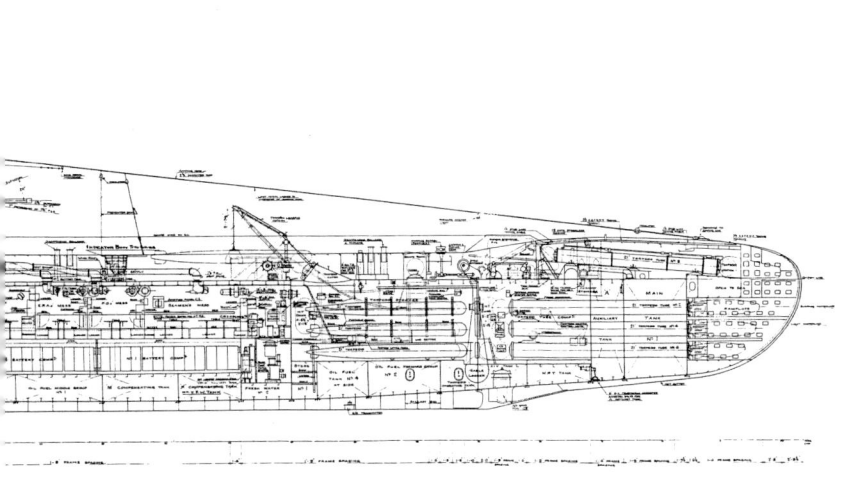

It took me several moments to regain my senses, and then I heard a cheer go up from those on deck, towering over me at what appeared to be a tremendous height. It was only then that I fully appreciated the height between the deck and sea level. Two or three of the crew were on the bottom rung of the ladder offering a hand to haul me out of the water, and we started to climb the ladder back on deck. 'What was it like?' they asked me. 'Terrible,' I said, 'don't do it.' That was good enough for them to change their minds. They all said 'well done', and with that I grabbed my towel and went below to wash and dress, and left them to it.

Going up the pole on *Forth* to correct a minor fault with a block was hair-raising enough, if you could stand the height and were especially careful. Diving off the side from such a height into the murky waters of the Clyde was a completely different scenario, and

Mull of Kintyre was a Maintenance and Repair ship, built in North Vancouver between 1944 - 1945 and was a familiar site in Rothesay Bay during 1946 and 1947. Her displacement 8,580 tons, length overall 439 feet, and beam 62 feet. This is how she looked in December, 1948.

Wright & Logan

Sister ship to Onslaught *in the "Onslow" class of destroyers, was* Opportune, *built by John I Thorneycroft & Co, Ltd, of Woolston. She was completed on 23 February, 1942, and was a fairly frequent visitor to Rothesay during 1947.*

one that was just plain stupid. Normally it was not in my nature to take part in such pranks, and I should have known better.

There was nothing in Regulations to say you couldn't jump or dive off the side, and by doing so, I gained absolutely nothing. There was no personal glorification, satisfaction or achievement in even attempting this, and I should have resisted being egged on to doing something against my better judgement. I was taking a tremendous risk in getting snarled up below, perhaps seriously injuring myself or worse, on some sunken submarine scrap, losing a limb and perhaps my life. As far as I could tell, I seemed to be unhurt, and I thanked God for it.

> The true strength of the Navy is not in the multitude of ships, but in the energies and alacrity of officers and crew.
>
> Thomas Cochrane, Earl of Dundonald – 1860.

Another view of the T-class boat Ambush *underway in November, 1947. She was commissioned on 20 May, 1947, by Lt-Cdr.G.E.Hunt, D.S.C. R.N. and entered service with the 3rd Submarine Flotilla, based on* Montclare *when I saw her frequently during the summer of that year.*

The Clyde Naval Review 6

Friday 18 July–Sunday 27 July 1947

MY COLLEAGUES and I heard through the grapevine that an important event was being planned around the last week of July. This was to take the form of a large-scale assemblage of naval craft and ships of the Home Fleet in the Firth of Clyde.

This did not come as a complete surprise to me, since I had read some advance notices announcing this in *The Buteman and West Coast Chronicle* on 11th October, 1946. The Lord Provost of Glasgow, Sir Hector McNeill, had taken the leading role with Lord Inverclyde in prompting the Admiralty to put on the show, and although it was stated that financial and other considerations ruled out organising a royal review of the Fleet, the Admiralty would arrange for a visit to be made of the Home Fleet 'augmented by as many other ships of the Navy as can be made available at the time'.

It was hoped to attract large numbers of tourists from the continent, especially from the Scandinavian countries, many of whom it was thought would probably find accommodation on the passenger ships bringing them here. This advance notice was intended to give 'all who cater for the visitor time to make their preparations'. The review was being staged to coincide with the Clyde yachting fortnight, and probably the Seawanhaka Cup.

As the event drew nearer, more news appeared in the *Rothesay Express* on 4th March, 1947.

This photograph, taken by me after great efforts to get close enough in a rowing boat, shows Montclare *dressed overall in readiness to leave for the review site.*

Montclare from a different angle shows up well here.

Apart from *Illustrious*, the other carrier attending the Clyde Naval Review was *Vengeance*, one of several in the "Colossus" class of Light Fleet Aircraft Carriers. Displacement 13,190 tons and class length overall around 695 feet. Her beam across flight deck 112 feet 6 ins. *Vengeance* carried between 39 to 44 aircraft, and a complement of around 1,400. She was built by Swan Hunter, Wallsend-on-Tyne, and building began in November, 1942, and completed 15 January, 1945. She was photographed here in September, 1949.

FROG MEN AT NAVAL REVIEW

Exhibitions by "frog men" whose exploits played such an important part in the invasion of Europe, will be a feature of the programme of entertainment to be staged by men of the Home Fleet during the Clyde Naval review this summer. The public will also see the ceremony of "crossing the line", drilling, diving and numerous other exhibitions.

The 80–100 vessels taking part in the review, headed by the flagship *Duke of York*, will anchor in the area bounded by Greenock, Helensburgh, Gourock and the Cloch. They will be open to visitors each afternoon.

With some 80–100 vessels reported to be taking part, this had all the makings of a very impressive and prestigious public showing of British naval warships and auxiliaries at its best, in addition to which it was to be a Royal occasion. King George VI, Queen Elizabeth and the Princesses Elizabeth and Margaret were to spend two days reviewing the fleet.

On 1st July, 1947, the *Rothesay Express* announced more details of the timetable of events, and stated that the Royal Family would spend 22nd and 23rd July with the fleet. They would inspect several of the principal warships, including the battleships *Duke of York* (flagship),

The battleship *Howe*, a sister ship to *King George V*, was built by Fairfield Shipbuilding and Engineering Co, Ltd, Govan. She was laid down in June, 1937, and completed on 29 August, 1942. This photograph was taken in May, 1947.

Wright & Logan

Anson and *Howe* and the carriers *Vengeance* and *Illustrious*. Other vessels open to the public would be cruisers, depot ships, destroyers, frigates, sloops, corvettes and submarines, as well as a variety of small craft.

By 11th July some of the vessels taking part in the line-up at the Tail of the Bank were arriving in Rothesay Bay. These included the destroyers *Onslaught*, *Onslow* and *Opportune*, the frigate *Woodbridge Haven*, and eighteen submarines.

While these vessels were gathering at Rothesay prior to leaving for the review site, the main fleet was making its way to take up position in the Clyde. In the days leading up to the opening itself, essential activities of the ship's company included vigorous washing, polishing, scrubbing and hosing down in order to make the entire ship spotlessly clean and ready for inspection. In the days before departing to take up our position *Montclare* was dressed overall.

Reporters from various newspapers and magazines covered this event to a greater or lesser extent, but none took a greater interest than the *Glasgow Herald*, who reported this event fully and in considerable detail. This paper's coverage is reproduced here with kind permission of Scottish Media Newspapers.

One of a number of "Bay" class frigates built was *Burghead Bay* pictured here in June, 1950. She was built by Charles Hill & Son, Bristol, and launched in March, 1945. Length was 307 feet 4 inches overall, beam 38 feet 6 inches, with a displacement of 1,600 tons. Complement 157.

126

Bicester, the "Hunt" class destroyer (Blankney No.2) Type in March, 1949, built by Hawthorne Leslie, Hebburn-on-Tyne, and launched in September, 1941. Displacement 1,050 tons, length overall 280 feet, and beam 31 feet 6 inches. She had a complement of 146.

Glasgow Herald
Friday, 18th July, 1947

HOME FLEET ARRIVES IN CLYDE

Tail of the Bank Spectacle Marred by Mist and Rain

MAJESTIC ASSEMBLY OF ARMED MIGHT

Seen here is *Sirius* in the "Dido" class cruisers. Built at Portsmouth, she was begun in April, 1938, and completed in 1942. She is pictured here in May, 1947.

The arrival of the Home Fleet at the Tail of the Bank this afternoon was almost blacked out by mist and light rain, as it had so often been blacked out by security during the war. Hardy spectators were rewarded by

Amongst the "Battle" class destroyers attending the Review, was *Sluys*, built by Cammell Laird and launched 28 February, 1945. June, 1948.

meagre glimpses of the grey-painted battleships and cruisers as they slid gently to their moorings. Later the weather cleared considerably.

Immediately after the ships arrived Vice-Admiral Sir Frederick H. G. Dalrymple-Hamilton, Flag-Officer Commanding, Scotland and Northern Ireland, went off from Princes Pier, Greenock, in his barge to call upon the Commander-in-Chief, Admiral Sir Neville Syfret, K.C.B., in his flagship the *Duke of York*.

Admiral Syfret then came ashore, accompanied by Vice-Admiral Dalrymple-Hamilton, in the Commander-in-Chief's green barge, which had been lowered from the flagship. He was met on Princes Pier by Captain G. A. Thring, R.N., Commanding Officer, Faslane, and by Colonel R. F. Cornwall, Royal Marines.

The Commander-in-Chief then left by car for Glasgow, where he paid a courtesy call on Sir Hector McNeill, Lord Provost of Glasgow, and later on the Provost of Greenock. Meanwhile Rear-Admiral Harold Hickling, Admiral Commanding Training Battleship, called on the Provost of Helensburgh, while Rear-Admiral A. H. Parker called first on the Provost of Gourock and later on the Provost of Dunoon.

Mighty Armada

As the mist gradually lifted, the spectators ashore were able to make out something of the carefully evolved pattern in which over 100 naval vessels lie displayed. Close to Greenock lie the three King George V class battleships – the *Duke of York* (which was originally to be named the *Anson*), the *Anson* (ex-*Jellicoe*), and the *Howe*, all of which were laid down in 1937. These battleships have each a complement of about 2000 men and a loaded displacement of nearly 45,000 tons.

Of these ships, the flagship, the *Duke of York*, was built at John Brown's Clydebank yard, and survived the Clydebank blitz while fitting out. The *Howe* was also built on the Clyde, by Fairfield at their Govan yard, while the third battleship, the *Anson*, was built by Swan Hunter on the Tyne.

Another destroyer in the "Battle" class attending the Review, was *St Kitts*, also built by Swan Hunter, and launched on 12 January, 1944. June, 1953.

The fourth ship in the line of "big ships" closest to Greenock is the light fleet carrier *Vengeance*, another Swan Hunter ship, which was commissioned only two years ago. This Colossus-class ship carries 39 to 44 aircraft and has a loaded displacement of 17,000 tons.

Behind the *Vengeance*, and moored alone, is the second aircraft carrier, the *Illustrious*, larger than the *Vengeance*, and first of the Illustrious-class, which was built at Barrow by Vickers-Armstrong between 1937 and 1940.

Opposite: Many corvettes were built in the "Castle" class, and *Flint Castle* shown here in May, 1947, was built by Henry Robb, Ltd, Leith, in 1943. Displacement between 1,060 to 1,100 tons, length 252 feet overall, beam 36 feet 8 inches.

A sister ship in the "Battle" class destroyers was *Gabbard*, built by Swan Hunter, and launched 16 March, 1945. August, 1949.

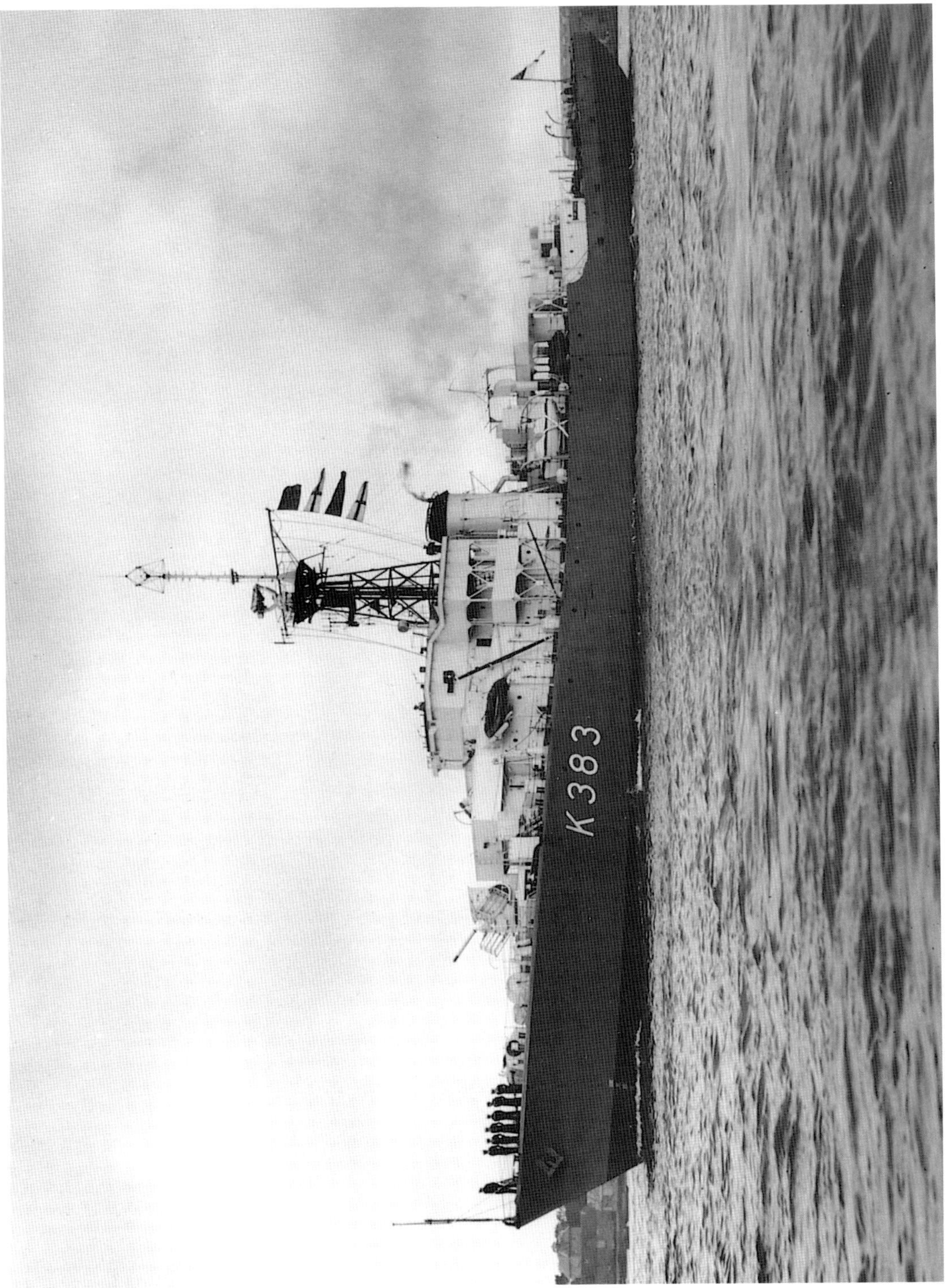

Wright & Logan

Pictured here is the "Fort" class ship *Fort Rosalie*, built by United Shipyards in Montreal. She was launched on 18 November, 1944, and completed 7 April, 1945. *Fort Rosalie* was used as an Armament and Naval Stores issuing vessel. November, 1947.

Lines of Ships

Most of the remaining ships are drawn up in a broad V, with its point towards the Kilcreggan shore, and having four lines of ships to the west and five (or, counting the big ships, seven) towards the east. In addition three lines of smaller ships are drawn up at an angle, to the east of the *Duke of York*.

The cruisers *Cleopatra*, *Sirius*, *Diadem* and *Dido* take up the centre of the front rank of the western ships, flanked by the flagship cruiser, the *Superb*, and by the submarine depot ships *Maidstone* and *Montclare*. Only one of these five cruisers, the *Sirius*, was built on the Clyde. She came from Scotts' yard in 1941 and is one of the Dido-class of 5500 tons displacement.

The western arm also contains a considerable number of destroyers, as well as the submarine target vessel *Woodbridge Haven*. Here, too, are the submarines, 20 in number, including a sizeable representation from the new A-Class. Behind them come the Royal Fleet Auxiliaries, which wear the blue ensign and are manned by merchant officers.

These are the oilers *Black Ranger*, *Prestol* (a familiar Clyde ship), and *Thornol*, the water boat *Petrobus*, and the depot ships *Fort Rosalie* and *Fort Duquesne*, whose typically merchantmen outlines look somewhat misplaced among the characteristic lean silhouettes of fighting ships.

Fort Duquesne, was also a Supply and Stores ship built by West Coast in 1944, and seen here in August, 1947.

CLYDE BERTHING PLAN

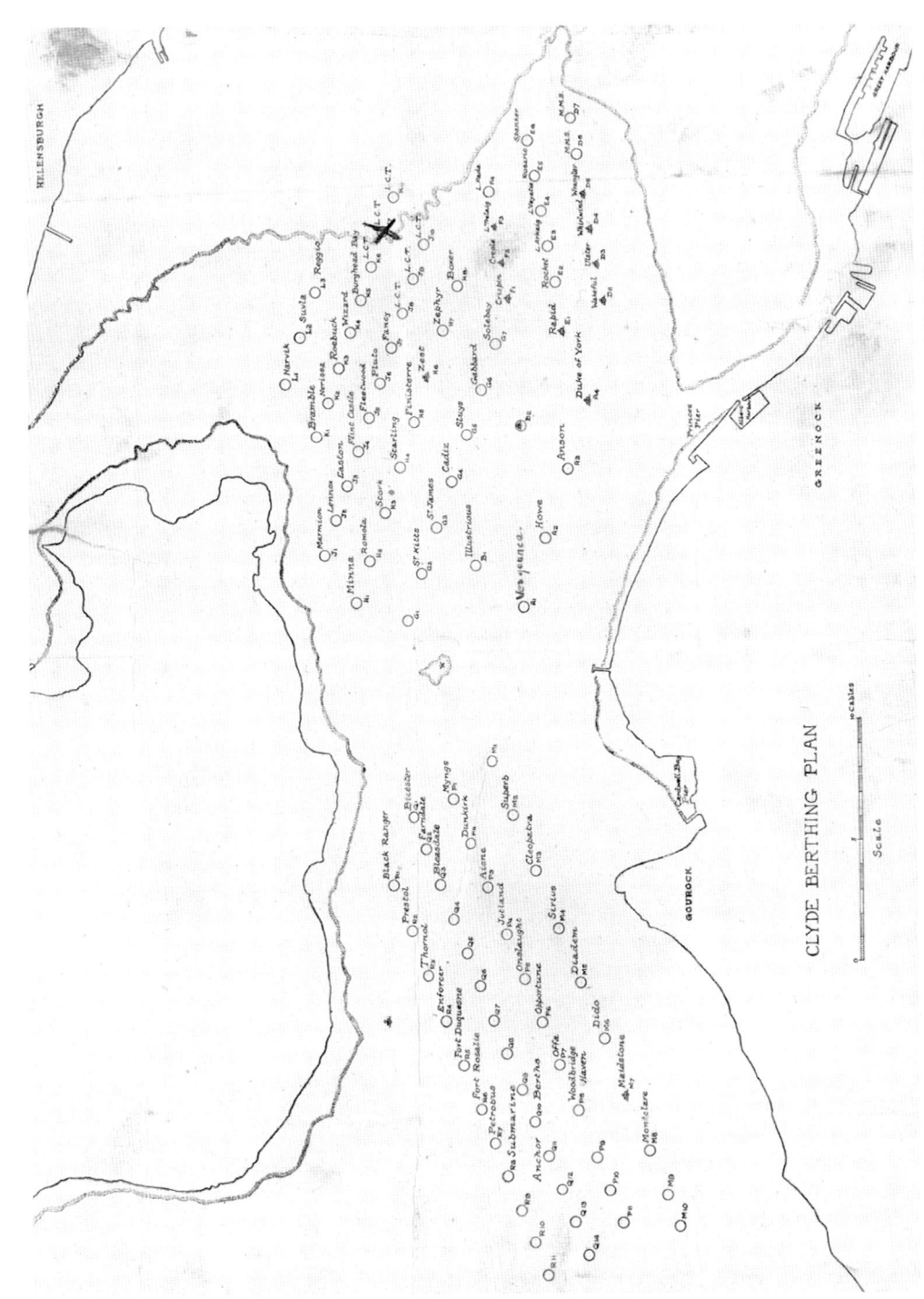

Clyde Visit Orders showing the Berthing Plan of vessels expected to attend the Clyde Naval Review in the Firth of Clyde 18-27 July, 1947. Several changes took place as the General Orders were amended as ships were added and cancelled. This Berthing Plan was kindly supplied by Charles Larter who was a stoker serving on LCT 4037 at the Review, which was berthed with others in the position marked with his cross.

A particularly fine picture of the T-class submarine *Taciturn*, coming into position. Officially described as a "Patrol type" submarine for general service. *Taciturn* was built by Vickers-Armstrong, Barrow, launched 7 June, 1944, and completed 7 October, the same year. Quite a number of T-class boats were on display, and these included - *Tradewind, Thule, Tactician, Thorough, Trump, Turpin* and *Trespasser. Tiptoe* is shown elsewhere.

Light Vessels

The eastern arm of the V, behind the "battlewaggons", consists of destroyers, including the *St. James*, which took such a battering while escorting the *Vanguard* on the first stage of her voyage to South Africa. Behind them are the radar training vessel *Boxer*, a number of sloops and minesweepers, one solitary corvette, the *Flint Castle*, and the Scottish Fishery Board's protection cruiser *Minna*, in addition to landing craft (tanks) and three tank-landing ships, the *Anzio, Suvla*, and *Reggio.*,

The three ranks drawn up at an angle to the main body to the east of the *Duke of York* consist of destroyers and frigates.

As the naval ships assembled merchant shipping began to sail out of the Clyde in the full tide, leaving Glasgow before the Fair Holiday interferes with working in the docks. Eleven merchant ships cleared outwards from Glasgow, including three in the colours of the Clan Line and the Henderson liner *Salween*, making her first voyage on reconditioning after war service.

The British Fleet Minesweeper *Pluto* in January, 1946. She was one of eighty-one in the "Algerine" class of minesweepers, and were regarded as being the fastest and most efficient minesweepers in the Royal Navy. They were frequently used as escort vessels. *Pluto* was built at Port Arthur Shipyards in 1944. Displacement between 950 and 1,040 tons, 235 feet overall, beam 35 feet 6 inches, and with a wartime complement 104-138. Nine of her sister ships were also at the Review, and these included *Fancy, Bramble, Lennox, Romola, Rosario, Nerissa, Spanker,* and *Marmion. Nerissa* and *Marmion* are shown elsewhere.

There were three Landing Ship Tanks (LST) at the Review, and one of them, pictured here, was *Anzio*, in the LST (A) class built by Vickers-Armstrong in 1945, but this picture of her was taken some years later in October, 1963.

Ready for Welcome

Burns Laird packets, inward bound, had their decks lined with passengers getting a priority view of the ranks of naval vessels. L.M.S. pleasure steamers were plying round the fleet within an hour of the ships' anchoring.

Ashore there was little sign of the Navy, and only a very occasional uniform was to be seen on the almost deserted streets. Between the maypole-like decorations of Port Glasgow's town hall to the last "Bon Voyage – Come Back" of Gourock Town Council lay a profusion of flags of all nations and colours, on public buildings and across the streets, while as the day wore on more and more private citizens were displaying bunting from – and in some cases right across – their windows.

Reggio LST(3) built by Davie in 1945, and photographed here in April, 1954, is named on the Berthing Plan, but was subsequently cancelled, but we include her here for illustration of these interesting type of vessels. Her place was taken by *Anzio*.

Boxer was built by Harland & Wolff in 1942. She was originally laid down as a large Landing Ship, and completed as a Fighter Direction Ship. Fully equipped with an unprecidented quantity of radio and radar equipment, she was the only vessel in the Royal Navy with four masts. In 1947, *Boxer* was a Seagoing Radar Training Ship attached to the Navigation School.

Aboard the ships, where a bustle of preparation could be viewed, and in the half-empty streets of Greenock, Gourock, and Port Glasgow, there was a feeling more of anticipation than realisation. Hidden in a curtain of mist the Fleet had moved silently to its appointed anchorage. Tomorrow the Fleet's visit begins.

Large crowds of navymen were given shore leave later in the day, and in high spirits they invaded Greenock and Gourock or travelled by train and bus to Glasgow. Local entertainments provided included dancing in Greenock Town Hall and in the huge R.A.F. hangar at the Battery Park. Two schools in Greenock and one in Gourock have been turned into dormitories to give accommodation for 1400 men on overnight leave.

ANCHORAGE SWEPT BY THUNDERSTORM

Visitors Disappointed

Thousands of people who went to the Greenock district last night to see the Fleet were disappointed, for the weather broke about seven o'clock and the anchorage was blotted out. The sky darkened and rain fell in torrents. Heavy peals of thunder and vivid flashes of lightning accompanied the rain, and those who were walking on the front were drenched.

Wright & Logan

Wright & Logan

Many buses arrived in Greenock and Gourock carrying passengers who had gone to see the Fleet at anchor, but so bad were the conditions that they were unable to leave the vehicles, which cruised along the waterfront. The passengers, however, could get only a restricted view of the warships nearest to the shore.

At the height of the storm visibility was so bad that the fog bell on Gourock Pier was sounded. Traffic had to use headlights for a time.

An extensive programme of attractions has been arranged in the Greenock area during the stay of the Fleet in the Clyde, but last night the only outdoor event was a band concert, and as the storm broke before this was timed to start it was cancelled.

The second LST on display was the LST(3) class *Suvla* shown here. She was built by Vickers-Armstrong (Canada), in 1945. She was broken up at Grays in 1960.

It was not the weather so much as the number of potential visitors that created problems in the ensuing days, resulting in headaches for the Scottish Tourist Board. It was said that 'at least 1,000 bookings a week for Clydeside had been turned down particularly for the period which included 22nd and 23rd July when the King visited the Fleet in Clyde waters'.

Between Friday 18th and Sunday 20th, it was reported, 6,750 passengers travelled to Bute and over 2,250 to Millport from Wemyss Bay. Normal steamer services proved inadequate, but it was claimed that no passenger had been left behind.

Narvik LST(3), Pennant L3044 was a Submarine Support Ship, and was photographed here in September, 1948. She was sold in 1971, and broken up at Antwerp.

The destroyer *Whirlwind*, seen here in February, 1947, was one of eight in the "Wager" class, and all launched in 1943. Displacement 1,710 tons, and apart from differing in armament, was the same specification as the 'C' and 'Z' classes. Built by Hawthorn Leslie, Hebburn-on-Tyne.

Whenever the King was not afloat various ships were open to the public, but those wishing to visit them found it difficult to do so because the local boatmen were quite unable to cope with the crowds. To ensure that boat hirers returned to take the visitors ashore the naval authorities refused to permit them to issue return tickets, and Gourock Town Council was moved to request that this restriction on the issuing of return tickets should be withdrawn or that the ferry services to the ships should be supplemented with naval craft.

The *Glasgow Herald* reported on the frustrations of sightseers who queued for hours to get a close-up view of the warships.

Sunday, 20th July, 1947

ROYAL FAMILY VISIT GLASGOW THIS AFTERNOON

Many holidaymakers were disappointed today when they were unable to visit the ships of the Fleet open to the public. Motor vessels plying from Greenock and Gourock were filled to capacity on every trip, but they could not fully cope with crowds, estimated by one harbour official to be 'the biggest seen here for many years'.

Long queues waited at every pier and jetty, and there was some grumbling among visitors who had travelled long distances when they realised that they had no hope of obtaining a passage. Many consoled themselves by going on cruises round the Fleet in motor boats provided by private hirers. Others joined the L.M.S. steamers crossing the Firth and obtained a close view of some of the ships.

Lyle Hill, above Greenock, was a popular point for sightseers, who had an unrivalled panorama of the Fleet and the Clyde estuary. The number of motor cars and buses in the area was thought to be the greatest in living memory. From Port Glasgow to beyond Gourock the traffic moved in an unbroken stream, and parking places were filled to capacity.

Every esplanade and beach was thronged with holidaymakers, and the gay dresses worn by many of the women introduced blue and white effects as befitted a naval occasion. Some tea-rooms and cafés remained closed, but most of them were open and received an unceasing demand for light refreshments.

For the benefit of the many naval ratings on shore leave a motor car equipped with loud speaker apparatus toured the streets announcing where canteen facilities were available. Cinemas were open in Greenock and Gourock, and there were also variety shows, while musical programmes were given by bands in the public parks.

The destroyer *Wrangler*, sister ship to *Whirlwind*, built by Vickers-Armstrong, Barrow, and launched December, 1943. Also attending the Review in the same class was *Wakeful* and *Wizard*. This picture was taken in January, 1948.

LCT 4039 attached to 93rd Training Flotilla, H.M.S. *Rosneath*. Photograph kindly supplied by Charles Larter.

"Loch" class frigates were built in large numbers, and four attended the Review. *Loch Tralaig, Loch Veyatie, Loch Fada,* and *Loch Arkaig. Loch Tralaig* shown here in 1952, was built by Caledonian Ship Building & Engineering, Co. Ltd, Tees. and launched in February, 1945. Displacement 1,435 tons, 307 feet in length, and beam 38 feet 6 inches. Complement was 103.

Helensburgh Busy

Throughout the day the Helensburgh shore was busy, although the congestion was not so great as at Greenock and Gourock. Between 5000 and 6000 people were estimated to have arrived by train and road traffic was heavy. The last trains from Helensburgh and Craigendoran were crowded, while extra S.M.T. buses were needed to carry all the passengers.

Two outings for naval men were arranged by Helensburgh Town Council:– One was to Rossdhu on Loch Lomond, at the invitation of Sir Iain Colquhoun, Bt., and the other to Ross Priory at the invitation of Major George Christie.

On Saturday evening a party of Royal Marines gave a demonstration of landing craft on the beach at Helensburgh.

Ships open to visitors today are H.M. Ships *Howe, Vengeance, Diadem, Maidstone, Sirius, Crispin, Loch Tralaig, Loch Veyatie, Offa, Onslaught,* and *Flint Castle.*

From *Montclare*, moored at position M8 in line on the western leg nearest the shore, it was possible to see quite a number of these splendid looking ships and submarines around us, and with the aid of binoculars one was able to determine the shapes of many more ahead of us towards Kilcreggan, all spread out across the length and breadth of the waters of the Clyde.

One could not but be moved by the sight before us and marvel at this armada of British ships all gathered together in one place at the same time, all motionless at their moorings. The weather had turned dull and murky, but in spite of this it was a truly magnificent sight, and indeed one that I might never have the opportunity of seeing again. If anything instilled in one a sense of pride, this did, seeing these giants of our time, unpretentiously displaying their strength and greatness, awaiting recognition for the part they played in helping to bring an end to the turmoil of the Second World War.

Many of the ships and submarines we were looking at had been in the thick of action in numerous war zones, whether patrolling our coastal waters or protecting convoys in the Atlantic, the Mediterranean, the Arctic, the Indian Ocean, or the Pacific. Most had been in battle, bombardment or supporting air strikes, and all had stories to tell.

One felt somewhat humbled in their presence. These were the ships that had been fighting to save our country whilst I was still a schoolboy, and during my early working life before National Service. Indeed, it was barely 12 months earlier that many of these ships were returning from the Far East at the very time I was completing my training, and my interest in all of them was such that I had to find out more about them.

The fleet carrier *Implacable*, for example, the largest and speediest of our carriers, completed in August, 1944, whose aircraft attacked targets in Japanese waters and took part in the bombardment of the Japanese base at Truk in the Carolines. Returning to Devonport from the Far East on 3rd June, 1946, she had covered 90,000 miles in just over a year.

Her sister ship, the fleet carrier *Indefatigable*, completed March, 1944, returned to British waters from the Far East at the same time. *Indefatigable* played a leading role with other carriers, including *Indomitable, Illustrious* and *Victorious*, together with the battleship *King George V* and a force of cruisers and destroyers, in completely destroying the Japanese aviation fuel refineries at Palembang in Sumatra in January, 1945. She also formed part of the strike force of British and US naval ships attacking the Pacific island of Okinawa, leading to the Americans securing the island in June, 1945. During the action of Okinawa *Indefatigable* and the carriers *Victorious, Formidable* and *Indomitable* were hit, but they were not seriously damaged due to their armoured flight decks. *Indefatigable* carried at least 100 aircraft and had a complement of 2,000 officers and men. After the surrender of Japan *Indomitable* brought home 1,000 troops and nurses who had suffered appalling treatment in Japanese camps.

These three photographs give a general view of the layout from where we were on *Montclare* anchored on the western leg of the review site.

These were the only photographs I was able to take during the days of the Review.

Maidstone, sister ship to *Forth*, is the main ship in the picture, and is dressed overall ready for inspection by King George VI and the Royal party. Around her, and as far as the eye could see, were dozens of ships and submarines at their anchorages towards Kilcreggan and beyond.

"RN Photographs"

On 14th June, 1946, one of our very latest carriers, the *Theseus*, which had been completed only in January of that year, returned to this country. It was expected that *Theseus* would be attending the Review, but as it turned out she was in Australia at the time. Some disturbing news about her visit there filtered through to us in a report in the *Glasgow Herald* on Monday, 21st July, 1947.

The A-class submarine *Alaric*, built by Cammell Laird, Birkenhead, launched 18 February, 1946, and commissioned 21 September, the same year.

Wright & Logan

An impressive view of the gathering of submarines at the Review. July, 1947.

EIGHT NAVAL MEN DIE IN CRASHES

Eight members of the Royal Navy were killed and two were injured in plane crashes during a farewell demonstration yesterday, Sunday 20th July, 1947, by the carrier squadron visiting Melbourne (Australia).

The first crash occurred (says Reuters) a few hours after the carrier squadron left harbour. Watched by a crowd of about 10,000, two Fireflies from the carrier *Theseus* interlocked in the air and crashed from a height of 1,000 feet into Port Philip Bay, killing five men and injuring two, one of whom died later.

Within an hour a Seafire landing on the *Theseus* narrowly missed the Flight Direction Officer and fatally injured a seaman. A Seafire from the carrier *Glory* bounced over the barriers in landing and crashed into parked planes injuring two mechanics, one of whom died later.

Another of the A-class boats on display was *Alcide*, pictured here, also built by Vickers-Armstrong, Barrow. Launched 12 April, 1945, and commissioned 13 August, 1946.

Wright & Logan

Posing for a photograph here, are the crew of *Alderney*, the A-class boat built by Vickers-Armstrong, Barrow, and launched on 25 June, 1945. She carried 159 tons of fuel, a crew of 61 and 20 torpedoes.

Sturdy, built by Cammell Laird, Birkenhead, was launched 30 September, 1943, and commissioned 29 November, the same year. She had a distinguished service record, serving mainly in the Far East. In December, 1946, she was re-commissioned for service with the 3rd Submarine Flotilla and was based at Rothesay and Londonderry. Between January, and May, 1947, she was one of eleven submarines supplying electric power to the dockyard at Devonport during the country's coal crisis.

The submarine depot ship *Maidstone* had been away for five years when she docked at Portsmouth in December, 1945. The battleship *Howe*, which arrived from the Far East in January, 1946, was the first ship of her tonnage to navigate the Suez Canal, first of the British Pacific Fleet to shoot down a Japanese suicide plane, and first of her class to enter Portsmouth.

On 14th June, 1946, the fleet aircraft carrier *Victorious*, completed May, 1941, a veteran of the war in almost every sea, returned to British waters. Among her many engagements was the pursuit of the German battleship *Bismarck* in 1941. She also covered the Torch landings in North Africa in 1942 and screened convoys in the Mediterranean and on the Russian route. In 1943 she was on her way to the Pacific where she operated with the US carrier *Saratoga* in the Coral Sea and supported landings by US troops in the Solomons in June of that year.

Among other aircraft *Victorious* carried the famous Fairey Swordfish two/three seat fleet torpedo-bomber-reconnaissance biplane which entered service in 1935, the prototype having first flown in 1934. Familiarly known as 'stringbags', they carried a crew of two for torpedo work or three for spotting and reconnaissance who sat in open cockpits as the pilot, observer and gunner/telegraphist. They were lightly armed with one .303" Vickers gun in the fuselage and one .303" Lewis gun in the rear cockpit. The Swordfish had a maximum bomb load of 1,500 lb. or alternatively an 18" torpedo or a mine could be carried. It had a maximum speed of 138 mph when loaded.

A very successful aircraft, the Swordfish had a distinguished record throughout the war. These aircraft were noted particularly for the part they played in the Norwegian campaign, in the devastating

Naval fighters and Bombers

Some of the numerous and varied types of Naval fighters and bombers of the Second World War. As a schoolboy, I remember hearing the names of some of them in news reports, as well as reading about them in magazines, but I was never fortunate enough to see any, only the carriers which supported air strikes with these remarkable aircraft.

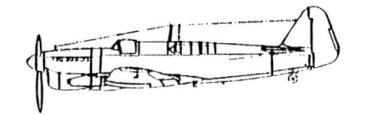

The Fairey Firefly
two-seater Naval day and night fighter

The Hawker Sea Hurricane - single-seat fighter.

The Supermarine Seafire, a ship-plane version of Spitfire IX - single seat fighter

The Blackburn ROC
two-seat fighter

The Fairey Swordfish - three seat Naval reconnaissance and torpedo-bomber

The Fairey Albacore - two/three-seat torpedo-bomber reconnaissance biplane

The Blackburn Skua - two-seat dive bomber and fighter

The Gloster Sea Gladiator - single-seat fighter

The Fairey Seafox - Fleet spotter and reconnaissance seaplane

The Supermarine Walrus - amphibian three-seat spotter reconnaissance seaplane

The Fairey Fulmer - two-seat Fleet fighter

The Grumman Avenger three-seat torpedo-bomber

The Grumman Wildcat - single-seat fighter

The Fairey Swordfish torpedo-bomber, a very successful aircraft which remained in service throughout the war. Notable among many, was the action against the Italian Fleet in Taranto Harbour on November 11-12 and in the action off Sardinia on 27 November, 1940, where the torpedoing was carried out chiefly by Fairey Swordfish biplanes. Torpedoes were known as 'Mouldies' weighing up to a ton, and containing around 500lbs of T.N.T. This photograph was taken in May, 1951.

raid on the Italian Fleet in Taranto harbour in 1940, in the Battle of Cape Matapan, and in the sinking of the German battleship *Bismarck*. Swordfish biplanes also covered convoys in the Mediterranean and Atlantic zones, and took part in actions against North Africa, Sicily and the Italian mainland.

The Swordfish was just one of many and varied types of Naval attack aircraft built during the war. I remember hearing the names of some of them in news reports as a schoolboy and reading about them in various magazines, but I was never fortunate enough to see any during my service days. My interest lay mainly with the carriers themselves.

Nevertheless, it would be remiss of me, I believe, to exclude the aircraft altogether when discussing the carriers and their wartime engagements. By including examples in profile form of only a few of these remarkable machines as representatives of Second World War naval fighters and bombers I may persuade the reader to find out more about them for themselves from the many excellent books of reference compiled by experts.

March 1945 saw the arrival of the British Pacific Fleet in the Far East, when carriers including *Formidable*, *Indefatigable*, *Indomitable*, *Victorious*, and later *Implacable* mounted air strikes on enemy bases in Japanese waters. These attacks led up to the cease fire on 15th August, 1945, and the surrender of Japan on 2nd September, 1945.

Ships of the Home Fleet at gunnery exercise in May, 1939. All the big ships took part including the "battle"-cruiser *Repulse*, which should have taken their Majesties to Canada. Here, a Swordfish seaplane is being hoisted into the water before use in the gunnery exercises. These aircraft acted as spotter planes for the big guns of the ships which could fire at an enemy out of sight. Aircraft gave the range and direction, and reported on the success of the shelling and on any change to be made in range. May, 1939.

The Albacore torpedo-bomber was brought into service as a successor to the Swordfish, but was less successful. The photograph here, shows the Royal Navy ground force folding back the wings of an Albacore as the plane is made ready to enter the blast shelter pen of an R.A.F. station in Malta in February, 1943.

The carrier *Illustrious*, completed in May, 1940, also returned to Britain at this time. She joined the Mediterranean Fleet in September, 1940, covering convoys to Malta and playing a leading role in supporting air strikes against the Italian Fleet at Taranto in November, 1940. Her aircraft bombarded enemy bases at Benghazi, Rhodes, Calato, Leros and Tripoli and attacked the Axis armies in North Africa. In January, 1941, while escorting a convoy a hundred miles west of Malta, *Illustrious* was dive-bombed by Junkers Ju87 Stukas with six 1,000lb. bombs. She was badly damaged, set on fire, and suffered severe casualties. In spite of this, however, she reached Malta six hours later under her own steam. While in the dockyard there, she was dive-bombed again, but managed to slip out of harbour on 23rd January, 1941, and reached Alexandria, again under her own steam. Her armoured flight deck saved her from disaster, but she was withdrawn from the Fleet, and later headed for the United States where she was repaired in American yards. Subsequently she supported actions in the Far East.

St James was one of many "Battle" class destroyers designed for operations in the Pacific. She was built by Fairfield Shipbuilding & Engineering, Co, Ltd, Govan, and launched 7 June, 1945. Class displacement varied from 2,315 - 2,325 tons. Length 379 feet overall, 40 feet 3 inches beam, and with a war complement of 337. This class of destroyer was well represented at the Review. In addition to those sister ships shown on other pages, in the line up also were *Cadiz, Finisterre, Jutland, Dunkirk, Barrosa* and *Corunna*. This photograph taken in June, 1953.

There were six S-class submarines at the Review, and shown here is *Seneschal*. Built by Scotts' Shipbuilding & Engineering, Co,Ltd, Greenock, she was launched 23 April, 1945, and commissioned 31 July, the same year. On completion, *Seneschal* joined the 3rd Submarine Flotilla and completed her trials at Holy Loch. In 1946, she took part in the Home Fleet Autumn Manoeuvres. Other S-class boats present at the Review were - *Spirit, Spiteful, Satyr, Sirdar,* and *Sturdy*, which is shown elsewhere.

News of the completion of the new battleship *Anson* was released on Trafalgar Day, 1942. She was what was called a Chatham ship. She arrived back at Portsmouth on 29th July, 1946, and was due for paying off, but then became a Training Ship at Portland. This accounted for the fact that at the time of attending the Naval Review in the Clyde, half the ship's company of *Anson* on parade were youths of between 17 and 19 years of age.

The battleship *Duke of York* (flagship), completed November, 1941, returned to home waters with a complement of 1,500 men. In 1942 *Duke of York* took Winston Churchill to America. With the cruisers *Norfolk, Belfast* and *Sheffield* she was in battle with the German battleship *Scharnhorst*, which was encircled by the Home Fleet and was finally sunk by the torpedoes of the cruiser *Jamaica* off North Cape in December, 1943.

The battleship *King George V*, completed December, 1940, made her debut arriving in the United States on 24th January, 1941, with Lord Halifax, Britain's new Ambassador on board. With the weight of her armour alone over 14,000 tons, having a thickness at the water line of 16 inches, together with her powerful armament, she was an awesome opponent, and played a leading role in numerous actions at sea, covering the North Atlantic and Russian convoys, taking part in the *Bismarck* action and heading a British Pacific Fleet task force at Guam in 1945 operating with the US Pacific Fleet.

A sister ship in the earlier "Dido" class cruisers, was *Cleopatra*. Built by Hawthorn, she was begun in January, 1939, and completed 20 November, 1941. She was photographed here in February, 1946.

Belfast, the largest cruiser of the Second World War, was completed in August, 1939, and served throughout the war. Besides patrolling the Arctic convoy route to North Russia, she played her part in the sinking of the *Scharnhorst* in the Battle of North Cape in 1943, and took part in the Normandy landings. She had fought the most brilliant disengaging actions in the records of modern warfare.

The outstanding record of the work carried out by the cruisers during the whole of the war years is well attested. *Dido*, *Diadem*, *Sirius* and *Cleopatra* for example, all of which attended the Naval Review, were among the many that were constantly in the firing line, and formed the protection screen in and after the landings in North Africa in 1942.

Forming part of the 15th Cruiser Squadron, *Cleopatra*, *Euryalas* and *Dido* protected convoys to Malta and covered the Fifth Army landings on the west coast of Italy, south of Rome, in January, 1944. *Cleopatra* was sent out from Britain in February, 1942, to strengthen the cruiser force in the Mediterranean, a month after she had become Admiral Vian's flagship when the *Naiad* was sunk by a U-boat.

The first seven ships built in the "Dido" class cruisers, included *Dido* (pictured here) built by Cammell Laird. Begun in October, 1937, she was completed in 1940. Displacement 5,450 tons, length 512 feet overall, and beam 51 feet 6 inches. *Dido* had a complement of around 550, and is seen here in May, 1947.

The cruiser *Diadem* was one of four in the later ships of the "Dido" class. Built by Hawthorn Leslie, Hebburn-on-Tyne, *Diadem* was begun in December, 1939, and completed 6 Juanuary, 1944. Displacement 7,400 tons full load, length 512 feet overall, beam 50 feet 6 inches, and she had a peacetime complement of around 550. This photograph was taken in December, 1945.

There were four A-class boats on display. *Alliance, Alaric, Alderney,* and *Alcide.* Here we see *Alliance* showing herself off, having only been commissioned on 11 March, 1947. The other three A-boats are shown elsewhere.

The Clyde Visit Orders named the destroyer *Offa* taking up position P7 on the Berthing Plan, but among numerous changes, her place was taken by *Onslow,* pictured here. *Onslow* was amongst the first destroyers to be built under War Construction programme in the "Onslow" class, and was built by John Brown, Clydebank, and launched in 1941. Displacement 1,540 tons, length overall 345 feet, and beam 35 feet. *Onslow* was sold to the Pakistani Navy in September, 1949, and renamed Tippu Sultan. Two of her sister ships were also at the Review, these being *Onslaught* built by Fairfield, and *Opportune* by Thornycroft, completed in 1942. Both were familiar sights at Rothesay during 1946 and 1947.

Early in September, 1942, Admiral Vian relinquished his command of the 15th Cruiser Squadron to Rear Admiral A. J. Power, C.B., C.V.O., the first Captain of the carrier *Ark Royal.* Admiral Vian had been continuously afloat in command of flotillas and squadrons since the war started. In the Mediterranean he had never taken his cruisers out to sea without some expectation of having to fight the Italian battle fleet.

Destroyers have been said to be the most beautiful ships of all, with both grace and power. In proportion to their size, they were very powerful which gave them impressive manoeuvrability as well as speed. There was scarcely a sea battle when destroyers were not involved. They formed the attack force in Narvik Fiord in April, 1940. Lieutenant-Commander Beattie rammed the lock gates at St. Nazaire in the *Campbeltown* and Captain Robert Sherbrooke in the *Onslow* led the 17th Destroyer Flotilla against a powerful force of German warships threatening an important Russian convoy. In the action, Captain Sherbrooke was badly injured and *Onslow* suffered severe damage to her funnel, bridge and hull; she had to be withdrawn, and was repaired in a Russian port.

Destroyers attacked and sank Italian cruisers, assisted in bringing home soldiers from the beaches of Dunkirk and Crete, and bombarded enemy shore bases in support of the army. Their main job was the protection of convoys and sinking submarines. With the smaller escort vessels, sloops, frigates, corvettes and cutters, they won the Battle of the Atlantic.

With the end of the Second World War new developments in training methods for RN recruits were instituted by the Training Battleship Squadron based at Portland, Dorset, consisting of *Howe*, *Anson* and *Nelson*. Easing the accommodation ashore and at the same time keeping those modern ships in commission without having to use full complements of trained personnel, the squadron gave elementary instruction in seamanship, gunnery and torpedoes for special service ratings. Each battleship had about 450 recruits during each 16-week course.

The *Glasgow Herald* continued its coverage of the Review on 22nd July with a description of the King's visit to the ships, which meant that vessels were not open to the public that day.

Tuesday, 22nd July, 1947

KING INSPECTS FLEET IN CLYDE

Destroyer's Action Demonstration

Every circumstance combined to make today's visit of the King and Queen, the Princesses Elizabeth and Margaret, and Lieutenant Philip Mountbatten to the Home fleet at anchor in the Firth of Clyde a naval event of special distinction.

It was the first time since the war that the Sovereign, himself a sailor, had been with such a large assembly of his ships of war. It was, too, the first occasion on which the officers and men of the Navy had had an opportunity of welcoming the serving sailor who has become the fiancé of the King's elder daughter.

Pictured here is the British Fleet Minesweeper *Nerissa*, built by Redfern Construction, Co, launched 25 November, 1944. She was one of eighty-one in the "Algerine" class of minesweepers, with a displacement of 950-1,040 tons, length 235 feet overall, and beam 35 feet 6 inches. *Nerissa* had a wartime complement of 104 to 138. *Rosario*, a sister ship in the "Algerine" class, also attending the Review, was built by Harland & Wolff and launched on 3 April, 1943. This photograph was taken in June, 1956.

"RN Photographs"

A nice view of *Maidstone*, depot ship of the 7th Submarine Flotilla, and one of the host ships listed for inspection by King George VI.

Stork, an escort sloop in the "Bittern" class was built by Denny Bros, Dumbarton, in 1936. Displacement 1,190 tons, length overall 266 feet, and beam 37 feet. *Stork* was built under 1934 Estimates as a Surveying vessel at a cost of £160,393, but was refitted as a sloop in 1939, and later formed part of the Fishery Protection Flotilla. This photograph was taken in January, 1946. *Stork* is named on the Berthing Plan, but in last minute changes to the Clyde Visit Orders, the Fleet Minesweeper *Marmion* took her place.

Friendships Renewed

For the Queen and the Princesses the occasion also meant the renewal of friendships made during their voyage to and from South Africa in H.M.S. *Vanguard*, for many of the officers in that battleship's complement are now serving on various units of the Home Fleet as at present constituted.

The visit was also notable because of the presence of the Prime Minister and Mrs. Attlee, who accompanied the royal family and shared with them a lively interest and obvious pleasure in the efficiency of the men and the immaculate appearance of the ships.

Only the very credulous would believe that such shining armament and spotless decks had been achieved without the most thorough effort, but officers and men had the satisfaction that the King and Lieutenant Mountbatten realised from their own professional experience what the routine entails in thought and work.

A capricious July, which has so often imprisoned holidaymakers in hotels and boarding-houses on the Clyde coast, was, today at least, moderately benign.

From early morning there were dark clouds over the Cowal hills, but meteorological reports were encouraging, and the senior officers of the Fleet rightly decided that there would be no need to limit the planned programme. Though clouds persisted there was spasmodic sunshine throughout the day, and there was no rain.

The Fleet Tug *Enforcer* photographed here in October, 1946, was one of five in the "Envoy" class, all built by Cochrane & Sons, Selby, and launched in July, 1944. She was 174 feet 6 inches in length, 36 feet beam, and displaced 1,332 tons. Her complement was 33. In various changes to the Clyde Visit Orders, *Enforcer*'s position was taken by the Fleet Tug *Saucy*. These powerful little tugs are worthy of including here.

Petrobus was a Petrol Carrier, built by Dunlop Bremmer in 1918. Displacement 1,024 tons, length 164 feet, beam 28 feet, and had a complement of 16. This picture was taken in March, 1934.

Twelve destroyers in the "Battle" class were present at the Review. *Barrosa, Corunna, Cadiz, St James, St Kitts, Sluys, Gabbard, Aisne, Dunkirk, Finisterre, Solebay* and *Jutland*. *Aisne*, pictured here in May, 1947, was built by Vickers-Armstrong (Tyne), and launched in May, 1945. Displacement 2,315 tons, overall length 379 feet, and beam 40 feet 3 inches. She had a peace-time complement of 250 and in war around 337. *St Kitts, Sluys, Gabbard,* and *St James,* are shown elsewhere.

Greenock Reception

The royal party were welcomed at Greenock by the Lord Lieutenant of Renfrewshire, Mr. A. A. Hagart Speirs, who presented Provost Daniel Morris, Greenock; Vice-Admiral Sir Frederick Dalrymple-Hamilton, flag officer commanding Scotland and Northern Ireland; and Chief Constable W. M. M'Kechnie.

As the royal barge left Princes Pier the largest ships of the Fleet fired a salute of 21 guns, each echoing salvo being accompanied by clouds of acrid smoke that spiralled and dissolved lazily before a light breeze. Simultaneously the Royal Standard was broken in the flagship of the Fleet, H.M.S. *Duke of York*, which was "adopted" by Glasgow during the war. The barge curtseyed to the swell as it veered in an arc to go alongside the flagship.

A shrill crescendo of boatswains' pipes accorded the King traditional honour as he ran lightly up the gangway. The Queen followed, then the Princesses, the Prime Minister and Mrs. Attlee and finally Lieutenant Mountbatten. As they stepped on board they were received by the Commander-in-Chief, Admiral Sir Neville Syfret, and the Royal Marine band played the National Anthem.

After a number of senior officers had been presented the royal party walked slowly round divisions, the King making a keen inspection of each flawless formation of sailors and marines.

Action Demonstration
Afterwards the royal party assembled on the starboard boat-deck to watch a demonstration of action drill by the ship's company of the new battle-class destroyer, H.M.S. *Aisne*, which was lying alongside. The King and Queen pressed against the guard rails to get the best possible view of the demonstration, which showed the action which would be taken by a ship in the screen of a convoy during an air attack.

The *Aisne's* 4.5-inch and Bofors armament were seen in action against imaginary sorties by high-level bombers and close-range attacks by rocket-firing aircraft. The measures which would be taken to combat damage and fire and to treat a splinter casualty were also demonstrated.

All the ship's company wore a new and compact type of action working dress which, with anti-flash clothing which is used at action stations, is designed to give the best possible protection against burns.

Throughout the demonstration Princess Elizabeth stood on one side with Lieutenant Mountbatten, who explained to her the sequence of action and the uses of the various guns.

The other ships visited were H.M.S. *Anson*, the flagship of Rear-Admiral H. Hickling, flag officer training battleships, the aircraft carrier H.M.S. *Illustrious*, and the destroyers H.M.S. *Myngs* and H.M.S. *Solebay*.

Two of the finest spectacles of the day were the march past of 1800 officers and men on the flight-deck of H.M.S. *Illustrious* to the strains of "Heart of Oak" and "Life on the Ocean Wave", and the march past of a large number of the ship's company of H.M.S. *Anson*, of whom half on parade were youths between 17 and 19 years of age with less than four months' naval service. The poise and precision of these young sailors evoked the admiration of the royal visitors.

Aircraft Inspected
In the *Illustrious*, from whose flight deck 22 Swordfish flew off to put out of action half the Italian Fleet in the famous attack on Taranto, the royal party inspected aircraft, including Sea Hornets, Seafires, Fireflies, and Swordfish.

"Battle" class destroyer *Solebay* Captain 'D' 5th Destroyer Flotilla, at Portland in 1947. Photograph kindly supplied by Alan Eyre, Acting AB on board for three months while undergoing training.

Myngs seen here in September, 1950, a sister ship to *Zephyr*, was also built by Vickers-Armstrong (Tyne), and launched in May, 1943. Both *Myngs* and *Zephyr* had a displacement of 1,730 tons, and the others in her class, 1710 tons. Apart from this, other dimensions were similar to 'C' class.

Afterwards they saw a completely different aspect of naval life—an aspect which would delight the eye and evoke the envy of any housewife. This was a handicrafts display to which officers and men from various units of the Fleet had contributed. It covered a multitudinous variety of articles such as toys, carpets, woodwork, small articles of furniture, paintings and drawings—one a study of the Prime Minister which the visitors, and Mr. Attlee in particular, viewed with marked appreciation—and needlework and tapestries wrought with delicacy and artistry.

The visitors also noted, when they descended from the flight-deck in one of the massive aircraft lifts, a commemorative inscription on a spot where the *Illustrious* sustained one of her battle scars at Pantellaria.

One of the most informal exchanges took place between the Princesses and a group of midshipmen on the quarter-deck of the *Anson*. The Princesses had met these young men during their passage to and from South Africa, and they recalled with vivacity happy friendships during those memorable cruises.

One of the midshipmen remarked to Princess Elizabeth:– "You are getting a good day, but aren't you famous for bringing good weather wherever you go?" Her Royal Highness's rejoinder was to cross her fingers and smilingly remark:– "Be careful what you say about the weather."

The 'C' class destroyer *Crispin*, was built by Samuel White (Cowes), and launched 23 June, 1945. Class displacement generally around 1,170 tons, length overall 362 feet 9 inches, and beam 35 feet 8 inches. Complement varied between 186 and 222. She was photographed here in June, 1953. *Creole*, a sister ship to *Crispin*, also at the Review, was built by Samuel White, and launched in November, the same year.

Ulster, a destroyer in the "Ulster" class of which eight were built altogether. Displacement 1,710 tons, length overall 362 feet 9 inches, beam 35 feet 8 inches. *Ulster* was built by Swan Hunter, and launched in November, 1942.
July, 1950.

Lilac Ensemble

The King was wearing the uniform of an Admiral of the Fleet. Her Majesty was dressed in a lilac ensemble, with a matching hat trimmed with a bow of tulle. She wore a treble row of pearls and carried over her arm a fox fur. Her white shoes were toe-less and heel-less.

Princess Elizabeth was in a turquoise woollen suit with a matching hat trimmed with white flowers and tulle. White gloves and white and brown wedge-heel shoes completed her ensemble. Princess Margaret wore an egg-blue linen suit with a bonnet-shaped hat, white and blue shoes, and white gloves.

In the evening the royal party again left Greenock in the royal barge to dine with the Commander-in-Chief on board the *Duke of York* and later there was a reception for 500 officers. The Prime Minister and Mrs. Attlee were also present.

Wednesday, 23rd July, 1947

NAVYMEN'S WELCOME TO THE KING

Royal Procession Through lines of Fleet in Clyde

For 65 minutes this afternoon the officers and men of the Home Fleet assembled in the estuary of the Firth of Clyde renounced the naval tradition of the "Silent Service." While the King and Queen, the

King George VI travelled through the lines of ships reviewing the Fleet in Motor Torpedo Boat V2016 shown here. Camper and Nicholson Type MTB's had a displacement of 115 tons, and a length of 117 feet, beam 22 feet 3 inches, with a Sea Speed of 26 knots. Armament included 4-18 inch tubes, 2-6 pdr, 6-20mm AA, and 1 rocket projector. Members of the Household were carried in V2017, and the B.B.C. used V5008, a Modified Fairmile 'D' Type, built by William King, Burnham on Crouch. All three boats had a complement of around 30 and were built in 1945.

I am very grateful to Lt.Cdr.B.Warlow, for supplying this photograph showing the Royal party passing between M and P lines (Cruisers and Destroyers) viewed from the destroyer *Dunkirk*, with the Submarine Depot Ship *Maidstone* in the background. The cruisers *Dido* lay astern of her, with *Diadem* nearest the camera just beyond the Royal party. Next in line were the cruisers *Sirius*, *Cleopatra* and *Superb*. My ship, the *Montclare* was in position M8 on the Berthing Plan next to *Maidstone*.

Princesses Elizabeth and Margaret, and Lieutenant Mountbatten made a 14-mile procession through the lines of the Fleet in a motor-torpedo-boat the navymen manned and cheered ships with lusty enthusiasm.

The rails and superstructures of the battleships and cruisers were lined by the men, the symmetry of their ranks and the blue and white of their uniforms making an impressive spectacle underneath triangles of flags stretched from stem to mainmast and from mainmast to stern.

On the smallest ships, such as the submarines with their complements in one single line and the tank landing craft with their restricted decks and utilitarian fitments, and on an assortment of auxiliary vessels the demonstration to His Majesty was no less fervent.

Here and there on the Dumbartonshire side of the Firth, merchant ships, also lavishly beflagged, greeted the royal craft sailing through the choppy waters.

Another splendid view supplied by Lt.Cdr.B. Warlow, showing MTB V2016 carrying King George VI and the Royal family as they pass the cruiser *Sirius*. Again taken from *Dunkirk*.

Beauty of Setting

The panorama afforded by the great weight of ships, from the 35,000-ton flagship *Duke of York* to the smallest supply unit, was invested with a special grandeur by the rugged beauty of the setting. Grey clouds overlaid the sky and hung low upon the hills on either shore, and a moderate breeze whipped the Firth into flurries of foam, through which the King's boat cut her way at a steady 13 knots.

There were two Motor Minesweepers at the Review, and M.M.S.84 was one of them. M.M.S.84 was an "Admiralty 105" Type, built by Wivenhoe in 1942. They were known as "Mickey Mouses", and were generally built of wood and used as a type of inshore minesweeper. Here she is in August, 1946.

The procession was led by a motor-torpedo-boat, on board which were the Northern Lighthouse Commissioners. They were claiming an ancient privilege of going ahead to ensure the safety of the Sovereign during his visit to Scottish waters.

Their approach was the signal for Royal Marine Bands on the larger ships to strike up the National Anthem, and when the King's boat drew level bosuns' pipes shrilled and the seamen, in response to stentorian orders to "off caps," began their robust "Hurrahs" in a moving gesture of hail and farewell.

Saucy, a Fleet Tug in the "Assurance" class, built by Cochrane & Sons, Selby, in October, 1942. Somewhat smaller than the "Envoy's", having a displament of 1,045 tons, length 157 feet, beam 35 feet, and with a complement of 31. She is seen well underway here in April, 1949.

Starling pictured here, was one of a number of Escort Sloops in the "Modified Black Swan" class, built by Fairfield Shipbuilding and Engineering, Govan. She was launched in October, 1942. Displacement was 1,430 tons to 1,490 tons, length overall 299 feet 6 inches, and beam 38 feet. Complement 192. This picture shows her underway in August, 1947.

Opposite: King George VI, Queen Elizabeth, and the Princesses Elizabeth and Margaret inspecting the crew on board the Submarine Depot Ship *Maidstone*. *Maidstone*, sister ship to *Forth*, was built at Clydebank, launched in October, 1937, and completed 5 May, 1938. Displacement 8,900 tons, length 574 feet overall, and beam 75 feet. Complement numbered around 502 which included 64 repair staff and 43 as spare submarine crew. Armament to both ships was the heaviest yet mounted in a British depot ship. Equipment included a foundry, coppersmiths, plumbers and carpenters shops, heavy and light machine shops, electrical and torpedo repair shops and plant for charging submarine batteries. *Maidstone* was the flagship of Vice-Admiral J.M. Mansfield, Flag Officer Submarines.

47 Years' Service

For an able-bodied seaman serving on board the King's boat the occasion had a special significance. "Jock" Lamont's proud record of almost 47 years' continuous service reached a climax when the King engaged him in an informal conversation and complimented him warmly. Able Seaman Lamont is 64, and holds the D.S.M. and Bar.

Before embarking in the motor-torpedo-boat the royal party watched from the deck of the *Duke of York* a demonstration of amphibious vehicles disembarking from three tank-landing-craft.

Sixteen emphibians entered the water, and one of them completed the realism of the spectacle by the tongue of flames projected from the flame-throwing apparatus that has scorched many a path for sorties on enemy shores.

Of the many grand scenes full of colour and unerring in precision, none during the past two days surpassed the march-past this afternoon on the spacious flight-deck of the *Vengeance*.

This was a sight which was shared by numerous parties who packed small craft which cruised so near the carrier at times as to warrant orders by vigilant patrol boats to maintain a wider berth.

Near the saluting dais on board the *Vengeance* were Viscount Hall, First Lord of the Admiralty, and Mr. A. V. Alexander, Minister of Defence. The royal party, who had come aboard by the starboard gangway, were conveyed to the flight-deck by one of the large aircraft hoists. As the hoist reached deck-level a Royal Marine band played the National Anthem. The last note had just faded when the officer in command of the Marine Guard marched forward, his sword held rigidly before him, and waited the King's pleasure as he spoke briefly to one of his entourage.

Then His Majesty walked forward to inspect the guard and to meet a number of senior naval officers. He also walked along a formation of officers commanding smaller ships of the Fleet before taking his place on the dais.

The Queen stood beside him, and the Princesses were a pace behind. Lieutenant Mountbatten stood almost at the back of the dais with Mr. Alexander, but later he stepped forward to speak to Princess Elizabeth.

159

160

King George VI inspecting the Guard of Honour on board the Submarine Depot Ship *Maidstone*, from which the Royal party watched a demonstration by the submarine *Tiptoe*.

Representing the "Rotherham" class of destroyers was *Rapid*, built by Cammell Laird, Birkenhead, in July, 1942. Displacement 1,705 tons, length overall 358 feet 3 inches, and beam 35 feet 8 inches. Here she is in October, 1946.

March Past

The march past of officers and ratings was representative of the Portsmouth, Plymouth and Nore Command ships, the First Minesweeping Flotilla, and the Fishery Protection Flotilla. For over half an hour the parade swung proudly past the dais in single file, each man saluting as he came level with the King.

The parade over, the King talked with officers of the *Vengeance*, and all the royal family recognised among them Warrant Catering Officer Tanner, who was chef for the royal party during the cruise to South Africa on H.M.S. *Vanguard*. Warrant Officer Tanner had been in the service of the King at Sandringham and Buckingham Palace for a time before joining the *Vanguard*.

The departure of the royal party from the *Vengeance* was as impressive as the arrival. The men on the flight deck lost sight of them as the hoist slowly descended, and did not see them again until the royal barge was heading across to the flagship, where the C-in-C., Sir Neville Syfret, entertained the visitors to luncheon.

Submarine Demonstration

The first ship visited today was the *Maidstone*, from which they watched a demonstration of submerging and surfacing by the submarine *Tiptoe*, which, they were told, is commanded by Lieutenant D. Cameron, who received the Victoria Cross from the King for his share in the torpedo attacks by midget submarines on the *Tirpitz* while she was seeking shelter

The "Swiftsure" class cruiser *Superb*, was one of our very latest. Building by Swan Hunter, Wallsend-on-Tyne, began on 23 June, 1942, and she was completed 16 November, 1945. *Superb* had a displacement 11,560 tons, full load, length 555 feet 6 inches overall, and beam 64 feet. Peacetime complement numbered around 867 and in war 1,000.

There were nine T-class boats on show, and one of them pictured here was *Tiptoe*. Built by Vickers-Armstrong, Barrow, she was launched 25 February, 1944, and commissioned 10 May, the same year. *Tiptoe* was the first of the T-class boats of all-welded construction, and the last of the T-class boats to serve in the Royal Navy. September, 1949.

in a Norwegian fjord. Lieutenant Cameron was taken prisoner.

From the *Maidstone* a visit was paid to the cruiser *Superb*, where the King walked round divisions which included representatives from all the cruisers in the Home Fleet and the Royal Fleet Auxiliary.

Before taking farewell of his ships and sailors the King, accompanied by the Queen, the Princesses, and Lieutenant Mountbatten, dined with the C-in-C. on board the aircraft carrier *Illustrious*, and afterwards attended a Fleet concert in the hangar.

No ceremony of the royal visit to the Fleet was more impressive than the 21-gun salute which tonight boomed across the Firth of Clyde as the King's barge left the aircraft-carrier *Illustrious*. The salvos were fired almost simultaneously from the largest ships at the anchorage, and the flashes of the many guns showed up in the half light.

Heavy rain was falling as the party disembarked. Four naval ratings carrying brightly coloured golfing umbrellas sheltered the royal guests as they passed from the landing-stage to the waiting cars. People on the pier sang softly "Will Ye No' Come Back Again" as the royal cars drove off to Princes Pier station where the royal train was waiting.

RECEPTION AT GOUROCK

The King and Queen, the two Princesses, and Lieutenant Mountbatten left Gourock pier this morning to spend their second day with the Fleet. After arriving at Princes Pier Station, Greenock, the royal party drove

Marmion (S.O.F.P.) seen here in September, 1947, was one of many in the "Algerine" class of Fleet Minesweepers. *Marmion* (ex *Orangeville*), was launched in June, 1944, and was built at Port Arthur Shipyards.

slowly through Greenock and Gourock streets, which were festooned with flags and banners of welcome and lined with cheering crowds.

The royal visitors were received by Provost Sloan Macmillan, Gourock, Admiral Sir Neville Syfret, C-in-C. Home Fleet, and Vice-Admiral Sir F. H. G. Dalrymple-Hamilton, Flag-Officer-in-Charge, Scotland and Northern ireland.

Queen's Dress
The King was dressed in the uniform of an Admiral of the Fleet. The Queen wore a cream-coloured frock under a buff-coloured coat, and a cream felt hat trimmed with yellow roses and tulle. She carried a fox fur. Princess Elizabeth was dressed in a pale blue lightweight suit and a pale blue flowered hat. Her shoes, gloves and handbag were of matching blue. Princess Margaret's primrose yellow dress was worn with fawn-coloured coat, pale yellow straw hat with primroses on the brim, and stone-coloured shoes.

As the royal barge sailed down the Firth to the first of the ships to be visited, the submarine depot ship *Maidstone*, large crowds on the beach at the western end of Gourock pier and along Gourock esplanade, waved and cheered.

When the royal procession through the Fleet was completed in the early afternoon considerable difficulty was experienced in manoeuvring the motor torpedo boat to the narrow steps at the western end of Prince's Pier.

After she had been tied up the King stepped on to the jetty, but as the Queen was preparing to land the boat started to roll slightly, and Her Majesty required the assistance of the King and a senior naval officer to enable her to jump on to the platform at the foot of the steps.

As the royal party were leaving at the end of their two-day visit on the Wednesday, Admiral Sir Neville Syfret received a message from the King:

The Queen, the Princesses and I have greatly enjoyed our two days with the Fleet. It gave us real pleasure to meet Officers and men from your Command, many of whom during the long years of war added glorious

Of the eight "Zambesi" class destroyers built, three of them were at the Review. *Myngs*, *Zest* and *Zephyr*. Pictured here is *Zephyr* (Capt. D) in June, 1948. She was built by Vickers-Armstrong (Tyne), and launched in July, 1943. Displacement 1,730 tons, length overall 362 feet 9 inches, beam 35 feet 8 inches, and with a complement around 186.

pages to the Navy's tradition of courage and efficiency. I was much impressed by the general bearing of the ship's companies and by the smartness of the ships. The Clyde has a magnificent record of Service to the Royal Navy and to the Merchant Navy during the war. It is fitting that the Fleet should pay tribute to that record. The Queen and the Princesses join me in wishing that every one in your Command, and your loyal friends ashore, will enjoy the remainder of your visit.
SPLICE THE MAINBRACE

Signed—George R.I.

There was an interesting footnote in the editorial diary of the *Glasgow Herald* on Wednesday, 23rd July.

THE AY'S HAVE IT

Although few aspects of the royal tour of the Fleet seem to have been left untouched, we felt that a word about the enthusiastic 'hip, hip, hurrays' marking the departure of the royal visitors from various vessels might be in order.

According to an A.B. who took part in the proceedings, an appreciable portion of his ship's company went through a diverting rehearsal of the greeting on Monday afternoon.

Emphasis was laid, he declares, on the fact that the correct phraseology is 'hip, hip, hurray', and not, as is generally believed 'hip, hip, hurra'.

Dwarf was a tender to Submarine Headquarters, Portsmouth, and was built by Philip & Son, Ltd, at Dartmouth, in 1936. *Dwarf* was 91 feet in length, beam 19 feet, and she displaced 172 tons. This picture was taken in May, 1937.

Photographs of their Majesties inspecting Divisions aboard H.M.S. *Duke of York* do not reveal an error in procedure in that the long rows of Navymen have 'caps off'.

Normally, however, Navymen parading before their Divisional Officer before embarking on the liberty boat are requested to remove their caps, not as a point of ritual, but in order to show whether their hair is of the regulation length and whether odd packets of cigarettes have been hidden in the headgear.

With the naval review behind them the King and Queen with the two princesses and Lieutenant Mountbatten paid a visit to Arran, where they received an enthusiastic welcome from islanders and holidaymakers alike. It was the first visit of a reigning monarch to the island since King Edward VII and Queen Alexandra had stepped ashore at the old quay of Brodick 45 years earlier.

On the same day that the Royal Family was visiting Arran in the cruiser *Superb*, Rothesay had its own visit from the Hunt class destroyer H.M.S. *Bleasdale*, which was moored in Rothesay Bay for three days. As soon as she arrived her Commanding Officer, Lieutenant-Commander L. E. Blackmore, R.N., came ashore to call on the Provost, who returned the visit in the evening. During the visit the eight officers and 140 ratings constituting the *Bleasdale's* company were invited to a dance in the Pavilion and given free access to the golf course and putting greens.

The Rothesay Express of 8th July, 1947, not only told of the ensuing visit but put on record the ship's war service in home waters, the Mediterranean and the Far East.

Bleasdale, one of eight in the Albrighton (No 3) Type "Hunt" class destroyers, was built by Vickers-Armstrong (Tyne), and was launched in July, 1941. Displacement 1,050 tons (1,490 tons full load), overall length 280 feet, beam 31 feet 6 inches. She carried 280 tons fuel oil and a complement of 168. A sister ship *Easton*, was also on display. November, 1948.

> H.M.S. *Bleasdale* is a Hunt class destroyer. Her armament is composed of two twin mountings, 4 ins. HA/LA guns: three twin Oerlikon mountings; one set of torpedo tubes: and one multiple 2 pounder Pom-Pom. She also carries depth charges, and anti-submarine devices, and is capable of 30 knots.
>
> During the war she was employed on south and east coast convoys and took part in numerous E-boat actions, and shot down two enemy aircraft. She also took part in the bombardment at Salerno, and made many attacks on enemy submarines.
>
> When the war in Europe ended, she was ordered to the Far East, and was one of the ships to enter Singapore when the Japanese surrendered.
>
> At present, the duties of H.M.S. *Bleasdale* include the policing of German waters. On 18th April she was the wireless firing ship in the destruction of the fortifications of Heligoland.

An impressive view of the Home Fleet at anchor off Gourock. This photograph was taken at midnight from Lyle Hill, above Greenock, with the Cross of Lorraine in the foreground.

James Hall

Saturday, 26th July was the last day of the Review, and the following day the vessels taking part began to disperse. On the hills above Greenock and on the sea front all the way down the Firth large crowds had gathered for the last view of Britain's might.

Visibility was good, enabling clamouring spectators to see whole lines of vessels on the move. All the ships were manned, and bands were playing. Watchers near Gourock Pier saw the cruiser *Superb* pass fairly close and heard the ship's Royal Marine band play 'Auld Lang Syne'.

Admiral Sir Neville Syfret's flagship the *Duke of York* cast off at 4.20 p.m. from her mooring buoy off Princess Pier, Gourock, and was canted to face down Firth. Other battleships, including *Anson* and *Howe*, followed suit, as well as the carrier *Illustrious* and others.

Meanwhile, the warships of the Second Cruiser Squadron lying off Gourock prepared to move. The five vessels of this group, *Superb*, *St. James*, *St. Kitts*, *Sluys*, and *Gabbard* moved off followed by the depot ship *Maidstone*. The remaining carriers, battleships, destroyers, cruisers, submarines and auxiliary craft all followed in turn, gradually clearing the Firth of Clyde, leaving it a vast empty space once more. *Montclare*, too, swung round and made her way back to Rothesay Bay.

With such a great Naval presence of immense seapower, coming together like this, it was a time for reflection. All the vessels attending had now left and were returning to their various bases, wherever that might be, policing our coastal waters or manning our bases abroad. Wherever the destination of these fine ships, this was the British Navy at its best, and one could rest assured our country was safe in their hands.

The Fleet of England is her all in all.

Tennyson

One of the four battleships in the "King George V" class, the *Duke of York*. She was laid down in May 1937, and completed 4 November, 1941. It was officially stated that the design of these great ships incorporated enhanced defence against air attack, including an improved distribution deck and side armour, more elaborate sub-division, and an improved system of underwater protection. Unofficial reports gave weight of armour as over 14,000 tons, and a water-line thickness as 16 inches.

The *Duke of York* was flagship of Commander-in-Chief, Admiral Sir Neville Syfret, K.C.B. at the Clyde Naval Review, and was photographed here in July, 1947.

*   *   *

Numerous changes to the Clyde Visit Orders were made right up to the event itself, and the following schedule is a likely summary of all the vessels attending

BATTLESHIPS
  King George V class, *Duke of York* (C-in-C), *Anson, Howe.*

FLEET AIRCRAFT CARRIERS
  Colossus class, *Vengeance.*
  Illustrious class, *Illustrious.*

CRUISERS
  Swiftsure class, *Superb.*
  Dido class, *Dido, Sirius, Cleopatra.*
  Modified Dido class, *Diadem.*

DESTROYERS
  Battle class, *Barrosa, Corunna, Cadiz, St. James, Sluys, St. Kitts, Gabbard, Aisne, Dunkirk, Finisterre, Solebay, Jutland.*
  C Class, *Crispin, Creole.*
  Zambesi class, *Zephyr, Myngs, Zest.*
  Onslow class, *Onslaught, Opportune, Onslow.*
  Wager class, *Whirlwind, Wrangler, Wakeful, Wizard.*
  Ulster class, *Ulster.*
  Hunt class, Albrighton (No 3) Type, *Bleasdale, Easton.*
  Hunt class, Blankney (No 2) Type, *Farndale, Bicester.*
  Rotherham class, *Rapid, Rocket, Roebuck.*

FRIGATES
　Loch class, *Loch Tralaig, Loch Veyatie, Loch Fada, Loch Arkaig.*
　Bay class, *Burghead Bay.*

CORVETTES, *Flint Castle.*

RADAR TRAINING SHIP, *Boxer.*

FLEET OILERS, *Black Ranger, Prestol, Thornol.*

LANDING SHIPS TANK (LST), *Anzio, Suvla, Narvik.*

LANDING CRAFT TANK (LCT), LCT 4037 and others.

FLEET MINESWEEPERS, Algerine class, *Fancy, Bramble, Lennox, Marmion, Pluto, Romola, Rosario, Nerissa, Spanker.*

MOTOR MINESWEEPERS (M.M.S), M.M.S.84.

PETROL CARRIERS, *Petrobus.*

DEPOT SHIPS, *Fort Rosalie, Fort Duquesne.*

FLEET TUGS, *Saucy.*

SUBMARINE DEPOT SHIPS, *Maidstone, Montclare.*

REPAIR SHIP FOR COASTAL CRAFT, *Woodbridge Haven.*

SLOOPS
　Aberdeen class, *Fleetwood.*
　Modified Black Swan class, *Starling.*

TENDERS, *Dwarf.*

SUBMARINES
　A-class, *Alaric, Alcide, Alderney, Alliance.*
　T-class, *Taciturn, Tradewind, Thule, Tiptoe, Trump, Tactician, Thorough, Turpin, Trespasser.*
　S-class, *Seneschal, Spirit, Sturdy, Spiteful, Satyr, Sirdar.*

MOTOR TORPEDO BOATS. A small number including V2016 carrying the Royal Party, V2017 with the Household on board and V5008 used by the B.B.C.

SCOTTISH FISHERY BOARD'S PROTECTION CRUISER, *Minna.*

Rothesay Ashore 7

2 August 1946–3 November 1947

FOR ME there was not another town like Rothesay, it was the idyllic place to be stationed. Advertised as the 'Premier holiday resort in the Western Isles of Scotland', Rothesay had everything one could have wished for, and one never tired of it.

The half-hour ferry crossing from the rail/ferry terminal at Wemyss Bay on the Clyde coast, easily reached by a short train journey from Glasgow Central to Rothesay, was always something to look forward to. On the return journey there were always feelings of regret.

The Isle of Bute, about 15 miles long and five miles wide at its widest point, unspoilt and beautiful in itself, is situated among some of the finest scenery that it is possible to find anywhere. Only a short distance away are many lovely places to visit: the Kyles of Bute, Loch Fyne, Loch Goil, Loch Striven, Loch Long, Loch Riddon, The Sound of Bute, Arran and Great Cumbrae Island, for example, are all easily accessible. No more difficult of access are Tighnabruaich, Tarbet, Inveraray, Dunoon and Balloch near the shores of Loch Lomond.

The Royal Burgh of Rothesay. King Robert III of Scotland presented Rothesay with it's first Charter as a Royal Burgh on the twelfth day of January, 1400.

A splendid view of the Paddle Steamer *Waverley* at Craigendoran, getting underway in the early 1960's. Postcard kindly donated by Donald Ferguson.

Although the advantage points for taking photographs of Rothesay has been established over many years, this splended postcard given me by Donald Ferguson, shows Rothesay, taken from Skipper Woods, as it was in the early 1960's.

Ferry companies operating when I was there in 1946/1948 included the London Midland and Scottish Railway and the Caledonian Steam Packet Company Limited, who advertised sailings from Rothesay on most days of the week to Lochranza and Campbeltown, Inveraray, Brodick, Whiting Bay, Largs and Millport, including a cruise to the Arran coast, the Kyles of Bute and Dunoon. Every day of the week the LNER ran sailings to the three lochs, Loch Long, Loch Goil and Loch Lomond, leaving Rothesay at 10.15 a.m. and arriving back at 6.15 p.m. The fare was 1st class and Saloon, 15/6d, 3rd class 13/2d and 3rd class rail and steamer 10/4d.

Steamers also visited Lochgoilhead and Arrochar with return saloon fares 6/2d. There were also Sunday cruises, and on 20th and 27th July, 1947, special sailings were laid on to cruise around the warships which were anchored off Gourock for the Clyde Naval Review.

Rothesay has been on the map for centuries. It was in April, 1398, that King Robert III of Scotland conferred the hereditary title of Duke of Rothesay upon his eldest son, David, in the Royal Castle at Rothesay; the Sovereign's eldest son Prince Charles holds the title to this day.

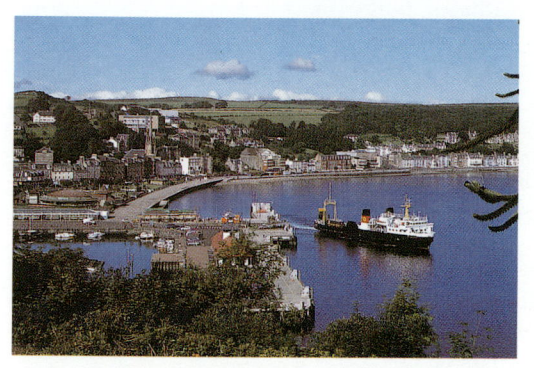

"Doon the Water" - Rothesay Bay. A very nice view of Rothesay taken within the last few years or so, from Skipper Woods overlooking the bay, pier and esplanade. Card donated by Alex Bennett, with kind permission from Whiteholme of Dundee.

Another postcard selected by Donald Ferguson, taken one summer in the early 1960's from Chaplehill, surely shows Rothesay at its best. The Promenade, Gardens and Pier have been built on land reclaimed from the sea. The original shoreline was some 200 metres inland.

In 1946, a British fleet minesweeper carried the name of *Rothesay*, and this was the second ship carrying the name. One of more than 30 vessels of the Bangor class, *Rothesay* was built by Wm. Hamilton & Co. Ltd, of Port Glasgow, and was launched in March, 1941. She was driven by geared turbines, and was 174 feet long overall and 28 feet 6 inches beam. Her displacement was between 605 and 656 tons and she had a complement of 60. *Rothesay* was broken up at Milford Haven in 1950, but she was followed by a third ship carrying the name, a frigate built at Yarrows at Scotstoun and launched in 1957 by the Countess of Selkirk. She was commissioned in 1960 and saw service on the South Atlantic Station, but after three commissions was taken in hand at Rosyth for a special refit to enable her to carry a helicopter. The third *Rothesay* was 370 feet in length with a beam of 41 feet and displaced 2,200 tons. Propulsion was by two steam turbines and she had a maximum speed of 30 knots. She was broken up at Santander in November, 1988.

The small town of Rothesay nestles quietly at the foot of rising ground which encircles the whole town at its rear, following the entire sweep of the Bay. On the hills above Rothesay from either Chapelhill at the northern end of the town or Skipper Woods at the other one can take in the whole panorama of the Bay of Rothesay, with the pier, esplanade, gardens, and the town itself.

The British Fleet Minesweeper *Rothesay*, was built by Wm. Hamilton, Port Glasgow, in 1941. She was one of a number built at this time and displacement varied between 605 and 656 tons. *Rothesay* was 174 feet overall, and beam 28 feet 6 inches. She had a complement of 60. Here she is in 1946.

The Isle of Bute, situated on the west coast of Scotland in the beautiful Firth of Clyde, is 15 miles long and 5 miles across at its widest point. The Boundary Fault which geographically divides the Lowlands of Scotland from the Highlands, passes through the centre of the island. Bute is green and fertile with flat coastal roads and light traffic. The island has no mountainous areas, the highest point being Windy Hill at 900 feet. The Isle of Bute has been occupied by man for over 5,500 years and traces of early civilisation can be found around the island in the way of stone circles, chambered cairns, cup markings and other mysteries. Bute is an unspoilt island in a perfect setting, unsurpassed in tranquility and beauty.

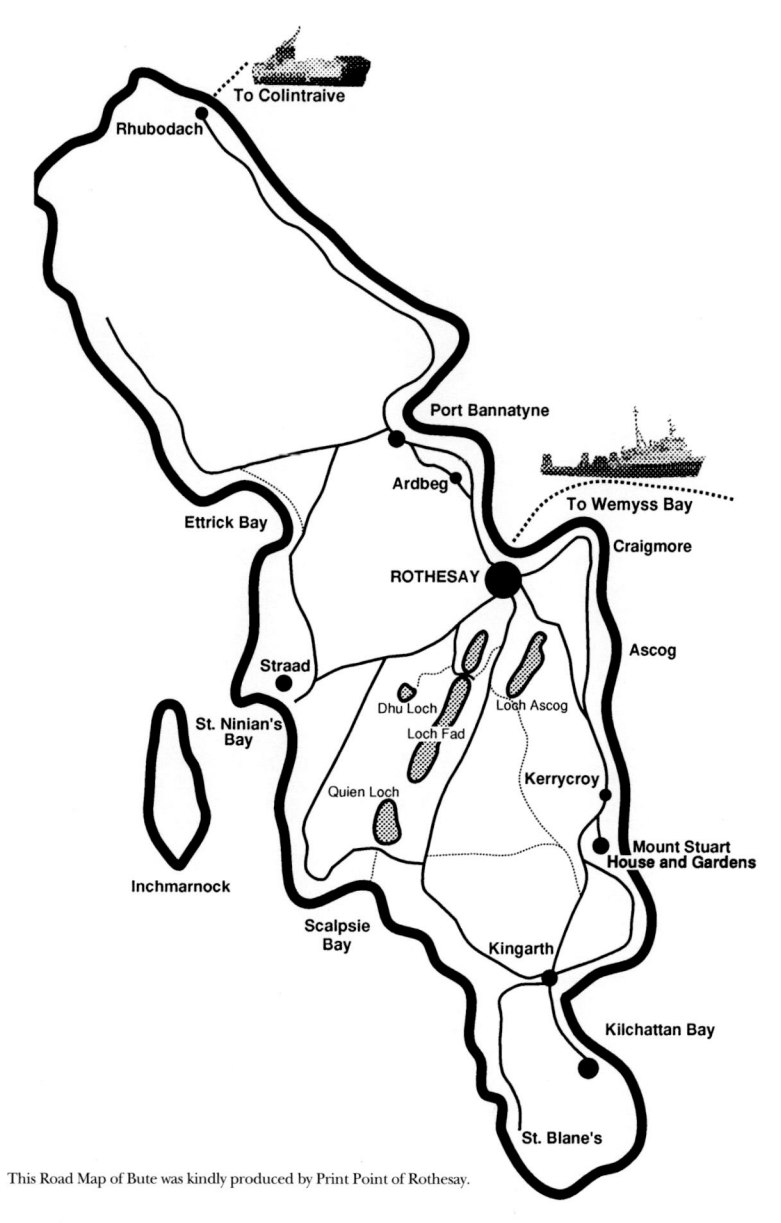

This Road Map of Bute was kindly produced by Print Point of Rothesay.

Rothesay comprises the main street fronting the town and numerous side and back streets, among which shops of every description support not only the livelihood and day-to-day requirements of the residents, but also varied accommodation and needs of those visiting and staying on the island. As I remember it in 1946, thousands of visitors descended on the town for weekends and one and two-week holidays. I recall the frontage of Rothesay being a pleasing blend of houses, shops and hotels. There was a choice of guest houses and boarding houses, as well as a variety of restaurants and bars, many of which enjoyed uninterrupted views across extensive landscaped gardens which merged planted borders with grass and paved verges, and beyond that the whole vista of the Clyde waters as far as the eye could see.

Between the gardens and the Clyde a broad esplanade runs the entire sweep of the bay. Conveniently situated in a central position to the town there is the well-proportioned pier, handling the constant transfer of cars, residents and visitors to the island by ferry.

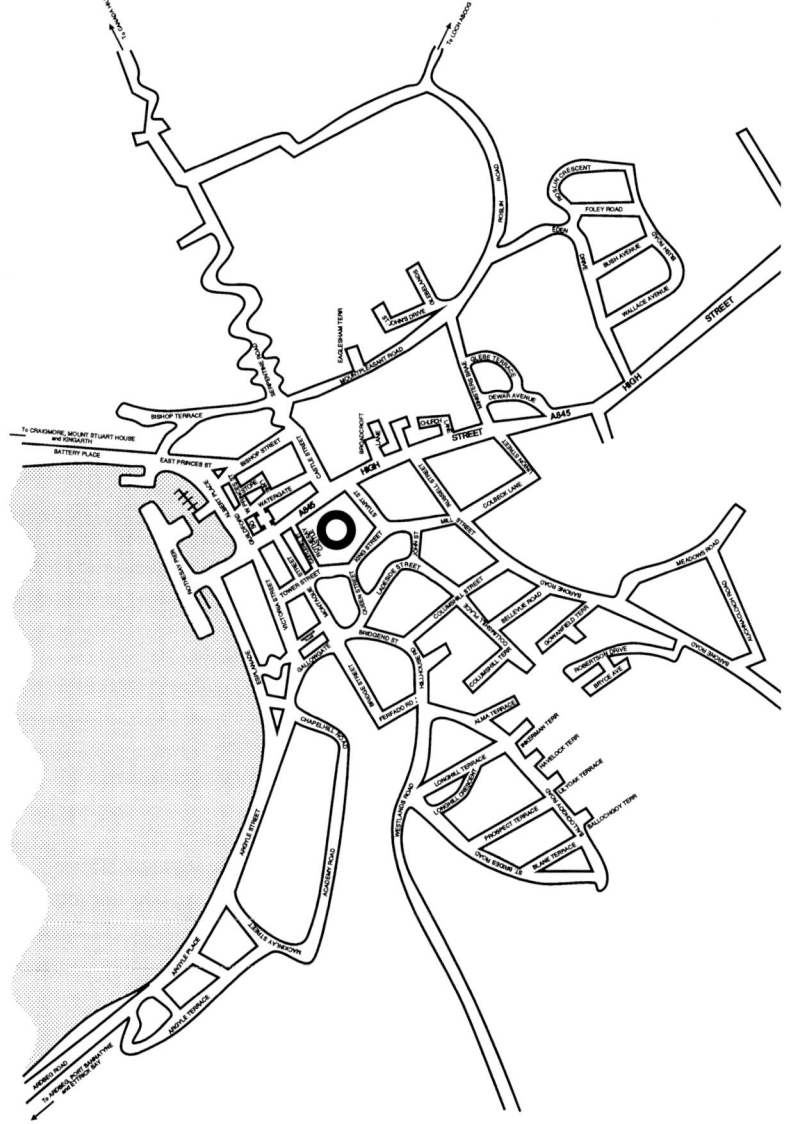

Rothesay is a delightful small town with around 6,500 permament population. With one street leading into another, everything is compact, convenient and easily accessible. The castle in the centre of Rothesay dates from Norman times, and the township became a Royal Burgh in 1400. The Prince of Wales currently holds the title Duke of Rothesay, first bestowed by King Robert III on his eldest son.

It was in the 1840's when Rothesay began to emerge as 'Scotland's Madeira', the favourite resort of Glaswegians, particulay during the Fair holidays. Rothesay has everything to offer the holiday maker, tucked away in a haven of completeness, its attractions have outlasted the many changes over the years, but remains today, a perfect place to visit and stay.

This Street Map of Rothesay was kindly produced by Print Point of Rothesay.

This photograph of the Winter Garden was taken in 1998, and although the attractions and functions provided today are different from those in 1946, when concert parties were staged twice nightly throughout the summer season, the building remains much the same as I remember it.

My thanks to Iain L. MacLeod for this photograph.

The entertainment facilities at Rothesay in 1946 and 1947 were second to none. For a young man ashore for the day, evening, or overnight, there was always plenty to do, many places to visit, and something of interest happening all the time. For a start there were three well-equipped cinemas, all showing a matinee if wet. The Palace, Regal and Ritz all changed their programmes every three days and showed the best films of the day. Over one week in early July, 1947, the Palace showed 'Dead Reckoning' with Humphrey Bogart and Elizabeth Scott, with a change to 'The Bowery', with Wallace Beery and Fay Wray. The Regal showed 'Margie', featuring Jeanne Crain, and 'Odd Man Out' with James Mason, and the Ritz 'First of the Few' with Leslie Howard and Rosamund John, followed by 'Easy to Look At' with Gloria Jean. Programmes began at 6.15 and 8.30 pm.

During the holiday season the Winter Garden on the esplanade presented concert parties. In 1947, for example, throughout the season, Fyfe & Fyfe 1947 Entertainers performed to packed audiences twice nightly at 6.45 and 8.45 p.m. The shows were produced by Jack Worth and the orchestra was directed by David Mackintosh. Prices (including tax) were 3/–, 2/6d, 2/– and 1/6d.

In other venues dancing was a regular feature of the week. Old time dancing was advertised by The Rothesay Tramways Co. Ltd. in Ettrick Bay Pavilion every Tuesday and Thursday, 8.00 to 11.00 p.m. Modern dancing was held every Monday and Wednesday in Port Bannatyne Hall from 8.00 to 11.00 p.m. and there was also dancing in Kingarth Hall every Wednesday and Saturday, 8.00 to 12 o'clock, admission 2/6d. The Rothesay Advertisers Association presented dancing every evening in the Pavilion Ballroom from 7.30 pm with music by Harry Gerrard, the resident dance band, with Les Morris.

Scottish dancing was also held in the town along with pipe bands, processions and charity balls. The Navy quite frequently took part in the carnival weeks, and there were special concerts and garden fetes to be enjoyed.

On one special occasion in July, 1947, a Grand Charity Theatrical and Carnival Ball was held at the Pavilion under the patronage of the Marquess and Marchioness of Bute in aid of the Soldiers', Sailors' and Airmen's Families Association. The programme of events included a Belle of the Ball Competition, an Old-time Waltz Competition, and Best Ladies' Hair Style Competition. One was invited to make up one's own set for an Eightsome Reel and enter an Eightsome Reel Competition for Boarding House and Hotel Parties. There was also a cabaret show, and the cafe and bar were open. Dancing was to the music of Harry Gerrard. Tickets were 10/6d each.

A regular feature for the children was Uncle Phil's Punch and Judy show at the Children's Corner. Uncle Phil performed at 11.00 a.m., 3.00 pm and 7.00 p.m. daily.

Apart from this type of entertainment, there were numerous other attractions and activities. Rothesay Tramway Company's buses organised drives to Ettrick Bay, 'two miles of silvery sand ideal for recreation and picnics—10d return', Kilchattan Bay by West Road, via Loch Fad and Loch Ascog, 1/6d return, Round Bute tour 2/6d. Another bus ride was Mount Stuart, via Craigmore and Ascog, 10d return, and there were others including special party bookings for Tighnabruaich on Tuesdays and Thursdays by bus to Rhubodach and motor boat to Tighnabruaich, leaving Rothesay at 10.30 a.m. and 2.30 p.m. Round Trip 5/–.

If you were interested in physical pursuits of any kind, there was plenty to choose from. Horse riding, indoor baths, tennis, cricket, snooker, golf, bowls, cycling, boating, fishing, and many others, including just walking the island.

At this time, also, there were 15 places of worship, including Good Templar

One can feel the friendly atmosphere of the town from this postcard of the Putting Green at Rothesay. This picture must have been taken during a hot summer, since the scorched grass is a little uncommon for Rothesay. Postcard supplied by Alex Bennett, with kind permission from Whiteholme of Dundee.

My thanks to Alex Bennett for this postcard of The Flower Gardens and Seafront at Rothesay, with kind permission of Whiteholme of Dundee.

A familiar view again of Rothesay from Chapelhill, in the mid 1980's. It is impossible to describe the pleasure derived from living in such a magical place as Rothesay. My thanks to Alex Bennett for supplying the card, and permission to use it 'by courtesy of Dennis Hardley photography, 01631 720 434'.

Hall, West-End Gospel Hall, Ardbeg Baptist Church, Rothesay Free Church, St. John's Church, Ascog Church, United Free Church, Trinity Church, West Church, St. Paul's Episcopal Church, Rothesay Congregational Church, Craigmore St. Brendan's, St. Colmac's & St. Ninian's, St. Bruoc Church, and the High Kirk of Rothesay. Many of these churches held bazaars and fetes with open admission.

All these varied functions and activities were included in the weekly programme of events, which kept Rothesay throbbing, stimulating enthusiasm and enjoyment for residents and visitors alike, every day of the week.

Since the Navy had shaped me into a proficient touch-typist, I thought it might be an advantage if I learnt shorthand to go along with it; not that there was any requirement for this on board, and it was purely a self-interest vocational pursuit. It was November by then, and the closed season for holidays on the island, so I considered it might be productive to spend one evening a week on learning something to advantage which might come in useful in the future. I enrolled during November, 1946, and joined a weekly Pitman shorthand class where there was around a dozen of us, all civilians except for myself.

I discovered I was not sufficiently dedicated to the course, which probably had something to do with the fact that I was the only Navy man there. Turning up regularly did depend in the first case on having shore leave on class nights, and secondly on whether there were other attractions going on in the town which could quite easily lure me away. It didn't help either, that class instruction finished early December and was not due to re-start until around mid-January, 1947, and this was the very time when *Forth* was due to leave Rothesay for Devonport for the transfer of the crew on to *Montclare*.

It was late May, 1947, when we arrived back at Rothesay on *Montclare*, the place was already buzzing with activity, and I never gave shorthand lessons another thought. Ferries were active in both directions carrying jubilant passengers in a continual flow to and from the island. Amidst the carefree frame of mind of the passengers, however, a warning was raised in some of the Scottish daily papers. On 25th June, 1947, it was reported that 'Mines were menacing the Clyde' and pleasure boats were warned to post look outs.

> Clyde pleasure steamers—now packed on almost every trip with holiday-makers—were amongst the ships which received an Admiralty 'Ware mines' flash sent out yesterday when mines were reported adrift in the Firth.
>
> One was located and destroyed in the Ailsa Craig area where the yacht *Aarla* was blown up in mysterious circumstances on June 17.
>
> The Admiralty warning went out from Portpatrick radio station to the scores of ships in the Clyde and the Irish Sea. By telephone, all harbour

and pilot authorities on both sides of the river were instructed to inform all ships and smaller craft that did not carry wireless.

The mine which was destroyed—first to be reported in the area for more than a year—was first sighted by the Burns-Laird cross-channel steamer *Lairds Isle*, on her daylight run from Ardrossan to Belfast.

It was afloat off Ailsa Craig, and the *Lairds Isle* gave its approximate position.

Within minutes the Royal Navy frigate *Woodbridge Haven* had put to sea from Rothesay Bay.

After a search of the area the mine was sighted seven miles off Ailsa Craig in the centre of a busy traffic lane.

It was sunk by gunfire.

"SCARE" MINE

A second mine, reported early in the afternoon, is thought to have been a 'scare'. A mine disposal squad from Faslane searched in vain for it over a wide area off Strone Point, which projects between Loch Long and the Holy Loch.

The admiralty then called off the search and sent out a signal late last night 'River is now clear of mines'.

Just before the search was called off the Naval crew located an empty depth charge case, rusty and encrusted with seaweed and limpets.

'This old depth charge must have given rise to the mine scare,' a Naval officer at Faslane said. 'It was not dangerous as apparently it had lain for a long time on some shore and the tides had gradually broken up the explosive material inside it.'

After receiving the warning, captains of all ships in the river yesterday cut down speed when in the vicinity of Loch Long and the Holy Loch entrances. Look-out men were posted on the bridge and on several ships forward in the bows.

Passengers were not told of the presence of a dangerous mine, and made the crossings of the river unaware of the search that was being made for it.

During the war years U-boats laid hundreds of mines in the Firth of Clyde below the boom defence which stretches across the river from Dunoon to the Cloch Lighthouse.

Tr.S.S. *Duchess of Montrose*. Built 1930.

Edward W. Paget-Tomlinson.

"WRITTEN OFF"

Although full details of their approximate positions were obtained from German U-boat commanders' records after the war and months were spent by the Navy's minesweeping flotillas in locating the mines and sweeping the channels clear, it is known that several of the German mines were never accounted for and, in Navy language, had to be 'written off'.

According to Naval officers, the most likely explanation for the blowing-up and sinking of the *Aarla* is that she struck a mine in the darkness.

The position in which the cross-channel steamer *Laird's Dale* saw an explosion and later wreckage in the water was not far from the spot where the first mine was sunk yesterday.

The theory for the presence of a mine in the river yesterday, however, is that it was carried north from the Irish sea by a strong south-west wind which has been blowing over the week-end.

In the Irish Channel, which was a heavily mined area during the war, there are several small mine-fields which have still to be thoroughly swept.

In Home waters, one of the most intensive minesweeping operations of the war was carried out in the Firth of Clyde—over an area of 1,000 square miles in a quest for moored magnetic mines laid by the U.218 on 18th April, 1945. At the end of July, three out of the 15 mines were still unaccounted for despite an intensive search made by 26 minesweepers with the co-operation of the U-boat's commander.

The important role of the Clyde steamers during the war was highlighted by *The Buteman and West Coast Chronicle* on Friday, 18th January, 1946.

THE CLYDE AT WAR—Steamers' Fine record

The immense contribution of the River Clyde to the war effort will no doubt one day be made known, but it is worthy at this time to recall the part played by the L.M.S. ports at the Tail of the Bank and by the Company's fleet of Clyde Steamers which in peace time conveyed millions of passengers to and from the famous holiday resorts on the Clyde coast. During the year 1938 they carried over four million passengers.

At the outbreak of war in September, 1939, there were 21 vessels, including the motor vessels *Ashton, Leven, Wee Cumbrae,* and *Arran Mail,* employed on the L.M.S. Clyde Coast services, and several of them were employed in the early days of September, 1939, conveying children under the Glasgow and District Evacuation Scheme to various coast towns.

Within two months of war being declared, the Admiralty took over nine paddle steamers and fitted them out as minesweepers; also three motor vessels for the conveyance of service personnel to and from the ships in the anchorage. Most of the paddle steamers were subsequently used as Coast Defence Auxiliaries, and three of them were lost in service.

Three of the Company's turbine steamers and a motor vessel were working to the requirements of the Sea Transport Officer, Gourock, being engaged in carrying troops and baggage between Gourock and Greenock (Princes Pier) and the troop transports in the Clyde Anchorages. For a period of 18 months one of these turbine steamers was employed at Stranraer conveying troops and baggage between Stranraer and Larne. This left the Company with only five steamers to maintain the Clyde Coast sailings.

Only essential services were maintained. No sailings were given from Gourock to places beyond Dunoon as a defence boom had been erected between the latter port and the Cloch Lighthouse; and no calls were made at Dunoon Pier after dark. During the winter of 1939/40, morning and evening calls on this section were made via Hunter's Quay, and in subsequent winters via Kirn, a buoyed channel to the latter point having been laid down by the Admiralty. Rothesay was served during the hours of darkness from Fairlie, but after the first war winter restrictions were relaxed and the morning and evening services resumed via Wemyss Bay.

The Arran service was transferred from Ardrossan to Fairlie and, acting under Admiralty orders, steamers for Millport and Arran sailed via the north end of the Cumbrae. The channel between the Holy Isle and the Island of Arran was closed and the steamer for Lamlash had to round the south end of the Holy Isle and pass through the gateway of the boom at that point.

The shortage of labour, the manning and coaling of steamers, presented difficulties which pre-war were non-existent, and occasionally after air raids the sailings were suspended for a few hours while the channel was mine-swept, but despite all the war-time problems which arose, the services were maintained with very little interruption. During the years 1939 to 1944 inclusive, over 17,000,000 passengers were conveyed by L.M.S. Clyde steamers.

In 1940, owing to enemy air activity, the Ministry of War Transport decided to utilise piers and harbours on the West Coast of Scotland for unloading deep-sea cargoes and to speed up the turn round of ocean-going vessels. A fleet of vessels was assembled at Gourock, sixteen of them under L.M.S. Management, to convey the dockers and other personnel to and from vessels which crowded the anchorages between Gourock Pier and the Dumbartonshire and Argyllshire coasts. Nearly 300,000 tons of cargo were unloaded and brought ashore in lighters and shallow draft vessels at these three ports, where facilities were available for the traffic to be loaded into railway and other vehicles.

With the defeat of the German Air Force and the re-opening of the ports in the east of England, the number of vessels using the anchorages in the Clyde for overside discharging of traffic declined. Operations at Fairlie ceased in 1943, and were tapering off at Bowling and Greenock towards the end of 1944. The large troop transports, however, continued to use the Clyde ports until after the end of the war with Germany.

The L.M.S. ports on the Clyde and the Company's fleet of river steamers have reason to be proud of the part they played in the greatest war in history.

An impressive view of the *Duchess of Montrose* at Rothesay in 1938. It was a common sight in 1946, to see the steamers packed to capacity with passengers.

Photograph with kind permission from "Paddle Steamer Preservation Society - Scottish Branch"

The additional pleasure derived from journeying to Rothesay was taking the ferry from Wemyss Bay. I remember sailing on three of these splendid steamers, the *Jupiter*, *Duchess of Montrose* and the paddle steamer *Waverley*.

My very first ferry crossing was on the *Duchess of Montrose*, which was one of the premier cruise turbine steamers on the Clyde for 35 years. The London, Midland and Scottish Railway company ordered her from Denny of Dumbarton and she joined their Caledonian Steam Packet fleet in 1930. In the thirties she gave excursions 'Round the Lochs' and 'Round Arran' and sailed as far as Ailsa Craig and Stranraer. During the Second World War she remained in home waters, serving mainly on the Wemyss Bay to Rothesay route. In 1946 the *Duchess of Montrose* returned to her excursion work, at first on the Arran via Kyles of Bute run and later sailing to Inveraray and to Lochranza and Campbeltown.

On many occasions it was the paddle steamer *Jupiter* that I boarded at either Wemyss Bay or Rothesay for the crossing on the Clyde. *Jupiter* was built by Fairfield at Govan in 1937 for the regular runs to Dunoon, Rothesay and the Kyles of Bute in connection with the trains at Princes Pier, Gourock, and Wemyss Bay. After war service, which included taking part in the Normandy landings in 1944, she was the first steamer to return to peacetime duties. There was a very interesting report about her in *The Buteman and West Coast Chronicle* on Friday, 15th February, 1946.

CLYDE STEAMER'S RETURN

After strenuous War Service

H.M.S. *Scawfell*, better known to thousands of holidaymakers as the L.M.S. *Jupiter*, has been demobilised, and has taken up the Gourock, Dunoon and Holy Loch service.

She was requisitioned by the Admiralty at the outbreak of war and served as a minesweeper on the Firth of Clyde, and later from Dover, Portland, and Milford Haven. Subsequently she sailed as an anti-aircraft ship on the Thames and on escort duty between the Tyne and the Humber. The *Jupiter* took part in the Normandy landings and can claim success in destroying enemy aircraft. Mr Herbert Branford, chief engineer of the *Jupiter*, who served with the vessel throughout the war years, has returned with her to peacetime duties.

The *Jupiter* has undergone extensive overhaul and presents a spick-and-span appearance. She was built in 1937 by the Fairfield Shipbuilding and Engineering Company, and prior to the war, with her two yellow black-topped funnels, the L.M.S. colours, was a familiar figure on the Clyde. She has accommodation for 1,200 passengers and has a speed of $17^1/_2$ knots. There are three decks, the promenade deck containing observation rooms, the main deck with tea-room and lounge facilities, and the dining-room and officers' accommodation. She is the second holder of the name to sail under the L.M.S. flag. Captain Lennox, recently master of the *Marchioness of Lorne*, is in command.

The *Jupiter* is the first of the L.M.S. Clyde fleet to return from the war. The *Caledonia* and *Duchess of Fife* are being refitted and it is hoped will shortly be available for service. Six others are awaiting refitting, and two are still on Government service. The return of these vessels will enable some of the steamers which have been carrying on valiantly during the war years to undergo overhaul. The L.M.S. are making plans to replace the steamers lost on war service.

Here we see *Jupiter* in the early days of loading cars at Dunoon. Dunoon Pier officially opened on 3 June, 1898, and was used as a port of call for the steamers. On 4 January, 1954, the Gourock to Dunoon route became the first major car ferry service in Scotland, with the introduction of the brand new MV "Arran" where cars were loaded by means of a vehicle hoist. Until MV "Arran", and her sisters "Bute" and "Cowal" arrived, cars had been loaded, tide permitting, over planks onto the conventional passenger steamers. Later, *Jupiter* and others became regulars on the route.

My thanks to Ian Young, the first Port Manager of Caledonian MacBrayne to have been appointed at Gourock, for this information, and to "Paddle Steamer Preservation Society - Scottish Branch" for supplying the photograph.

Although taken a couple of years after I left Rothesay, this superb photograph embraces everthing as to how it was in 1946-1948. The steamer *Jupiter*, with her decks crowded with passengers steaming into Rothesay. Behind her to the left, is my ship, the Submarine Depot Ship *Montclare*.

"With kind permission from Ian McCrorie"

P.S. *Jupiter*. Built 1937.

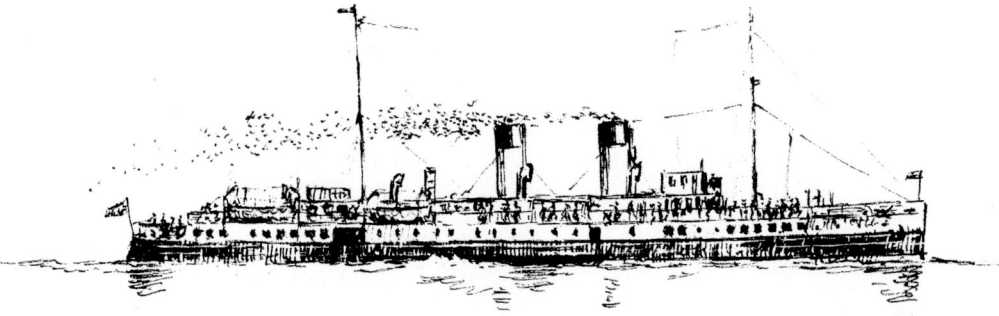

In July, 1947, *The Buteman* reported that two Naval officers and six ratings were drifting in a liberty boat on to rocks a mile north of Wemyss Bay pier. They were saved by the L.M.S. steamer *Jupiter* which after two attempts to take the boat in tow—the first towline broke— safely brought her to Rothesay Bay where she was handed over to the submarine depot ship *Montclare*. The liberty boat, her engine broken down, dragged her anchor when a strong wind started up and was seen by the *Jupiter's* captain drifting in heavy seas.

In the summer of 1947, the Scottish Press reported 'Clyde Steamer Aground All Through The Night'. The *Duchess of Montrose* ran aground on the rocks between Hunter's Quay and Kirn, at 5 p.m., with 300 day-trippers and week-enders bound for Dunoon.

For an hour the L.M.S. steamers *Marchioness of Lorne* and *Duchess of Hamilton* tried without success to pull her off, so motor ferry boats were brought out to take the passengers off in the dusk. At midnight, her lights blazing, the *Duchess of Montrose* was still there, her bow high and dry on the shore and her stern low in the water.

Up to a late hour sightseers travelled in buses from surrounding districts to see her. The cause of her grounding was a freak fog that lifted as quickly as it had descended. The impact as the vessel grounded was so slight that until distress signals were made few passengers realised that the ship had gone aground.

Edward W. Paget-Tomlinson.

The World's last sea-going Paddle Steamer *Waverley*, celebrated 50 years of paddling on 16 June, 1997. On many occasions I was one of the crowd lining her decks. This superb photograph was supplied by Iain L. MacLeod, with kind permission from "Paddle Steamers Preservation Society - Scottish Branch".

Waverley on a maiden voyage in the glorious summer of 1947

A Year of Celebration Cruises aboard The World's Last Sea-Going Paddle Steamer

for further information - Tel: 01 446 720656 or 0141 221 8152

Waverley, on a maiden voyage in the glorious summer of 1947, celebrating in 1997, her Golden Jubilee. With kind permission of the "Paddle Steamer Preservation Society - Scottish Branch".

A third steamer that I enjoyed sailing on was the *Waverley*, the successor to a famous paddle steamer that had been built in 1899 by A. & J. Inglis at Pointhouse to the order of the North British Steam Packet Co. Ltd. and had been lost by dive-bombing on her return from the Dunkirk beaches in 1940. The new vessel was ordered by the London & North Eastern Railway from the same Clyde yard that had built the former *Waverley*, and the keel was laid on 27th December, 1945.

Launched on 2nd October the following year, she made her maiden voyage on 16th June, 1947. The LNER ships were traditionally given names from Sir Walter Scott's novels, and the *Waverley* took hers from the hero Edward Waverley, whose head adorned her paddle boxes. Unlike most steamers of her era the *Waverley* is still afloat and still carrying passengers not only on the Clyde but much further afield.

Fitted with a triple expansion engine that gives her a speed in service of 14.5 knots, she has an overall length of 239.6 feet and can accommodate 1,350 passengers. She has comfortable dining saloons and observation lounges with deep windows providing passengers with clear views of the passing scenery.

From early spring until late summer, many thousands of visitors came to Rothesay. There was a constant flow of coming and going, shops, hotels, bars, restaurants and places of enjoyment never ceased from satisfying the seemingly unsatiable demands of the holidaymakers. The town was always vibrant with excitement and exuberance, and once ashore, you couldn't help but be part of it.

Another view of *Waverley*, steaming gracefully, fully loaded with passengers and carrying the banner "ROTHESAY ISLE OF BUTE".

Photograph kindly supplied by Iain L.MacLeod. With kind permission from "Paddle Steamer Preservation Society"

In the 'Local Jottings' of *The Rothesay Express* in July, 1947, there were several interesting snippets of information: 'At a cost of about £70, Rothesay Town Council is ordering 700 yards of all-wool bunting streamer pennants in preparation for Carnival Week'—'Applications for accommodation during July have been exceptionally heavy, according to the Information Bureau at the pier, which states that they have been inundated with requests for bookings from England, especially for Glasgow Fair fortnight'—'Watergate is the busy street these days. In addition to its normal activities, Bute Wholesale and Distributing Agency's new and up-to-date ice cream factory is running full blast, and with the arrival during the week of herring in good quantities, Barr's Kippering Stores are busy curing'.

Weekends at Rothesay were one round of pleasure and enjoyment from start to finish, with dancing on Saturday evenings and concerts on Sundays. This mixed in with a visit to the cinema, a meal in one restaurant, tea and cakes in the Grand Marine Hotel, and a drink at a bar, was indeed something to look forward to.

Next door to the Pavilion (to the extreme right in this picture) is this large building which used to be the Grand Marine Hotel, a regular haunt of mine for teas, snacks and dancing. The outside of the building is much the same as it was, but has now been renovated into flats. The hotel was originally the Queens Hotel - the part next to the Pavilion was the headquarters of the Royal Northern Yacht Club, in the halcyon days of super yachts.

My thanks to Iain L. MacLeod for the photograph, and background information from Kathleen Clegg, Bute Museum.

The Pavilion, Rothesay, in 1998. My family and I spent a few days in Rothesay in the summer of 1999, and I couldn't resist calling here several times. The entrance hall, the twin staircases and swing doors into the stage and dance floor were all there. Each time I called, there was no-one about, but I could feel the atmosphere of the place, just as if everything was waiting to return to those times that I remember so well. My thanks to Iain L. MacLeod for this photograph.

Clare - Rothesay, May, 1947. Wearing my new 'Tiddley' uniform for the first time. Note the full width to the bell-bottom trousers and the seven ironed creases supposedly to represent the seven seas.

One exceptionally popular venue of entertainment, particularly for young people of my generation, was the Pavilion Ballroom, where most young visitors on holiday, as well as those living on the island, gathered in the spacious and well-appointed ballroom for regular Saturday night dancing, with music provided by Geraldo, presenting Harry Gerrard and his music, the resident dance band for the season. The well-proportioned stage, draped with a heading and plush heavily lined side curtains in a striking deep shade of blue, provided the setting for frequent Sunday evening concerts, when many well-known artists presented a comprehensive and varied programme of entertainment.

The Pavilion Ballroom had a welcoming feel about it, the atmosphere was always friendly, the decor was attractive, and it was run and maintained to a high standard. It was promoted by the Rothesay Advertising Association, whose advertisement carried the slogan 'Scotland's Premier Ballroom—Dance at the showplace of Rothesay'. Aside from the ballroom and changing rooms, there was a comfortable lounge area laid out with tables and chairs where one could relax between dances and enjoy refreshments.

The Pavilion was a recognised venue where the boys met the girls, and more often than not friendships made there continued over the following few days during the girl's holiday period, and then it was good-bye.

Some relationships lasted longer than this. My 1946 girl friend was Jean, who lived at Coatbridge. We met in early September at the Pavilion and spent much of the evening dancing together. We continued writing to each other regularly, and met from time to time in Glasgow, where our meeting place was usually under the clock at Queen Street station or at the Shell Display at Glasgow Central.

In September, 1946, Rothesay was buzzing with holidaymakers, and Jean and I had planned a weekend towards the end of the month, when she was free to come over to Rothesay for a few days. On 24th September, however, she wrote to me to say that in spite of trying very hard she was unable to find any accommodation. All the hotels, guest houses and boarding houses were full, and none of them could give any hope of offering a room. As a result, we agreed to meet in Glasgow, and spent our time enjoying the various pleasures the city had to offer, visiting her home, and dancing at Dennistown Palais. We were, however, able to meet again at Rothesay in October, when the town had become a little quieter.

It was never easy for any friendships made in Rothesay to be anything other than a holiday romance. For any longer relationship to last, there was always a number of hurdles to overcome. In the first place, it was not easy to arrange appropriate shore leave, and particularly weekend passes, to coincide with one's girl friend's family ties and commitments. There were also difficulties to do with her employment, perhaps, and holiday entitlement. Finding accommodation at Rothesay (if that was how meetings were planned), could be difficult, and then there was the time involved in journeying from the mainland with the sea crossing, and the numerous costs involved. All those difficulties usually led instead to writing letters to one another as the only means of keeping in touch.

Neither did it help much when *Forth* left Rothesay for Devonport in January, 1947. Although none of us knew at the time, we were to remain there for nearly five long months. This interval of time was too long for any budding romance to succeed. Inevitably interest gradually waned, friendships faded, and letters stopped.

On returning to Bute on *Montclare* in the spring of 1947, Rothesay was as lively as ever, and if anything even livelier than in 1946. The delights of the town, and the pleasures of the island itself were there as ever just for the taking, and the ship's company did just that.

On one Saturday evening in June, 1947, I had the last and only dance of the evening with Janette. She casually mentioned that she was staying at a hotel along the front and was due to return home next morning, having spent a few days on holiday at Rothesay. I had no idea where home was, neither did I know the hotel where she was staying, nor the time she was leaving to catch the ferry. We said goodbye at the entrance of the Pavilion, and as she left with her sister Agnes I noticed that Janette was wearing a green coat.

Next morning around 1030 I was manning the bridge of *Montclare*. It was a bright, sunny day, the air so clear and fresh with just a gentle breeze blowing off the sea, and it was very easy for me to imagine I was relaxing on the deck of a luxury cruise liner rather than manning the bridge of one of His Majesty's warships. In an idle moment, I swung the powerful telescope to point towards the Rothesay esplanade, moving it slowly from left to right scanning the activity ashore. There was just a chance, I thought, that I might spot Janette, perhaps coming out of her hotel, on the pier awaiting the ferry, or walking towards the town.

After persevering with this several times, suddenly, there she was wearing the green-coloured coat, walking with her sister, carrying suit cases. They were coming out of the George Hotel, one of the hotels situated in a prominent position on the frontage, overlooking

"In Rothesay I met Bunty,
Just for a day or so,
And then went out with Margaret,
Once to a midnight show".

Jean and I spent many happy times together over the four months I knew her, until early January, 1947, when *Forth* left Rothesay for Devonport, where we remained until May, 1947, awaiting transfer onto *Montclare*. I don't know why, but leaving Rothesay seemed to end our association, and we never corresponded or met again. More than once she reminded me of an old Scottish saying - "What's for ye'll no gang by ye". Here she is in Rothesay, October, 1946.

After our brief first meeting at the Pavilion Ballroom, Janette returns to Rothesay to hear my song 'Is it Love' being played by Harry Gerrard at the Sunday Concert. This early photograph of Janette was taken in July, 1947. My depot ship Montclare *is in the background.*

the gardens and esplanade. I couldn't believe my eyes as I followed them on their short walk to the pier. I lost sight of them among the crowd of people gathered on the pier however, and although I continued looking for them on board the ferry *Jupiter* it was impossible to pick them out among all the passengers lining her decks.

I noted the name of the hotel, however, and decided to call at the George during my shore leave later that day and ask the hotel if they would give me Janette's name and address. This I did, and the proprietor, Mrs. Miller, after hearing the sequence of events, thought that it was so romantic that she broadcast my story to all the guests in the lounge at the time. I was quite embarrassed over it all.

The result was that Janette and I had many happy times when she was able to get time off from work (she was employed in the Tracing office of the Shipyard Typing Office of John Brown, the Clydebank shipbuilders) to come over to Rothesay, or when I was able to see her at her home in Balloch, or at the Shell display (a mounted exhibit of a First World War shell casing) at Glasgow Central Station.

During the Clyde Review one of the ships open to visitors was one of our latest, the Swiftsure-class cruiser *Superb*, completed in 1945. I received a letter from Janette on 27th July in which she told me 'one of our visits was to HMS *Superb* and I found it most interesting, seeing some parts of the ship that I type about, although sometimes not having the slightest idea what they are used for. I even looked through one of the telescopes and now I realise how powerful they are'.

Before National Service I was taking piano lessons at home. I composed a song and had someone in London score it for me into 16 band parts, and I brought a copy of the piano score with me when I joined up. One Sunday early in July, 1947, I asked Harry Gerrard, the dance band leader at the Pavilion, if he would play it at one of his Sunday concerts. He said he would, and suggested I arrived at the concert the following Sunday about an hour or so before doors opened, so the band could run through it, and this I did.

Janette and I were there, of course, and the concert was reported in both *The Rothesay Express* and *The Buteman*.

VISITORS ENJOY CONCERT—Tuesday 8 July 1947

A few bars of music - 'Is it Love' composed by Anthony J. Walker, and played by Harry Gerrard and his Orchestra at the Pavilion, Rothesay, on Sunday 6th July, 1947.

July holiday-makers, who have arrived in the town in large numbers, made up the greater part of a big audience which attended the Sunday evening concert in the Pavilion. The concert also attracted many Navymen who had a special interest in a musical composition written by one of their shipmates and featured by Harry Gerrard and his Orchestra who were supported on the programme by three talented guest artistes, Mary Ferrier, soprano, Margo Henderson, impressionist, and George Hutchinson, entertainer.

The musical number 'Is It Love', composed by Signalman A. J. Walker, H.M.S. *Montclare*, made 'a hit' with the audience, and Signalman Walker on being introduced by Gerrard was enthusiastically applauded.

I wasn't the only one to present Harry Gerrard with a musical composition. A month earlier, a local man's music was featured by the band, which was also reported in *The Rothesay Express* on 17th June, 1947.

LOCAL MAN'S MUSIC

To be featured by Harry Gerrard

A musical composition 'The Stalag Red Cross Blues' by Mr Walter Dale, who is employed as a bar tender in a local hotel, is to be featured by Harry Gerrard and his Orchestra at next Sunday evening's concert in the Pavilion.

Mr Dale wrote the song and the music while a prisoner of war in Germany. The other day he showed it to Gerrard who was so impressed with the score that he decided to feature it in his next programme.

Mr Dale was a prisoner of war for five years, and prior to enlisting in the Forces he served as a steward on several Clyde steamers. His brother, Tommy, now appearing at the Beach Pavilion, Aberdeen, has written songs for several well-known comedians, his last song being 'Rothesay at the Fair', featured by comedian Tommy Morgan.

Commander Hamilton tells me that in 1943 Eric Morley, of Miss World fame, arrived in Rothesay. He was in a Boat Company with the Royal Army Service Corps, whose job was to run a 'taxi' service between Military transports and the shore and to carry stores and mail between the shore and the ships.

In 1944 Lieut. Eric D. Morley, R.A.S.C., produced 'The Navy and the Army's first pantomime, Sinbad the Sailor', which was presented 'by kind permission of Capt. B. Bryant, D.S.O., D.S.C., R.N. (of submarine *Safari* fame) and Lieut-Col. T. E. Southwell, R.A.S.C. The

Concert held in the Pavilion in 1942. Organised by HMS *Titania* with Wrens from HMS *Cyclops* and officers and ratings from both ships of the Third Submarine Flotilla.

My thanks to Kathleen Clegg, Bute Museum, for this photograph.

pantomime was staged at the Pavilion, Rothesay, on Sunday, 24th December, 1944, and at the Winter Garden on 29th and 30th December, 1944, and 1st January, 1945. Programmes were sixpence, and all proceeds were donated to the Rothesay Welcome Home Fund and local Navy and Army Funds.

In 'Tales from Rothesay at War' in *The Buteman* of 27th June, 1998, Commander Hamilton recalls rumour has it that when Eric Morley first suggested to some local girls that he would like to organise a dance he was told 'Oh, Eric, you couldn't run a dance, leave it to us'.

By 17th March, 1946, Morley had been promoted Captain, and was Entertainments Officer of the Waterborne Training Centre at Rothesay. He produced several concerts during his time at Rothesay, and copies of his programmes are with the Bute Museum Library.

I cannot over-emphasise the popularity of Rothesay as a holiday resort during the years I was there. It was not only apparent from the number of people about, but we were constantly being reminded of the fact by regular newspaper reports in one way and another:

The Rothesay Express—Tuesday, 8th July, 1947

ANGRY TRIPPERS

Extra passengers taken aboard at Rothesay and Dunoon last Sunday caused two hundred day trippers to Dunoon to be left behind when the all-the-way steamer made its return journey. Demonstrating at the pier booking office, the travellers protested against alternative transport offered—a steamer to Gourock and rail journey to Glasgow—on the grounds that it involved them in an extra outlay of 2s 2d. Dunoon Town Council has decided to make representations to the Railway company to stop booking passengers for the single journey, to the exclusion of return ticket-holders from Dunoon.

Although Rothesay was well catered for with wide choices of hotels and alternative places to stay, visitors when planning a holiday on the island had to book well in advance of their holiday dates due to the permanent demand for accommodation.

On 16th July, 1947, the Marquess and Marchioness of Bute were sponsors of a fete at Kames Castle in aid of the Soldiers', Sailors' and Airmen's Families Association. The President of the West of Scotland Branch was the Duchess of Montrose. An invitation arrived on *Montclare* for three representatives of the ship to attend, and the invitation was passed to myself and two of my colleagues in the Communications Branch. We duly accepted and joined in the festivities. Teas were available in the Castle, and the day was to finish with a dance at Ettrick Bay. When asked if we would be going on to the dance, however, my colleagues and I politely excused ourselves since we had made other plans for that evening.

St Andrews Day concert in the Pavilion - 30 November, 1952, kindly supplied by Kathleen Clegg, Bute Museum.

Around the same time as this a dance was arranged on board *Mull of Kintyre*, and this was reported in *The Rothesay Express* of 8th July, 1947.

DANCE ON BOARD SHIP

A large and representative company attended a party and dance held recently on board H.M.S. *Mull of Kintyre* by Commander Egan and the ship's officers. The guests included Captain Slaughter (H.M.S. *Montclare*), Captain Everard, Commander Hunter-Blair, Commander De Chair (H.M.S. *Roseneath*), Lady Nina Martin, Huddersfield, Mrs. T. Dyson, B.B.C. news commentator, and Miss Jean Macaulay, *Evening News*. Local guests included Provost and Mrs. Muir, Captain Tudman and Mrs. Tudman, Mr. W. Reed, Pavilion Manager, Mr. Harry Gerrard, Pavilion dance band leader, Mr. and Mrs. R. A. Chrystie, and Mr. and Mrs. Ralston. Members of the cast of Rothesay Entertainers also attended. Dancing was enjoyed on deck under an awning until the weather broke when it was continued inside. The music was provided by the Revellers Dance Band.

There was an extremely useful facility ashore that was provided exclusively for the use of the submarine crews and crews of the depot ships *Forth* and *Montclare*, and indeed before them *Cyclops*. Ships' companies on overnight shore leave were offered accommodation in

A typical scene during the summer of 1947. Leaving the pier at Rothesay, the paddle steamer *Jupiter*, with her decks lined with passengers at the end of their holiday, passes close to *Montclare*, depot ship of the 3rd Submarine Flotilla, for the half-hour crossing to Wemyss Bay.

what was known as the 'Church of Scotland Huts'. During the war years, the crew of *Cyclops* used this accommodation continuously, and Commander Morgan, speaking at the *Cyclops* Farewell functions stated that the maximum number of sleepers for one night had been 500. When I was there in 1946/47 I was shown a bed in the same hut every time, and Commander Hamilton has confirmed to me through an ex-Wren who was a book-corrector on *Cyclops* that there were in fact two such huts, each accommodating about 50 men. He has also reminded me that they were beside the Church Hall in Argyle Street, the Church Hall being used as a Canteen.

E.W. PAGET-TOMLINSON
NOV 1999.

The Church of Scotland Huts were well managed, clean and inexpensive, and one could just turn up; the availability of a bed was pretty well assured. In addition there were washing facilities and a light quick breakfast was provided for those who wanted it.

In view of all the various functions going on in the town and around in those days, the huts were usually open all night, certainly until the early hours of the morning. These sleeping arrangements ashore provided a very useful and worthwhile service in catering for Naval men by offering overnight accommodation after enjoying themselves in the various delights of the town, instead of having to

Painting by Edward W. Paget-Tomlinson.

The Shell display at the entrance to Glasgow Central railway station, July, 1999. This was the meeting point for numerous friendships made at Rothesay, but not in its current position. I can remember the Shell being more in the concourse of the station area, nearer to the entrance to the platforms, and between the last main line train platform to the right and the line to Wemyss Bay.
'Happy to meet
Sorry to part
Happy to meet again'.

scramble back to the ship by dashing to catch the last liberty boat that night.

Because of the cramped and over-crowded sleeping conditions on *Forth* and *Montclare*, due mainly to inadequate hammock space. I used the hut's sleeping arrangements ashore frequently.

Since my first day in uniform on joining *Royal Arthur* my civilian clothes had become superfluous, and we had had the opportunity of packing them up and sending them home at the expense of the Admiralty, but I did not do so. Instead, I folded them carefully into the cardboard box the Admiralty had supplied and humped them around with the rest of my kit. Once on *Forth* and *Montclare* I carefully stowed these inside my locker.

One day it occurred to me that it would be nice to wear a civilian suit now and again when ashore rather than being in uniform all the time. It wasn't anything to do with not liking or wanting to wear uniform, but I thought it would be refreshing sometimes to don a suit instead. I was not aware of any regulations forbidding crews to be out of uniform when ashore, so I thought I would make some enquiries as to how and where I might be able to change ashore.

On the esplanade, near the Winter Garden, there was a very well maintained public convenience which contained a wash and brush up room. The building was supervised by Joch, backed up with his relief Jim, one of whom was always in attendance during the daytime. The general facilities were always available, but the wash and brush up area was only open from about 9 a.m. until around 9.30 p.m., when this section was locked

Neither Joch or Jim had been approached before with such a request, but they were both agreeable to an arrangement for me to leave my civilian clothes in this room and to change into them when I wanted, and to change back into uniform later in the day before returning to the ship or staying overnight in the Church of Scotland Huts.

The arrangement worked well for several weeks, until one night I turned up well before 9.30 p.m. to change back into uniform, and the place was closed, at least Joch's room was, and I had no access. I waited impatiently for some twenty minutes or more, becoming more desperate by the minute. I had to be back on board that night since I had no overnight pass, and the last liberty boat back to the ship was 2330, but how could I return to the ship out of uniform?

To my great relief, Joch came running up, sincerely apologised and explained that he hadn't forgotten, but something had come up at home and he had had to close up early. As it turned out, everything was all right, but I realised I daren't take the chance of that happening again.

Obviously if I wanted to continue changing ashore I had to make some alternative arrangements, and my enquiries led me to a small hotel situated in a side street where the proprietor said she had an empty wardrobe in a small room off the landing that was never used. This was ideal, and a much more reliable arrangement, permanent

The building I used for changing from uniform to civilian clothes, was in the same position as the public convenience block in this photograph, situated in the landscaped gardens near the Winter Garden. I cannot be sure that this is the same building, since this looks fairly modern, and it is likely this has been modernised over the years. This photograph was taken in July, 1999.

and secure, and enabled me to continue the life style I had been enjoying.

Regardless of all the tributes and fond farewells exchanged between the town officials of Rothesay and the officers and men of *Cyclops* on her leaving the island in 1946, there was a groundswell of opinion ashore during the summer of 1947 that the Admiralty should be asked to move its submarine depot ship to a position more distant from the pier. Reports in the *Rothesay Express* revealed that the Rothesay Harbour Trust was intending to ask the Admiralty to shift the *Montclare* some three cable lengths (600 yards) north to north-east of the position she then occupied.

The Harbour Trust said that the *Montclare* interfered considerably with the navigation of passenger steamers approaching and leaving the pier and that garbage, ashes and sewage from the ship were polluting the shore of the West Bay. It was even said that because of the pollution the local council had been unable to open up the bathing station there, though one member of the Trust retorted that it was actually a shortage of time, labour and materials that had influenced the council in its decision not to reopen the bathing station that year.

It became clear that there were differences of opinion between those who not only wanted the *Montclare* moved to a more distant mooring but would not be sorry to see her removed from Rothesay Bay altogether, believing that her presence deterred holidaymakers from coming to the town, and those who believed that the town benefited greatly from her presence. One of the latter pointed out that each week personnel of naval vessels moored in the bay spent more than £2,000 in the town.

Answering those who complained that the pollution in the bay came from the *Montclare*, one councillor, Duncan Dewar, said he would rather have a dirty face and a pound in his pocket than have a clean face and be stony broke.

There should only be three of us in this picture - the other guy is pushing his luck. Perhaps he thinks I am only a civilian. Rothesay, June, 1947.

This view, taken from above the roof of the Winter Garden, shows how close *Montclare* was moored to the shore. Note the crowded deck of the ferry. Photograph taken about 1947/1948, and kindly supplied by Cdr. I. Hamilton.

The situation was complicated by the laying of a buoy for use by the London, Midland and Scottish Railway steamers, and there was a suggestion that the Admiralty should pay for that mooring buoy to be moved to a position further away from the *Montclare's* mooring. On the one hand some of the protagonists pointed out that it was the obligation of vessels arriving at or leaving the pier to proceed with caution and at slow speed and on the other there were people who saw the great bulk of the *Montclare* as a blot on the Rothesay landscape.

The discussion went on for some weeks. The *Montclare* was too close to the shore and she should be moved at least half a mile away, said some. The presence of the ship spoilt Rothesay as a holiday environment, she was a danger to navigation and it was her presence that led to increased pollution along the shoreline.

Those who wished to present a contrary view said it would make no difference if the ship were moved, that the ship's presence was good for the town, bringing in visitors and revenue, and that if the controversy resulted in her leaving it would be a great loss to Rothesay, particularly in the winter.

After a great deal of argument the Harbour Trust changed its mind and decided not to ask the Admiralty to move the *Montclare's* mooring. After all, it had been pointed out that the ashes along the shoreline could not have come from her; her boilers were oil fired.

To coincide with the Clyde Naval Review at Gourock my parents arranged a tour of Scotland, and their holiday plans included a stay at Greenock so they could see the Fleet, and my ship *Montclare*. I was able to arrange for a few hours shore leave to meet them, and our rendezvous was a restaurant in the town of Greenock. I remember we ate whalemeat. This was not something any of us would normally have chosen, but we selected this from a somewhat restricted menu. I'm not sure any of us enjoyed the meal, but at least we were able to meet and spend some time together.

Cdr. Ian Hamilton

The crowds were immense, thousands of people in the area at that time arriving for the festivities surrounding the Clyde Review. The demand for accommodation was so great that restaurants were forced to include whalemeat on the menu to supplement dwindling supplies of more traditional dishes.

From Greenock my parents travelled to Rothesay and stayed at the Glenburn Hotel for two nights. They timed this to fit in with the return of *Montclare* to Rothesay, and on their second night there I dined with them at the Glenburn. We did not eat whalemeat this time.

The Glenburn Hotel was probably the largest hotel on the island, situated on high ground above the southern end of the town with a commanding view of the bay and the pier. One could clearly see *Montclare* anchored in the bay, and at night she looked quite magnificent with all her lights shining through the portholes and the reflection glimmering on the water.

In the immediate post-war period *Forth*, followed by *Montclare*, had a permanent presence at Rothesay. The submarines as well as all the other vessels coming and going were a great attraction for holidaymakers and day trippers visiting the island. The popularity of Rothesay as a holiday resort, and the fact that the Navy were there, offered the possibility of having a good time, with a touch of romance as well, and this was almost assured.

It goes without saying that this worked the other way round for the ships' crews, since there was an endless stream of girls arriving every week, at the same time as others were saying goodbye. There were no plausible excuses for not having a girl friend in Rothesay.

This was also true, of course, of *Royal Arthur* and *Scotia*, and to a lesser extent at *Glendower*, since these Training Establishments had also become permanent bases over the years, and when the Fleet's in port, so are the girls.

Janette and myself in a hurry. Rothesay - September, 1947.

The unrivalled position of the Glenburn Hotel, with its commanding view over Rothesay Bay.

Postcard supplied by Alex Bennett, with kind permission of Whiteholme of Dundee.

T'was Skegness where we did our training
That first I quickly fell
For this young lady pictured here
Her name was Isobel.

In Ayrshire it was Molly
(that's Molly on the right)
And Anna, Cath, and Florence
Before a dance one night.

In Rothesay I met Bunty,
Just for a day or so
And then went out with Margaret
Once to a midnight show.

Another Margaret walked along
She really was quite sweet
Then rescued Clare when she was being
Chased by H.M. Fleet.

I met this Jean when dancing
She was the best so far
She asked me home one evening
To meet her Ma and Pa.

An unfinished poem
Montclare, Rothesay—June, 1947.

Throughout the whole of my time in the Navy I was never unwell, ill or needed to report sick. I treated my training and work seriously, and believe I carried out my duties proficiently and responsibly, and indeed because of this, I was promoted. I had experienced a mock-battle at sea, and taken part in the largest assembly of Naval warships since the war in the presence of King George VI. I had also been amongst many of our finest ships which formed part of our battle fleet during the war, and had seen many others, as well as some of our very latest ships and submarines.

On looking back, as I have done in writing this book, my time was well spent, on board and ashore. I enjoyed life to the full, and as a young man of eighteen and rising, what more could I have wished for?

My candle burns at both ends;
It will not last the night;
But ah, my foes, and oh, my friends—
It gives a lovely light!

Edna St. Vincent Millay.

Discharge 8

4 November 1947–3 January 1948

IN THE latter part of October, 1947, I was on duty, sitting in front of my teleprinter on *Montclare* reading through some messages I had just received, when the teleprinter started up again. It was quite a short message:

Replacement being sent for Signalman T/P Walker 4 November 1947

C/JX 791680

It went on to say that I was to report to H.M.S. *Pembroke*, RNB Chatham, for release from Service.

I stared at the message in front of me almost in disbelief. I read it over and over again, not really wanting to believe it was my name in the message. It came as a bombshell. I was numbed and shocked by it, even in revolt at the very idea of them sending a replacement for me when I hadn't asked them to.

Never had I given it a moment's thought that my National Service days might be coming to an end. I added up the months that I had been in the Navy—yes, come 4th November I would have served 21 months, the statutory period being around 18 months. This must be the end of it all, and I didn't know whether I was pleased or sorry.

I couldn't think of anything else at that moment, everything flashed through my mind all at once. Yes, It would be nice to go home, of course it would, but it would also mean saying goodbye to everything here, the life I had become used to and which I was enjoying so much, my colleagues, and Rothesay. And I wouldn't be seeing Janette any more. That had been a rather special friendship.

Perhaps worst of all, I would be out of the Navy for good. Did I want that? I asked myself.

In July, 1946, whilst at Chatham Barracks awaiting drafting, I was walking along a road one day when quite by chance I bumped into a friend of mine from my home town. Jim and I had been friends at school, and unknown to me he too had joined the Navy. We chatted for quite a time, and he asked me whether I would be interested in investigating the possibility of a Commission. I told him it had occurred to me but under National Service I doubted whether it was possible.

It turned out that we were able to organise a short leave at the same time, and together we arranged a visit to the Admiralty in London. My qualifications made me eligible, but the obligatory requirement was signing on for five years. Both of us having been in the Navy for only a few months at that time, we felt that we had not sufficient experience yet of Navy life, and were reluctant to commit ourselves further at that stage, so we both abandoned the idea.

The full meaning of the message in the machine was real enough, and told me my National Service days were at an end. There was nothing I could do about it. There was no procedure for requesting to 'stay on a bit longer' or 'perhaps until next spring'. In any case, even if it were possible, everything was arranged for another to take my place on *Montclare* and I would undoubtedly be drafted elsewhere, and I wouldn't want that either.

With the news of my release coming out of the blue like that, I immediately felt annoyed, depressed and downhearted. With all the people I had met, the friendships made, the Navy, and Rothesay itself, I believed my life to be complete, and I wanted it to go on for ever.

Wearing my demob suit, with my brother David at our family home around springtime 1948.

On 4th November, 1947, I said goodbye to my messmates, a few of whom had been with me on *Forth*. Some of the others who had been on *Forth* had left over the past few days to be drafted or released, and their replacements had arrived; for the new men, their time was just beginning, and I felt quite envious of them. I collected together my kit-bag, hammock and attache case, said my goodbyes to others on board with whom I had made friends, and climbed into the liberty boat for the very last time.

I felt very sad as I waited on the pier for the steamer to arrive to take me across to Wemyss Bay for the final journey. Over the months I had been stationed there on *Forth* and *Montclare* I had acquired very strong attachments to everything to do with Rothesay, with everyone

I had met, the places where I had spent many happy hours, and the good times I had enjoyed. It was an emotional moment which remained with me for a very long time.

The steamer *Jupiter* arrived all too quickly. Everybody waiting with me boarded her, and in no time we were off. I stood against the rail at the fore-end as I had done all those months ago when I was anxiously looking for the first sight of *Forth*, my first ship, but this time it was different, I wanted to take in the full sight of *Montclare* for the last time, as we passed her on her port side. There were four submarines alongside, and no other vessels in the bay at all. As we drew level with her, I hesitatingly raised my hand and emotionally murmured to myself 'goodbye *Montclare*, goodbye'. I stood gazing at her, and as we pressed ahead I walked to the stern of *Jupiter* to get one last look at her. I stood there until she was completely out of sight.

From that moment on it was goodbye all the way, at Wemyss Bay, the train ride to Glasgow Central, and the Shell Display at the station, the happy meeting point for renewing friendships I had made at Rothesay. One day soon, I told myself, I would return.

I arrived at Chatham Barracks later that day, and during the next three days I completed the procedure for my release. My Certificate of Service states that my actual release date was 3rd January, 1948. I had two months' pay in lieu of service when I was released Class A.

Lieutenant Birch completed my Signal History Sheet on 7th November, 1947, confirming my Character during Service 'Continuously Very Good (1946–48)' and General Efficiency in Carrying out Duties 'Satisfactory'. Efficiency on Discharge was assessed as 'Satisfactory'. His special remarks stated that I was 'a conscientious, reliable, pleasant and extremely polite young man, who has worked well, and one who was an asset to the department'.

The Certificate of Service S-459 assessed character on discharge on the basis of 'V.G., 'Good', 'Fair', 'Indifferent' and 'Bad'. Efficiency on discharge was judged as being 'Superior' (above average efficiency), 'Satisfactory' (average efficiency), 'Moderate' (less than average efficiency), and 'Inferior' (inefficient).

The final act came on 8th November, 1947, when I travelled to No. 2 Civilian Clothing Depot, RAOC, Infantry Barracks, York, where I was kitted out with civilian clothes. One brown two-piece double-breasted suit, one Raincoat, one Trilby hat, one pair Brown Shoes, two pairs socks, two shirts and a tie.

From York I travelled home, wearing my new demob suit and carrying my uniform and attache case. The Navy had dispensed with my services, and I was a civilian once again.

Out of uniform - early 1948.

> As generation succeeds generation in our historic Navy, may each age learn to live up to and imbibe the high traditions of its predecessors.
>
> Admiral Sir Doveton Sturdee
20 November, 1918.

Epilogue

GUINEA-PIG SUBMARINE LEAVES FOR ARTIC. The 'guinea-pig' submarine *Ambush*, left Rothesay on 12 February, 1948, for endurance tests in the Arctic. *Ambush* was fitted with the British adaptation of the German Schnorkel breathing device ('the snort') and remained submerged for several weeks while the effects of severe cold on the vessel and crew were noted. 12 February, 1948.

I HAD joined the Royal Navy at a time when the numbers of Training Establishments, personnel and ships were being scaled down. The war had been over six months, and there was no longer a requirement to maintain the wartime strength of personnel. Much of the organisation as I had known it during my training days was becoming superfluous; indeed, as soon as the war had ended contracts for new vessels were postponed or cancelled. The cost of the war was being addressed not only by the Admiralty but by all the armed forces.

My first Training Establishment, *Royal Arthur*, Skegness, which became the Central Reception Depot for most Naval entrants in February, 1944, was paid off in 1946. I had been one of the last hundred or so new entrants to pass through. *Glendower* at Pwellhi was also paid off in September, 1946, just five months after I finished my training.

The submarine depot ship *Cyclops* which, for most of the war was stationed in Rothesay Bay, was taken in tow in the early days of July, 1947, from the Clyde to the Bristol Channel, where she was to be broken up. Three months earlier, *Cyclops* was brought back to the Clyde after breaking away from her tugs in the Irish Sea. Source unknown.

British Naval units of the Far East Fleet operated with the United Nations Naval Force in support of land forces in Korea and in the control of local sea communications. The British Naval units together with units of the Royal Australian Navy, The Royal Canadian Navy, and the The Royal New Zealand Navy, have co-operated as partners with the navies of other nations in patrolling, escorting and giving flank support to the land forces. This picture was taken from the Bristish Aircraft Maintenance carrier *Unicorn*, which transported the first contingent of British land forces to Korea, and shows the cruiser *Belfast* perfectly against the rugged coastline. Photograph 1950/51.

A nice view of *Forth* with her flotilla of British submarines moored alongside her in St Angelo Creek, Malta. 7 May, 1951.

Looking as splendid as ever, *Forth* arrives in Malta after her first summer cruise. The depot ship won the Regatta of the Royal Navy's Mediterranean Fleet held earlier in the Levant. *Forth* beat H.M.S. *Liverpool*, by 42 points to 40, 16 July, 1951.

Training at *Scotia*, Doonfoot, Ayrshire, ceased altogether on 20th December, 1947, and the Establishment was paid off 19th January, 1948, the same month as my release from service.

In 1947 National Service was reduced from eighteen to twelve months, and the final intake was in 1959. The National Service Act was repealed in 1963; the last National Servicemen left the Royal Navy in 1961.

In spite of the toll taken by the war, by 1946 we had a modern Fleet with up-to-date ships and equipment, a Fleet which was unsurpassed in strength and sea power, a Navy which was held in high esteem and pride by the nation. Yet, as modern as we were then, some of our old traditions and ways of doing things had not at that time been swept away. Hammocks, for example, were still being used almost without exception on most of the older ships, and I was told that on *Forth* it was not until her refit in 1962 that hammocks were replaced with bunks. The daily issue of rum was not abolished until July, 1970.

Some of the ships that had helped win the Second World War for us at sea were soon to be in action again. The Korean war broke out in 1950, and lasted three years. In June, 1950, Britain despatched troops, ships and Naval aircraft in support of the US Marine Forces off the West Coast of Korea, and the British contribution included

Another imposing view of *Maidstone* (sister ship to *Forth*) at Portland Harbour, with submarines from left to right - *Tradewind, Sleuth, Scorcher, Scythian* and *Sidon*. During her stay at Portland, she was with the Seventh and Second Submarine Flotilla and then became Flag Home Fleet in September, 1956 - March, 1958. She was reconstructed between 1958-1962, to support nuclear submarines of the Third Submarine Squadron at Faslane between 1962-1968, and from 1969-1977, she was used as an Accommodation and Prison Ship at Belfast. *Maidstone* was finally sold on 4 May, 1978. This picture was taken sometime in 1950. Source unknown.

Below: After refitting at Devonport in 1947, *Forth* was in Malta and Suez between 1948-1951, as depot ship of the First Submarine Flotilla. She was back in Devonport in 1959, as depot ship of the Second Submarine Flotilla. Between 1962, and 1966, *Forth* was refitted at Chatham to support nuclear submarines with increased accommodation, and was then in Singapore between 1966-1971, as depot ship of the Seventh Submarine Squadron. She returned to Devonport in June, 1971, and on 17 February, 1972, was renamed *Defiance* at Devonport Fleet Maintenance Base, and became depot ship of Second Submarine Squadron. *Defiance (Forth)* was placed on the disposal list in 1978, and in April, 1985, she was sold and broken up at Kingsworth on the River Medway.

Here we see *Forth* in 1966 after her refit at Chatham, looking bran new but with some very noticeable alterations.

Submarine depot ship *Montclare*, looking as splendid as ever when she was photographed here in June, 1953.

Hawker Sea Furies preparing to take off from the flight deck of *Illustrious* to join in the NATO exercise "Operation Mainbrace" off the Norwegian coast. *Illustrious* was scrapped at Faslane in 1952 . Photograph 26 September, 1952.

Overhead view of *Montclare*, taken 5 February, 1955, when she was drifting west of the Scilly Islands in an Atlantic gale while under tow from the Clyde to Portsmouth. She broke her tow lines in all four times until the final attempt was made to fix the tow again, and she was expected to reach Portsmouth the next day. *Montclare* ended her days being broken up at Inverkeithing in 1958.

light fleet carriers carrying Fireflies and Sea Furies, in addition to cruisers, destroyers and frigates. Britain's naval role was primarily blockade, air strikes and bombardment.

Within a few years of the ending of the Korean war the ships that had served during the Second World War, many of which I knew during my service career, were out-of-date and at the end of their useful life. The battleship *Anson* was scrapped in 1957, and *King George V* along with *Duke of York* in 1958. The battleship *Howe* was placed in reserve, destined to be scrapped, in 1958 and *Vanguard* was due to be broken up at Faslane in August, 1960. The carrier *Illustrious* was scrapped at Faslane in 1956, *Indefatigable* was broken up at Dalmuir the same year and *Implacable* at Inverkeithing in 1955. *Theseus* followed in 1962.

The end came for the destroyer *Opportune* at Milford Haven in 1955, for *Bleasdale* in 1956 at Blyth and for *Zephyr* at Dunston in 1958. The later destroyers of the Battle class lasted a little longer with *St. James* being broken up at Newport in 1961, *Solebay* at Troon in 1967 and *Aisne* at Inverkeithing in 1970.

"WEEKS UNDER WATER - Submarines Experimental Cruise"

The Rothesay Express - 16 December, 1947

The new 'A' class submarine *Alliance*, which arrived at Portsmouth on Friday from Rothesay, after an experimental cruise to Freetown, remained under water for a period, which the Admiralty do not specify, but which they said was "several weeks". Previously, the submerged time of any one dive has been limited to days.

The *Alliance* which is attached to the Third Submarine Flotilla, will be returning to Rothesay after the Christmas leave.

The Admiralty on Sunday stated - "H.M.submarine *Alliance*, has recently completed a cruise to Freetown during which she called at Gibraltar, Bathurst, and Gambia. The purpose of the cruise was to test living conditions aboard a submarine during prolonged dives in tropical waters.

A doctor made the cruise, but the crew's health was excellent. Only one man reported ill, and he recovered in a few days. While under water, the men saw films, and heard gramophone records and recordings of B.B.C. entertainments. The only effect, they said, of being submerged for so long, was that when they came to the surface, they "smelt like fish".

Submarine *Alliance*, as she is today on blocks as a permament display at The Royal Navy Submarine Museum, Gosport. After numerous modernisation refits over the years, she bears little resemblance now, to the *Alliance* as I knew her in 1947. Copyright - Royal Navy Submarine Museum.

The cruiser *Dido* was put into reserve in 1947 and later broken up at Barrow, the *Superb* was broken up at Dalmuir in 1960, and the cruiser *Cleopatra* was placed in reserve in 1953 and later broken up at Newport. One of the other cruisers, *Diadem*, was sold to the Pakistani Navy in June, 1954, and renamed *Babur*. The *Woodbridge Haven* was broken up at Blyth in 1965 and the *Mull of Kintyre* was broken up in 1969.

A number of submarines underwent refits, modernisations and conversions in the years after I left, but eventually their end was in sight. In 1965 *Teredo* was scrapped at Briton Ferry and *Aurochs* at Troon in 1967. *Alaric* was broken up at Inverkeithing and *Astute* at Dunston, both of them in 1970. *Ambush* was broken up at Inverkeithing in 1971 and *Taciturn* at Briton Ferry the same year. In 1974 *Alcide* was broken up at Hull, and in 1975 *Aeneas* at Dunston.

The passing of time destroyed or dispensed with nearly everything I knew and took pleasure in when a National Service Sailor. Pretty well everything has been consigned to history, having given way to the advanced techniques and technology of today.

Time had run out for these great ships of the day, and one by one they were placed on the disposal list. The *Duke of York* shown here for example, was scrapped in 1958.

Maidestone, depot ship of the Fourth Submaine Flotilla at Portland Harbour, with the battleship *King George V* in the background. 1948/1949. Source unknown.

In one of the tugs, the "Warden", four men were injured when the lines parted. Surg.-Lt. J. Sutherland was lowered from another helicopter to give medical treatment, and later the St.Mary's (Scillies) lifeboat shown here, was launched to take off the injured men. (painting by Edward W.Paget-Tomlinson from a picture published in The Daily Telegraph, 6 February, 1955 - source unknown).

Of all the ships and submarines I came across during my Navy days, I know of only two which are being preserved by trusts, preservation societies or museums. The A-class submarine *Alliance* was new when I first saw her within days of her commissioning in March, 1947. One of the last A-class to be built for action in the Far East, she was placed on blocks in 1979 to form a centrepiece of the Royal Navy Submarine Museum at Gosport.

In her peacetime role *Alliance* travelled far and wide on exercises and sea trials of equipment and endurance. Apart from patrolling Home Waters, she visited many places overseas, including Gibraltar, the Canary Islands, Canada, South Africa, Aden, across the Arabian Sea, Hong Kong, Singapore, Malta, Lisbon, Spain and Tangier. She had refits in 1948/49, 1950 and 1953, and another between 1953 and 1955, all at Portsmouth. In October, 1958, she was brought to Devonport for extensive modernisation, which transformed her from the *Alliance* I knew. An Asdic dome was fitted on the bow, her hull was streamlined, all external torpedo tubes removed, the conning tower was converted into a 26.5 feet high fin, and all guns were removed. Between 1965 and 1966 *Alliance* was at Devonport for another refit and in 1969 she was taken out of service for yet another refit. She ended her sea-going career in 1973 and became a static display at H.M.S. *Dolphin* at Gosport, before becoming a museum exhibit and a memorial to the officers and men of the Submarine Service.

Montclare, 19,600 ton submarine depot ship adrift with only 52 men on board, being towed again off Land's End, on 5th February, 1955, after many hours adrift in an Atlantic gale. While under tow from the Clyde to Portsmouth for refit, the lines parted when she was west of the Scilly Islands. A helicopter was used to help to reconnect the ropes. (painting by Edward W. Paget-Tomlinson from a picture published in the Daily Telegraph, 6 February, 1955 - source unknown).

NAVAL ARTIC EXPEDITION

The British light fleet aircraft carrier *Vengeance* is pictured here in an Arctic setting from a helicopter during her voyage to far Northern waters. *Vengeance* returned to Britain on 7 March, 1949, with other naval units which accompanied her on a six weeks cruise to test men and equipment under conditions of extreme cold. Taken sometime in 1949.

The cruiser *Belfast*, the largest cruiser of the Second World War, was saved for the nation in 1971 as a unique and historic reminder of Britain's Naval heritage in the first half of the 20th century. Moored just above Tower Bridge in London, *Belfast* is open to the public seven days a week.

She was launched on 17th March, 1938, and completed 3rd April, 1939. Her displacement was 10,000 tons, length 613 feet 6 in, beam 63 feet 4 in. Heavily damaged by a mine in the early months of the war and practically rebuilt, she played a leading part in the sinking of the German battleship *Scharnhorst* at the Battle of North Cape. She also served on the Arctic convoy route and took part in the Normandy Landings. After the war she supported United Nations Forces in Korea, and remained in service with the Royal Navy until 1965.

Thankfully also being preserved is the C-class destroyer *Cavalier*, which was built by J. Samuel White & Co. Ltd. of Cowes

Another superb picture showing *Vengeance* (in foreground), and ships of the Home Fleet moored in the harbour at Gibraltar, during their autumn exercises. *Vengeance* went to Brazil in 1961, and was reconstructed 26 September, 1950.

Associated Press

"DIVERS TRY TO SOLVE RIDDLE OF THE AFFRAY"

The Affray: its disappearance in 1951 prompted almost daily press reports and theories which included its theft by the Russians

The Daily Telegraph - 27 July 1998. By Tim Butcher.

SPORTS divers using new deepwater techniques have reached the wreck of the Affray, the Royal Navy submarine in which 75 sailors lost their lives almost 50 years ago in a disaster that remains shrouded in mystery.

The divers were the first to see the wreck, which lies at about 270ft in one of the deepest parts of the Channel, since members of Royal Navy underwater recovery units in the early Fifties.

Aware that the site remains the last resting place of the crew, the team of eleven divers, led by Christina Campbell and Innes McCartney, took nothing from the site other than video footage.

The video has been requested by Royal Navy experts anxious to solve the mystery behind the cause of the worst British submarine accident since the Second World War.

"I was one of the first pair to go down the guide rope lowered onto the site," Mr McCartney said.

"It really was the most impressive sight to go down to that depth where there is no ambient light only to turn on a lamp and see the unmistakable shape of the submarine.

"She is a most magnificent sight, towering almost 30ft clear of the seabed and looking as formidable as she did in her heyday.

"She remains a significant and salutary reminder of our Naval heritage".

By not tampering with the wreck or removing any artefacts the divers did not contravene the Protection of Military Remains Act which was drawn up after the Falklands war to protect sites including naval wrecks.

SUBMARINE MISSING IN THE CHANNEL
"The 'A' class submarine *Affray* has not surfaced as expected after diving while on exercises" reported the Admiralty on April 17, 1951. "She sailed from Portsmouth last night April 16, unescorted, and dived at 2115 hours, south of the Isle of Wight. She was proceeding westwards and submerged at a speed of 4 ½ knots. She was expected to surface this morning but no surfacing signal has been received and her position is unknown. Destroyers and aircraft including helicopters, are searching for the submarine and efforts to contact her by radio are being made."

Numerous Royal Navy submarines and U-boats lost in shallower parts of the channel are often visited by divers but it was only with special gas mixtures including helium that the Affray could be reached.

Martin Rowden, an experienced wreck diver from Australia, said the danger increases exponentially at depths greater than 100ft with a consideable risk at the depth of the Affray.

Mr McCartney said the submarine was intact on the seabed and the right way up with only a slight lean to port.

The wooden letters of her nameplate have long since decomposed but the shape of her 281ft hull was unmistakable.

The loss of the Affray caused sensation when it was reported missing on 17 April, 1951, a day after sailing from Portsmouth.

As well as its normal crew of 61, it carried two classes of submarine officers under training and a small party of Royal Marines.

After failing to transmit a routine report, the Royal Navy began its procedure for dealing with lost submarines and for several anxious days hopes remained that Affray could be found and the submarine recovered.

There were stories of tapping noises and Morse messages being picked up by the searching vessels but, as the days went by and more ships took part in the search, hopes began to fade.

As the weeks passed rumours circulated of the A-class submarine being stolen by the Russians and the press reported almost daily as the search of thousands of square miles of seabed continued.

After two months the submarine was eventually found 37 miles from its last reported diving position. The loss of life represented one of the worst in the history of Royal Navy submarines and the Admiralty was anxious to establish the cause. Remote-controlled television cameras were used for the first time and they found damage to the snort mast used when submerged to draw in air for the diesel engines to run.

The mast appeared to have snapped, allowing water to flood into the submarine but mystery remained as to the cause of the break.

Experts recovered part of the mast and carried out tests that established metallurgical faults but theories about possible collisions or on-board explosions remained.

Mr McCartney's divers could shed little light on the issue, although they could confirm there was no other damage to the hull and all hatches and torpedo tubes remained sealed.

Perhaps the only way to establish exactly what happened would be to raise the Affray but with no other A-class boats in service there is no military logic to carrying out a salvage as nothing could be learnt to protect other vessels.

Mr McCartney plans to lead another expedition to find the M-1, one of the earliest Royal Navy submarines, which mounted a vast 14-inch gun on its hull".

©Telegraph Group Limited, London 1998

and launched in April, 1944. Funding for her preservation is being sought to restore her to her former glory, when she will serve the country again as a reminder of how the Second World War was won.

Caledonian MacBrayne is a name synonymous with sea travel to 23 islands off the West Coast of Scotland, and 1998 saw the silver jubilee of the formation of the company in its present form.

Caledonian MacBrayne was formed on 1st January, 1973, but its roots go back for almost a century and a half, the MacBrayne empire being traceable back as far as 1851. The Caledonian Steam Packet Company was formed in 1889.

The company's vessels today range from small ships with capacity for 50 passengers and six cars to vessels with certificates for 1,000

THESEUS EN ROUTE HOME
This unusual-angle photograph shows the light fleet carrier *Theseus*, veteran of the Korean war, en route home to Britain. She was for many months actively engaged in operations in the war zone and during this time was awarded the Boyd Trophy - given annually for the finest feat of aviation in the Navy - for outstanding flying and maintenance. The carrier reached Portsmouth on May 29, 1951, where she received the Boyd Trophy from the First Sea Lord, Lord Fraser. *Theseus* was broken up at Inverkeithing in 1962. Photograph 23 May, 1951.

An impressive view of the Fleet Aircraft Carrier *Illustrious* as she sails from Portsmouth heading for the Mediterranean with troops of the Third Infantry Division aboard. 5 November, 1951.

passengers and 120 cars. Many of the larger vessels have self-service restaurants, fully-licensed bars and shops, and many others have facilities for teas, coffees and snacks. Sailings are all year round, with vessels carrying over five million passengers and one million cars each year.

Besides providing pleasure trips and day cruises from mainland ports to many of the islands, the ferries convey produce of the islands not only to markets on the British mainland but to continental Europe.

The paddle steamer *Jupiter* which I remember well from those immediate post-war days is now no more. When the car ferries were built in 1953 *Jupiter* was retained to supplement the busy Rothesay service, being converted from coal to oil burning in 1957. At the end of the 1957 season she was withdrawn from service, and was towed to Dublin and broken up in 1961. Today, however, there is another *Jupiter* among the many vessels in the Caledonian MacBrayne fleet, a motor vessel that carries 531 passengers and 36 cars.

The turbine steamer *Duchess of Montrose*, the very first of the Clyde steamers I travelled on from Wemyss Bay to Rothesay on joining my ship *Forth*, also is no more. She was withdrawn at the end of the 1964 season, and a year later was towed to Belgium, where she was broken up.

The *Waverley*, now billed as 'The world's last sea-going paddle steamer', celebrated 50 years of paddling on 16th June, 1997. After nationalisation of the railways in 1948 she came under the control of the British Transport Commission, who transferred her in late 1951 to the flag of the Caledonian Steam Packet Company, which became Caledonian MacBrayne on 1st January, 1973. In a cost-cutting exercise at the end of 1973 Calmac decided to retire *Waverley*, and sold her to the Paddle Steamer Preservation Society. Waverley Excursions Ltd. of Anderston Quay, Glasgow, now offer an extensive and varied programme of sailings and it is heartening to know that this very same paddle steamer on which I enjoyed numerous cruises is still very much operational today.

Today there are several ferry service operators in and around the Clyde, from whom almost unlimited choices are available for conveyance of passengers and cars to umpteen destinations in the region. For me, the ferries were always part and parcel of the enjoyment of being in Rothesay. At the departure point at Wemyss Bay, the excitement of merely being in the area began. I can't think of a more pleasant way of beginning and ending a journey.

Fairey Firefly aircraft are ready on the flight deck of the British Fleet Aircraft Carrier *Illustrious,* to take off for a dawn strike against 'enemy' forces in Norway, during the recently-completed NATO "Operation Mainbrace". An examination by senior officers of the success of the "Mainbrace" operation took place in Oslo on Sunday 28th September, 1952.

Holywell Isolation Hospital, Watford, late September, 1949. We had a few very warm days, when some polio patients were wheeled outside. The lady in the wheel-chair was paralysed from the waist down, the little girl was affected down the left side, and couldn't move her left arm or her legs, and I had sandbags placed around both legs to prevent me from moving and the virus spreading further. It was unfortunate that directly opposite the hospital at this time, was a sewage farm, and dozens of flies used to invade the building and cubicles. The nursing staff used to give us rolled up newspapers to brush the flies away as they continually landed on our faces. It was all some of us could do to wield the newspaper rolls with a flick of the wrist.

The Polio virus affected the use of their arms of these two toddlers. Raising a smile for this photograph in October, 1949, at Holywell Isolation Hospital, but reality set in once at Stanmore Orthopaedic, when we found we were unable to stand, let alone walk.

In the summer of 1998, Her Majesty the Queen visited Arran, arriving on board the Royal Yacht *Britannia* which anchored in Brodick Bay. Her Majesty came ashore in the Royal barge, and landed at Calmac's Brodick Pier. Amongst those to greet her on board were Caledonian MacBrayne's chairman Rear Admiral Neil Rankin, and former managing director Colin Paterson, now retired.

Her Majesty's previous visit to the island was on 24 July 1947 when as Princess Elizabeth she accompanied King George VI and Queen Elizabeth, and Princess Margaret in reviewing the Fleet of 100 Naval vessels assembled in the Firth of Clyde.

In the months following my release from service in 1948, I thought many times about arranging a holiday to Rothesay and spending some time there and with Janette at Balloch, but somehow I could never seem to manage it. Having been away for two years, one needed time to adjust to being at home again. Quite apart from this, there seemed to be so many social and domestic issues in which I soon became totally involved. In any case, I felt I needed a few weeks to properly settle down in what was really a new beginning; the very thought of 'working for a living' sounded humdrum, unexciting, and the last thing I wanted to contemplate in a hurry.

In September, 1948, I met Janette's sister Agnes when she came to London, chaperoned by her aunt Mary, to sit for her ARCM Class Teaching exam at the Royal Academy of Music in Marylebone Road. They stayed at Cranston's Ivanhoe Hotel in Bloomsbury. Agnes wrote to me on 25th September, 1948, saying she had passed the examination and could now append LRAM after her name.

After two or three months of being at home, my father arranged an appointment for me to attend an interview with a major firm of timber importers, Gabriel Wade & English Ltd., in Aldwych, London. I accepted the job offered, and duly returned to a working life in London, which I found I thoroughly enjoyed, my responsibilities taking me to various parts of the City and the London docklands. However, my new career was destined to be short lived.

Around the middle of 1947 an outbreak of Infantile Paralysis was beginning to emerge, and numerous brief announcements started to appear in the daily newspapers gradually drawing the attention of the general public to an impending health threat. The virus gathered pace over the ensuing months, spreading to epidemic proportions over the following few years.

My story really ends here, since it was my misfortune to catch the virus myself in September, 1949. Poliomyelitis had become widespread, causing the death of dozens and bringing disablement in one form or another to many, children and adults alike. Any lingering thoughts I had of revisiting Scotland and pursuing a career came to an abrupt end. I was faced with weeks in Isolation Hospital, followed by on-going treatment at Stanmore Orthopaedic, and many months of learning to walk again.

After an interval of several months due to the severity of my disability Janette and I resumed an exchange of letters. A great day arrived in April, 1950, when Janette and her friend Ella came to

London with the Glasgow Orpheus Choir, and during her short visit they came to our family home in Rickmansworth for a day. Following this happy reunion, we continued writing until I received a last letter from her on 25th November, 1951.

Around this time my progress was steady but slow, and my confidence generally was building as well. Regular sessions of physiotherapy and visits to the Watford Swimming Baths assisted greatly in restoring mobility. I was almost back to my normal self, and this encouraged me to arrange a holiday in Scotland, but not until around springtime or early summer, 1955, when I intended to make a surprise visit to Balloch.

I was able to meet Agnes, who had married David and was the mother of toddler, Fiona. She told me that Janette had also married and was now living in Canada.

In considering my own unfortunate predicament over the previous few years, and the fact that during this period neither of us, for whatever reason, had kept in touch, too much time had elapsed. A poignant reminder, perhaps, that personal circumstances change along with the pace of time and events, and we are left with only the realisation that lost moments seldom return.

A romance which began one evening in Rothesay in June, 1947, had finally ended.

In the garden of our family home in Rickmansworth, April, 1950. Although well supported here, recovery was painfully slow, and at this time, I could only just stand up on my own.

> Is it but a dream now
> Those years so long ago,
> And was I really there
> To see them come and go.
>
> And did they really happen,
> But how can I be sure,
> And did I fall in love,
> A hundred times and more.
>
> Dream on, Oh timeless dreamer
> Imprisoned in the past.
> Time's savage hand takes all
> And nothing ever lasts.
>
> Those very special moments,
> Glow bright as twilight nears,
> But nothing can destroy
> Those precious yesteryears.
>
> Anthony Walker

It was great seeing my favourite girl friend again.

Sequel

As THE months passed whilst writing this book, I never envisaged that there would be the need for a Sequel to my story. An Epilogue, yes, to bring to an end that which had a beginning, or a presence, material or otherwise, that was all part of the scene, and which was my world for such a short period of time. Not for a moment did I contemplate that I would ever return to Rothesay after so many years have passed.

Quite by chance, the opportunity arose in July, 1999, when my daughter Deborah and her husband Philip, and little James, asked my wife and me to accompany them on a holiday to Scotland. At my request, we planned to spend just a few days at Rothesay.

I have only ever lived in two places, my home town of Rickmansworth and Rothesay, and over all these years, although I had never returned there, I have always regarded Rothesay with affection as my second home. I desperately wanted to visit Rothesay again following my release, as I have written earlier, but was physically prevented from doing so. After this unhappy period of convalescence, I felt I no longer wanted to return there but instead to retain the memory of it all, just as it was when I left.

We stayed at Cannon House Hotel in Battery Place—I could not count the number of times I must have walked past Cannon House in my Navy days. From our bedroom window we were fortunate to see the steamer *Waverley* come and go conveying passengers just like the old days, and she looked as marvellous as ever.

Several visits to the Pavilion was a priority, of course, and this brought back many happy memories. It all looked pretty much the same as it did then, the entrance hall, the twin staircases and the doors into the dance hall, and the stage itself. I could feel the atmosphere just as if everything was waiting to return to those times I remember so well. The Winter Garden had memories, too, the Esplanade and the flower gardens, the Grand Marine Hotel, now converted into flats, held special memories, so too did the Glenburn Hotel, the layout of the town itself, Ettrick Bay, and much else.

There was a moment, as I was sitting on a bench on the Esplanade amongst the beautifully kept lawns and flower borders, when my thoughts became totally preoccupied with the past. I was gazing towards Rothesay Bay, looking out to the Admiralty buoy, still there, to which my depot ships had been moored. I was able to enjoy, for a few moments only it seemed, many memories which chased one another in rapid succession, as my blinkered stare concentrated on the Admiralty buoy, in total oblivion to everything else around me.

Awareness returned soon enough, when a ferry came into view steaming towards the pier, manoeuvred and tied up. How different from 1946 and 1947, I thought, when the decks were crowded with passengers and excited holidaymakers poured into the town, whilst dozens of others waited to embark. As I watched about half a dozen cars and a Safeway box van had lined up for boarding, with a number of foot passengers waiting to disembark, and as my eyes veered towards the town there was not a sailor in sight.

It is extraordinary how the turn of events have come full circle after so many years. I could have returned to Rothesay at any time over the past fifty years, but didn't, and I could have written this book many years ago, instead of leaving it until now.

Whatever the reasons, those unforgettable times of the past have found their way to the present, via a sequence of events reminiscent only of a world that once existed, but one which in comparison now is almost incomprehensible; a world that time has all but obliterated, with only memories remaining.

Memories of those post-war years under National Service for some will now be fragmented, the passing of time having dimmed the memory, recalling only certain events but forgetting others. Many others, no doubt, consider their National Service days a total waste of time, regarding them as no more than an intrusion into that particular time of their lives, gaining nothing from the Service in which they served, and concerning themselves only with an early release. As for the rest of us, our National Service days remain as vivid as ever, and we feel privileged to have at least taken part.

I am convinced that the training, discipline and experience gained under National Service provided a sound foundation for our future in many ways, and instilled in all of us, whether we fully realise it or not, an acceptable standard and a code which has stood us in good stead throughout our lives.

Whilst sitting on the bench seat on the Esplanade at Rothesay all these years later, one could be forgiven for thinking those days might just be a daydream after all, with everything seemingly so different from how it was in the late 1940s. I have never forgotten how much I enjoyed my National Service in the Royal Navy, and the time I spent at Rothesay, and how everything was then interesting, exciting and rewarding. For me, far from it all being an illusion or a dream, it remains reality itself.

From 1939, for more than 25 years, Rothesay had a strong Naval presence, with a resident depot ship in the Bay, a flotilla of submarines, and various other Naval warships visiting the area from time to time. Naval personnel poured into the town, and men dressed as sailors would be seen everywhere.

Understandably, today, many people visiting the island are ignorant of Rothesay's past claims, and would see little to tell them how important Rothesay had been as a Naval base. But for me, probably the most symbolic reminder of all, is the Admiralty mooring buoy, still clearly visible in the Bay, to which all the depot ships in turn were anchored. This photograph was taken in July, 1999.

Associated Press

The "Daring" class destroyers came into service after I had left the Navy, but their new construction embodying novel features in ship and engine design, together with improved fire power, was completed in February, 1945, and announced under 1947 Estimates. The "Daring" class were to be an expansion of the "Battle" class, having a standard displacement some 500 tons greater at 2830 tons, with a length overall 390 feet, 43 feet beam, and a complement of more than 300.
Defender (D114) pictured here in July, 1959, off Tigne Point, Malta, was built by Alex Stephens & Sons, Ltd (Govan), laid down 22 March, 1949, and completed 5 December, 1952. She was broken up at Inverkeithing in 1972.

Appendix one

RECOLLECTIONS OF D-DAY—AND THEREABOUTS!

I AM not anxious. I am not even nervous. On the contrary, I am elated. I am privileged. At this moment I would not change places with anyone. I am standing on the bridge of H.M.S. *Rodney* as we steam towards the coasts of Normandy on this, the morning of 6th June, 1944, and I see unfold before my eyes one of the great events in the history of our time. Nothing like it has happened before; nothing to equal it is likely to happen again. We are part of the Second Front. We are about to break the Atlantic Wall!

I am sorry for most of our ship's company, closed up at 'Action Stations' in the engine room, in the boiler room, in the gun turrets, in the transmitting stations, in the damage control parties and in the first aid parties. Their horizon is limited to the bulkheads of the compartments in which they are closed up and they have to rely on reports given from time to time over the P.A. system by the Chaplain of what is going on outside the confines of their own little world.

A few days earlier I had written home: 'We've been entertaining recently. First, we had General Montgomery on board. He walked round the ship and also made a short speech. He spoke very well. The troops just lapped it up. How, when he was in Italy, he had seen *Rodney* bombarding the Italian Coast, how the newspapers spoke of a "Second Front", but it was his and our Fourth or Fifth Front; an appreciation of the German soldier today, and how we were certain to win. It was all sound psychology—how good we were and how he would like us to support him again. It certainly was a morale-raiser.'

Our assembly point was the Firth of Clyde. There were hundreds of ships in the anchorage. We sailed on 4th June, escorted by a group of motor minesweepers. The following day we were dismayed to be informed that D-Day had been postponed because of bad weather, and we passed what seemed to be an endless day slowly circling off

Rodney in action. These were the guns which bombarded the Italian coast, saw action against the German battleship Bismarck, and poured 16-inch. shells on enemy batteries and concentrations on the Normandy coast on D-Day, 6 June, 1944.

This photograph was supplied by Commander Ian Hamilton, and on the back of which was fastened the following Naval Message. "From C.in,C.HOME FLEET. AFLOAT.
= 081504

For many months I have watched with admiration and pride the officers and men of the Home Fleet carrying out their many arduous, and often monotonous, tasks with unfailing zeal and thoroughness.

Now at last victory has come without our being given the chance of bringing the Enemy Fleet to action at sea, but the very fact that he has allowed his ships to be put out of action separately in harbour is a great tribute to the way in which the Home Fleet has carried out its tasks.

Ships of the Home Fleet may be called on to carry out tasks to help in the settlement of EUROPE in the near future and I have no doubt that you will tackle these with similar enthusiasm and efficiency.

I wish to convey my congratulations and thanks to all officers and men who have served so well in the Home Fleet."

In Transit - 8 - 5 - 1945

Signal ends.

the Welsh coast, fearful that the whole operation might be abandoned. However, with no further news of postponement we realised that the long-awaited Second Front would be launched the following morning, 6th June.

We proceeded on our way. In the early morning we heard the Allied aircraft flying overhead—remember, they flew 10,000 (some say 13,000) sorties that day. Many were firing their guns. We could see no hostile aircraft and soon realised that they were merely testing their guns.

D-Day dawned bright and clear, though there was quite a heavy swell. We were not among the early arrivals, and by the time we approached the beaches there was already a swept channel marked by gaily painted buoys with little flags on top. The closer to the shore we got the more congested things became. Groups of landing craft continued to cross our bows, causing us to make violent changes of course. These changes seemed only to lead us into further danger of collision. Eventually Captain Fitzroy declared, 'We'll keep to our course. They will have to take their chance!' There must have been many anxious moments among the tail-enders of groups of landing craft as they saw the bows of *Rodney* bearing down on them. On a later sortie from Portsmouth, at night, we ran over a landing craft. *Rodney* gave a slight wobble, the landing craft and her crew were gone forever.

As we proceeded to our allotted station, I remember a Signal Boy, horror-struck yet fascinated, peering through his binoculars at bodies floating past, some headless, then going to be sick in a bucket in the corner of the bridge. Hundreds of dead cuttlefish and squid floated past, killed by the concussion of shells exploding in the water.

The scene around was quite astonishing. Nothing like it had ever been seen before. 1,213 Naval ships took part in the assault and over 4,000 landing craft. As far as the eye could see there were ships coming and going. Also arriving were tugs towing strange-looking objects. We would now describe them as being like small oil rigs. Only later did we discover that they were to form part of the artificial harbour already being constructed around our anchorage.

Shortly after our arrival a returning force of landing craft close to us was shelled by a German battery near Le Havre. The landing craft were soon hidden by a smoke-screen and we fired two rounds of 16-inch shell at the battery. Their shelling ceased.

To our great disappointment we were informed we were 'surplus to requirements' and ordered to return to Portsmouth until required. As we retired that evening heavy firing still continued away to the West, and to the East at Ouistreham our destroyers were firing away at close range at a group of houses presumably still held by machine-gunners and snipers. On the shore directly ahead of us what had appeared like a disturbed ant-hill was now more like columns of warrior ants snaking away inland.

We had scarcely returned to Portsmouth when we received orders to return to the Beaches. There followed three days in which we fired 300 rounds of 16-inch shell, 450 rounds of 6-inch shell and countless rounds from our multiple pom-poms and Oerlikon guns. Our targets were enemy batteries and concentrations of armoured fighting vehicles. Even without making direct hits the blast from our exploding 16-inch shells was fearsome enough to knock a 45-ton Tiger tank over on its side and to obliterate personnel not behind armour. We were hammering tank concentrations as far inland as Caen, without any possibility of response. It must have been devastating to the morale of the German tank crews.

Memories of small incidents flood back. The artificial harbour, Mulberry, was almost complete, consisting of the sections towed out from home and of naval and merchant ships used as block-ships. We got a call one day from a young Royal Marine officer who had left us a few months before to take charge of a motor boat squadron running what appeared to be a kind of taxi service. He had taken up residence in the partly flooded hold of one of these merchant ships. When the tide rose a body floated up from a corner of the hold to join him. As it receded the body disappeared, to rejoin him with the next tide.

An alarm! Someone saw bubbles appearing from the ship's side. Suspicious of a limpet mine being placed on the hull, the alarm was sounded and a small charge dropped over the side. Investigation proved that someone had left the pump for a bathroom sump running, and after clearing the water it was pumping air out.

A Guards officer, immaculately dressed, leaving the ship with two newly-baked loaves wrapped in tissue paper under each arm.

Our Supply Officer, Commander Greswolde Ozanne Davis, a small wiry Channel Islander, wearing steel-rimmed glasses, was not to be deflected of his custom of thirty years by a small matter like a Second Front. While the rest of us in the Wardroom wore white overalls and rank shoulder-boards, he dressed for dinner each night. Dressing in his stiff shirt and bow tie in his cabin, he walked the thirty feet or so to the ship's main safe, turned the combination, pulled open the heavy door and took from the safe, the safest place in the ship, his Mess Jacket, donned it, and entered the Wardroom in time to have his 'standard' drink before dinner. He also had his very own Oerlikon gun. Whether he ever had to go to 'Action Stations' in his Mess Dress I do not know, as I would be otherwise engaged. It would make an incongruous spectacle, someone in Mess Dress manning an Oerlikon gun repelling a German air attack.

On one occasion we received a signal to fire 75 rounds on a German A.F.V. concentration on a map reference which was a position near Caen. We opened fire and continued with the bombardment. We then received a peremptory signal from Flag Officer Gold—'Cease firing. Report why you have fired so many rounds.' Captain Fitzroy, who was enjoying himself, inquired—'How many rounds have we fired?' 'Sixty-eight, sir.'

'We might as well complete the seventy-five. Carry on firing!' When we completed the firing, we puzzled over the Flag Officer's

Associated Press

This striking picture shows the main fire power of the battleship *Rodney*, which, with her sister ship *Nelson*, were the only ships in the Royal Navy to mount 16-inch. guns. Nine 16-inch. guns in three turrets, all of which could be fired on either beam. With a broadside weighing nearly 10 tons, their salvos could hit a target at a range only bounded by the limits of vision. These were the biggest guns ever mounted afloat with one exception, the 18-inch, an experimental gun used in *Furious* and certain monitors during the Great War, but were discarded for Naval purposes. The cost of Rodney's guns and turret armour was around £3,000,000, and the cost of firing a triple salvo £700.

signal. The signalman was summonsed. 'Did you get that signal from Flag Officer Gold correctly?'.

The Signalman looked at his pad. 'Yes, sir. Fire fifteen rounds of 16-inch H.E. shell at A.F.V. concentration, map reference ———.'

'But the signal says "Fire seventy-five rounds."'

'No, sir. Fifteen rounds. I always make my ones with a tick at the front!'

Our Chaplain managed to 'borrow' three trucks from the Army and advertised a 'Free Trip of the Battlefields'. The offer was vastly over-subscribed and the successful 'tourists' were picked from a hat. I was unsuccessful, but I got their story on their return. The appearance of three trucks of matloes rubber-necking from a ship caused no little astonishment among the troops trudging up to the front, and there were many ribald remarks—'You're going the wrong way'; 'Can you not take it any more on the sea?' and indelicate suggestions as to the reason for the run ashore!

They finished up within a few hundred yards of the German position, having a 'picnic lunch' with an Anti-Tank Battery, dug-in and camouflaged at the side of a road. There was a little alarm when they noticed that the guns were pointed along the road from whence they had come! When we got the signal to return to Portsmouth everyone was quite happy. Whilst our destroyers and frigates had done a good job in keeping German E-boats and other enemy surface craft away from our anchorage, we had been disturbed every night by enemy aircraft flying over dropping bombs and mines among our ships. We had brought down at least one Junkers 88. We were looking forward to getting some undisturbed sleep, some mail and re-ammunitioning and re-provisioning. However, we were infuriated when we heard the B.B.C. attribute all our successes and efforts to our arch-rival, H.M.S. *Nelson*, who, we grumbled, had spent the last fortnight 'swinging round a buoy at Milford Haven', and there was not a word about *Rodney*!

In a letter I sent home on 16th June I wrote: 'Well, we happened to be on the spot from D-day, and pretty often since, the big ships firing away at the coastal batteries and M/T inland; the destroyers flattening buildings that were being used by snipers; thousands of landing craft in a continuous stream and squadron after squadron of aircraft passing overhead. The R.A.F. were first-class, they gave us complete air cover except for odd German fighter-bombers which sneaked in once in a while.

'We have had a very mixed bag—coastal batteries, field batteries, tanks, motor transport, troops and villages—all in our own time and with scarcely any opposition.

'We haven't been issued with the seasickness pills. I gather that they are now really a success.

'We had a Russian Commander on board for a few days, now we have a Chinese Lieutenant named Wong. Typical Chinese too—always smiling. He says he likes our food better than the Chinese food.'

Ian Hamilton,
Commander, RN (Retd). 6 June, 1944.

Battleship - *Nelson*.

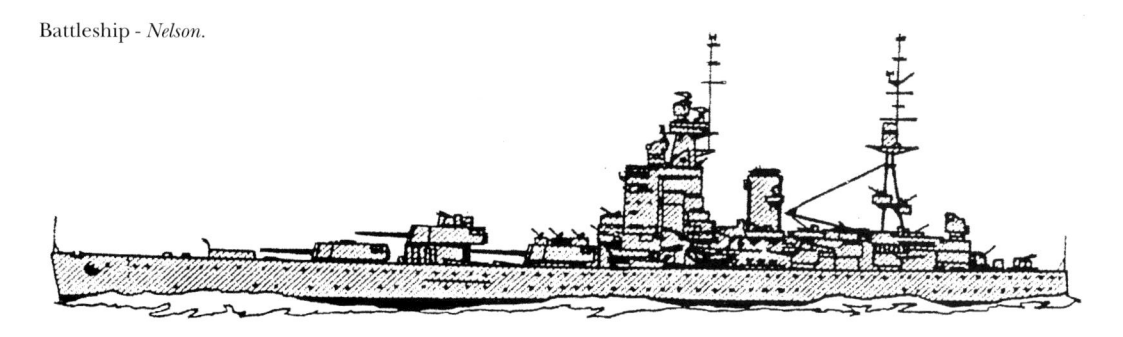

Jane's Fighting Ships, 1946/1947, with the kind permission of Random House UK Limited.

A superb view of *Truculent* making headway in May, 1946. One of a number of T-class boats built by Vickers-Armstrong (Barrow), laid down 28 December, 1941, and commissioned 31 December, 1942. After completion she was in action off Norway carrying out anti U-boat patrols in the Arctic convoy routes, and in September, 1943, was at Loch Cairnbawn from where she sailed to take part with HMS/ms *Thrasher, Stubborn, Syrtis, Sceptre,* and *Seanymph* in "Operation Source", the attack by X-craft on the German battleship *Tirpitz. Truculent* was assigned to tow X-6. In October, 1943, *Truculent* was in the Far East, and became the sixth T-boat in the Trincomalee flotilla using H.M.S. *Adamant* as the depot ship. *Truculent* had a distinguished service career throughout the war, but disaster struck in January, 1950, when she sank after colliding with a Swedish tanker in the Thames Estuary. Some of her crew were killed on impact, a small number were rescued by the tanker, but most were swept away by the tide and died in the freezing cold water.

Appendix two

MIDGET SUBMARINES

ALTHOUGH I was stationed at Rothesay for almost sixteen months, I never knew much about H.M.S. *Varbel*, the shore base of the Experimental Submarine Flotilla, situated in the Kyles of Bute Hydropathic Hotel at Port Bannatyne, on the Isle of Bute, only a short distance from the town of Rothesay.

The Kyles of Bute Hydro was taken over by the Admiralty in August, 1942, under the command of Commander David Ingram and became the headquarters of the 12th Submarine Flotilla, and it was from here that the midget submarine operations began. In addition to the Kyles of Bute Hydro, a satellite base was established at Ardtaraig House, a very substantial shooting lodge at the head of Loch Striven. This was taken over by the Admiralty in August, 1942, renamed *Varbel II*, and became the home of many of the 12th Flotilla personnel.

While initial training of X-craft crews was carried out in Loch Striven, which was closed to all other traffic not under the control of *Varbel*, an advanced training base was established in Loch Cairnbawn around a former Clan Line steamer converted to a depot ship, H.M.S. *Bonaventure*.

During the war midget submarines were built for the Admiralty, in conditions of great secrecy, by three inland firms, at Chesterfield, Gainsborough and Huddersfield. In the guise of motor-boats, these midget submarines were conveyed to the railway stations, where special trains were waiting to take them to the Clyde.

The first midget submarine, X-3, was built at the Varley Marine Works near Southampton and was launched in March, 1942. X-3 weighed 22 tons, was 43 feet long and had a crew of three. She could

The Hydro, pre-1909, when the building was partly burned down. The extension was added at the time, and the Hydro re-opened in 1911. Just visible at the bottom left of the picture, the Port Bannatyne Pier, looking a very flimsy wooden structure which was used by the Clyde River Steamers. Photograph kindly supplied by Commander I Hamilton.

make six knots on the surface, and five knots submerged, and she was armed with two detachable side charges, each containing two tons of explosive with delayed action clockwork fuses. Trials were so successful that she was taken to Faslane and towed to Loch Striven.

After the first prototypes X-3 and X-4, six more were built. These were larger at 27 tons, 51 feet long and had an outside diameter of around 5 feet 6 inches. They carried a crew of four and were named X-5 to X-10.

These craft called for crews of exceptional courage and daring. They were used on special missions where secrecy and stealth were vital, and where they could travel undetected right under the noses of the enemy to lay their explosive charges on targets of strategic importance and military value which were a threat to our country and our allies.

In September, 1943, two midget submarines, X-6 and X-7, carried out a daring attack on the German battleship *Tirpitz*, moored in the heavily protected anchorage of Kaafjord, North Norway. Through miles of fjord patrolled and protected by anti-submarine and torpedo nets, the Commanders of these two midgets manoeuvred their tiny craft after a passage of at least 1,000 miles from their base, and from a perilous position within the screen of nets protecting the *Tirpitz* and from a range of only 200 yards they got to work. So small and cramped were these craft, with insufficient room for the crew either to lie down at full length or to stand up properly,

This splendid picture of the Kyles of Bute Hydro, was the headquarters of H.M.S. "Varbel", the shore base of the Experimental Submarine Flotilla, at Port Bannatyne, on the Isle of Bute. This was established in August, 1942, to coincide with the arrival of X-3, the first of the flotilla midget submarines. Source unknown.

(RNSM)

that the placing of the charges proved difficult. Nevertheless, their mission was successful. There was an enormous explosion which lifted the 45,000-ton battleship five feet into the air; all three main engines were damaged, the electrical supply failed and her port rudder rendered inoperable. Much general damage was sustained as well, putting her out of action for many months.

The two Commanders of X-6 and X-7 scuttled their craft to prevent them falling into the hands of the enemy, and, with most of their crew, were taken prisoner. The Victoria Cross was awarded to Lieut. B. C. G. Place, D.S.C., R.N., commander X-6, and to Lieut. D. Cameron, R.N.R., commander X-7, for their bravery.

It was usual for these X-craft to be towed by submarines for a distance towards their target. Six X-craft were to have taken part in the raid on 11th September, 1943. They left Loch Cairnbawn under tow, the plan being that X-5, X-6, and X-7 were to attack the *Tirpitz* and X-9 and X-10 were to attack the 26,000-ton *Scharnhorst*, while X-8 was to attack the pocket battleship *Lutzow*.

X-5 was sunk either by gunfire or depth charges, X-8 broke loose from her tow, X-9 disappeared completely and X-10 developed a series of mechanical faults and had to abort her part of the mission.

On 10th April, 1944, X-24 got into Bergen Harbour and laid a charge under the 7,500-ton merchant ship *Barenfels*, which was berthed at a coaling jetty. The explosion sank the ship and caused considerable damage to harbour installations. Then in September the same year X-24 managed to re-enter Bergen Harbour and sank a floating dock, the explosion also sinking a small merchant vessel alongside it. For his daring achievement in sinking the *Barenfels* the commander, Lieut. M. H. Shean, R.A.N.V.R., was awarded the D.S.O. The Commander-in-Chief, Home Fleet, described the operation as 'a

Taken over by the Admiralty in August, 1942, was this very substantial old shooting-lodge, 'Ardtaraig' situated at the head of Loch Striven. Re-named 'Varbel II' it was a satallite to the Kyles Hydro, and the home of many of the 12th Flotilla personnel. Source unknown.

Shown here is the X-24 Midget submarine, with Sub-Lieut.John Britnell (Passage Crew CO) on the casing, flying the Jolly Roger. X-24 was laid down in 1943, but it is not known when she was commissioned. Her length was 51 feet 7 inches, beam 5 feet 9 inches (without charges). Surface displacement without charges 27 tons and submerged 29.5 tons. The X-24 carried 2 side charges each containing 2 tons of explosive and her maximum surface speed without charges was 6.5 knots. She had a crew of 4 including the Diver. X-24 is now on permament disply as a memorial at The Royal Navy Submarine Museum, Gosport, Hampshire. Source unknown.

magnificent achievement, ably planned and most daringly carried out'. Lieut. H. P. Westmacott, D.S.C., R.N., commander of X-24 in the attack on the floating dock, was awarded the D.S.O., and the D.S.C. went to Sub-lieut. Beadon Dening, D.S.O., R.N.V.R., for his part in this operation, 'Operation Heckle'. These honours, amongst others, were awarded 'for great gallantry in a most hazardous operation'.

Another type of midget submarine, larger than the X-craft, were the XEs. XE-3 attacked two Japanese cruisers, the *Takao* and *Myoko*, anchored in shallow waters in the Johore Straits off Singapore, and the XE-5 took part in the daring mission to cut the submarine telegraph cables in Lamma Channel off Hong Kong.

In addition to dangerous missions such as these, X-craft were used as defence markers during the Allied Landings in Northern France. They were actually the first vessels of the Royal Navy off the French shore, and lay submerged for 48 hours before the first landing craft approached the coast.

Debbie Corner of The Royal Navy Submarine Museum, Kathleen Clegg of the Bute Museum, and Commander Hamilton, who have all kindly provided background information to this section, have drawn attention to the fact that the crews of the 12th Submarine Flotilla of midget submarines totalled about 200, of whom 39 died. They were awarded 4 V.C.s, 3 C.B.E.s, 11 D.S.O.s, 10 D.S.C.s, and over 100 'Mentioned in Dispatches'—probably the most-decorated body of men in the British Services.

The enemy had midget submarines as well. One such type inspected by British experts was a two-man midget U-boat. This prefabricated type was 39 feet in length, with a displacement of 16 tons, and had an approximate endurance of 275 miles at 8 knots, plus about 50 miles at 3 knots submerged. Eighty-one midget U-boats were sunk or captured.

As well as training midget submarine crews, H.M.S. *Varbel* trained men for human torpedo operations. Human torpedoes were approximately the same size as ordinary torpedoes, 21 inches in diameter, 18 feet long, and were driven by electric batteries; they were manned by a crew of two who wore diving suits and sat astride the body of the torpedo. Approaching the target at slow speed, they dived below it, detached the explosive head from the main body, and fixed it to the bottom of the enemy ship. Time fuses were set and the human torpedo, now minus its warhead, was driven away in order to be clear of the target area before the explosion occurred.

Human torpedoes successfully penetrated the strongly defended harbour base at Palermo in January, 1943, and sank the Italian Regolo-class cruiser *Ulpio Traiano* and severely damaged the 8,500-ton transport *Viminale*. The human torpedo which sank the cruiser was manned by Lieut. R. T. G. Greenland, R.N.V.R., who was awarded the D.S.O., and Ldg. Signalman A. Ferrier, who gained the C.G.M. Sub-lieut. R. G. Dove, R.N.V.R., and Ldg. Seaman J. Freel, crew of the craft which damaged the *Viminale*, gained the D.S.O. and C.G.M. respectively. With others who took part in the operation they were made prisoners of war.

In this picture, Sub-Lieut. Frank Ogden is bringing back XE-3 into Labuan Harbour, North Borneo, after "Operation Struggle", the attack on the Japanese cruisers *Takao* and *Myoko* in the Johore Straits off Singpore, at the end of July, 1945. It is not known when XE-3 was built, but her length was 53 feet, beam 5 feet 9 inches, and her maximum speed 6.5 knots surfaced. She carried 2-explosive charges, and had a crew of 4/5. She was built by Vickers-Armstong, Ltd, Barrow.

For this daring exploit, the Commander, Lt.I.E. Fraser DSC (RNR), and Leading Seaman J.J.Magennis, were awarded the Victoria Cross. Sub.Lieut. W.J.L.Smith (RNZNVR) recieved the D.S.O. and ERA C A Reed received the CGM. XE-3 was scrapped in Australia, after the 14th Submarine Flotilla was disbanded 11 September, 1945. Source unknown.

HEROES OF THE HUMAN TORPEDOES—Extract from The Buteman, 13.11.1998

A Rothesay man, originally from near Hastings in Sussex, Lieut. Commander Bill Smith, volunteered for the Navy at the age of 17 and then for Special Service, where he was posted to H.M.S. *Varbel* early in the war. In October, 1944, a dangerous mission was planned to carry out a 'human torpedo' sortie against enemy ships in Phuket Harbour, Thailand. Two chariots named *Tiny* and *Slasher* were launched from the submarine *Trenchant* on the evening of 27 October. Their objectives were two ex-Italian merchant ships being repaired by the Japanese—the 5,000 ton *Sumatra* (attacked by *Tiny*) and the 5,272-ton *Volpi* (the target of *Slasher* with Smith as the Driver and Able Seaman Bert Brown as his diver). It was the last chariot operation of the war and one of the most successful. Brown was injured and his suit flooded, but both targets were sunk and all four charioteers safely recovered, although their chariots were scuttled. Smith and Brown were both awarded the D.S.M.

An unidentified submarine making headway in a rough swell, and flying the Jolly Roger. This picture has been in my attache case for more than fifty years, and depicts a wartime operation.

Appendix three

HOME FLEET REVIEW. July 1947 CLYDE 18.7.47–27.7.47

Source—Admiralty Pink Lists 14.7.47, 21.7.4
       Held by Naval Historical Branch MOD

HOME FLEET
2nd Battle Squadron   *Duke of York* (C-in-C, Home Fleet).
Training Battleships   *Anson, Howe..*
2nd Cruiser Squadron   *Superb* (C.S.2), *Cleopatra, Diadem, Dido, Sirius.*
4th Destroyer Flotilla   *Myngs* (D.4), *Dunkirk, Aisne, Jutland.*
5th Destroyer Flotilla   *Solebay* (D.5), *Gabbard, Cadiz, Sluys, St. James, St. Kitts.*
Fishery Protection Flotilla   *Marmion* (S.O.F.P.), *Lennox, Romola.*

NORE FLOTILLA   *Bicester, Bleasdale, Farndale.*

PORSMOUTH COMMAND
    Illustrious (Training Carrier).
Portsmouth Local Flotilla   *Finisterre* (Gunnery Firing Ship)
    Zephyr (Capt. 'D')
    Zest (Torpedo training)
    Opportune (Submarine Target Ship attached 5th Submarine Flotilla),
    Starling (Navigational training ship)
    Boxer
    Fleetwood
    Easton } 3rd Escort Flotilla
    Flint Castle
    Onslow (Submarine Target Ship attached 7th Submarine Flotilla)

PLYMOUTH COMMAND
Plymouth Local Flotilla   *Wizard, Burghead Bay, Roebuck* (Air Target Ship).
    Bramble } 1st Minesweeping Flotilla
    Nerissa

SUBMARINE COMMAND—CLYDE
3rd Submarine Flotilla   *Montclare, Dwarf, Alaric, Alcide, Alderney, Alliance, Satyr, Spiteful, Sturdy, Taciturn, Trespasser.*

5th Submarine Flotilla	*Woodbridge Haven* (Target Vessel), *Sirdar, Tactician, Thorough, Thule, Trump, Turpin.*
7th Submarine Flotilla	*Maidstone, Seneschal, Spirit, Tiptoe, Tradewind.*

ROSYTH COMMAND

Rosyth Local Flotilla	*Wakeful, Ulster, Whirlwind, Wrangler* (all Boys Training). *Rapid* and *Rocket* (Air Target Ships). *Onslaught* (Submarine Target Ship attached 5th Submarine Flotilla).
4th Escort Flotilla	*Crispin, Creole, Loch Arkaig, Loch Fada, Loch Tralaig, Loch Veyatie.*
	Spanker ⎫ Lochinvar Training Flotilla *Rosario* ⎭

Mike Cox, M. COX INFO SERVICES 'ORBATINFO'

Camper & Nicholson type MTB-V2015 photographed here in May, 1946, was similar in all respects to V2016 which attended the Clyde Naval Review in July, 1947, and was used by the royal family in reviewing the lines of ships. There were a number of these vessels in attendance, but it is uncertain whether V2015 was one of them.

Appendix four

DIVISIONAL ORGANISATION AND ARRANGEMENT OF WATCHES

THE PRIMARY consideration for the organisation of any of H.M. ships is, and always has been, her fighting efficiency. The secondary consideration is naturally her working efficiency, and it will be seen that these two go hand in hand.

In time of war, the most efficient method of keeping the ship in a constant state of readiness to engage the enemy is to have the men 'closed up' at their fighting positions or 'action stations' the whole of the time that the ship is at sea, but if the ship is at sea a long time in the hope of meeting the enemy, it is obvious that individual efficiency will be impaired by the tiredness of the men. Therefore, a Watch system is required.

The routine work of a ship still carries on even in wartime, and a Watch system is necessary both in harbour and at sea. At sea, because one watch is closed up at their 'cruising stations' while the other watch does the work necessary and rests. In harbour, because one watch is on shore leave and the other on board to do the necessary work, and, in the event of a ship receiving 'immediate' sailing orders, to take the ship to sea and be capable of fighting her.

The ship's company is divided into two halves called the Port and Starboard watches. Each watch is again divided up into two halves, called the 1st and 2nd Parts of the watch. In ships which have a large complement, generally speaking cruisers and above, the parts of the watch are still further subdivided into two parts called the 'sub' (subdivision) of watch.

Port Watch	1st Part	1st sub.
		2nd sub.
	2nd Part	3rd sub.
		4th sub.
Starboard Watch	1st Part	1st sub.
		2nd sub.
	2nd Part	3rd sub.
		4th sub.

Red, White and Blue watches are only used in ships with a large complement, where not more than one-third of the ship's company is closed up at 'cruising' stations and the other two-thirds are employed in their part of the ship, or resting. Generally this is only used when the ship is at sea. The engine-room personnel nearly always use the three-watch system both at sea and in harbour.

As an additional means of obtaining working efficiency the ship is divided up into 'parts of ship', the number depending on the size of the ship, and an officer, generally of lieutenant rank, is placed in charge of each. He is referred to as the Divisional Officer, and is responsible for the general welfare, requests and discipline of the

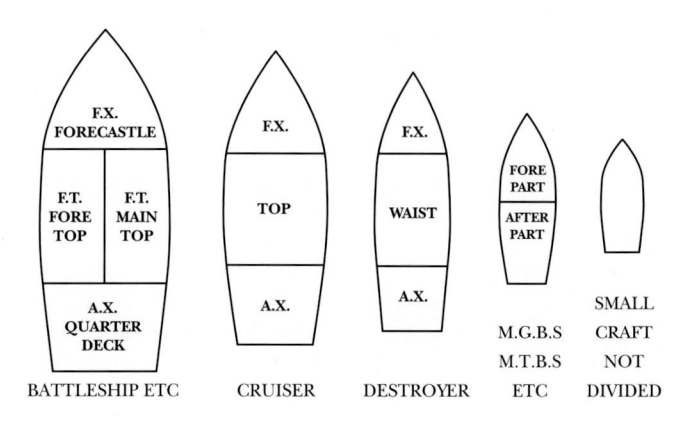

BATTLESHIP ETC	CRUISER	DESTROYER	M.G.B.S / M.T.B.S ETC	SMALL CRAFT NOT DIVIDED
F.X. FORECASTLE / F.T. FORE TOP / F.T. MAIN TOP / A.X. QUARTER DECK	F.X. / TOP / A.X.	F.X. / WAIST / A.X.	FORE PART / AFTER PART	—

men in his division. The ship's company is divided equally between each 'part of ship', so that there are equal numbers of higher ratings (i.e. C.P.O.s, P.O.s, Ldg. Seaman, etc.) and equal numbers of gunnery rates in each part of ship. The men in each part of ship are divided equally among the watches.

My Station Card on *Forth* stated my 'part' as C.C.O. (Communications Office) and 'part of ship', Comms.

Battleship - *Vanguard*.

Cruiser - *Belfast*.

Destroyer in the "Zambesi" class.

Jane's Fighting Ships, 1946/1947, with the kind permission of Random House UK Limited.

Appendix five

ROTHESAY BAY AND APPROACHES, SURVEYED BY CAPTAIN H.E. PUREY-CUST, RN. H.M.SURVEYING SHIP *TRITON*, 1904, WITH CORRECTIONS TO 1956, SHOWING THE WARTIME ADMIRALTY BUOYS.

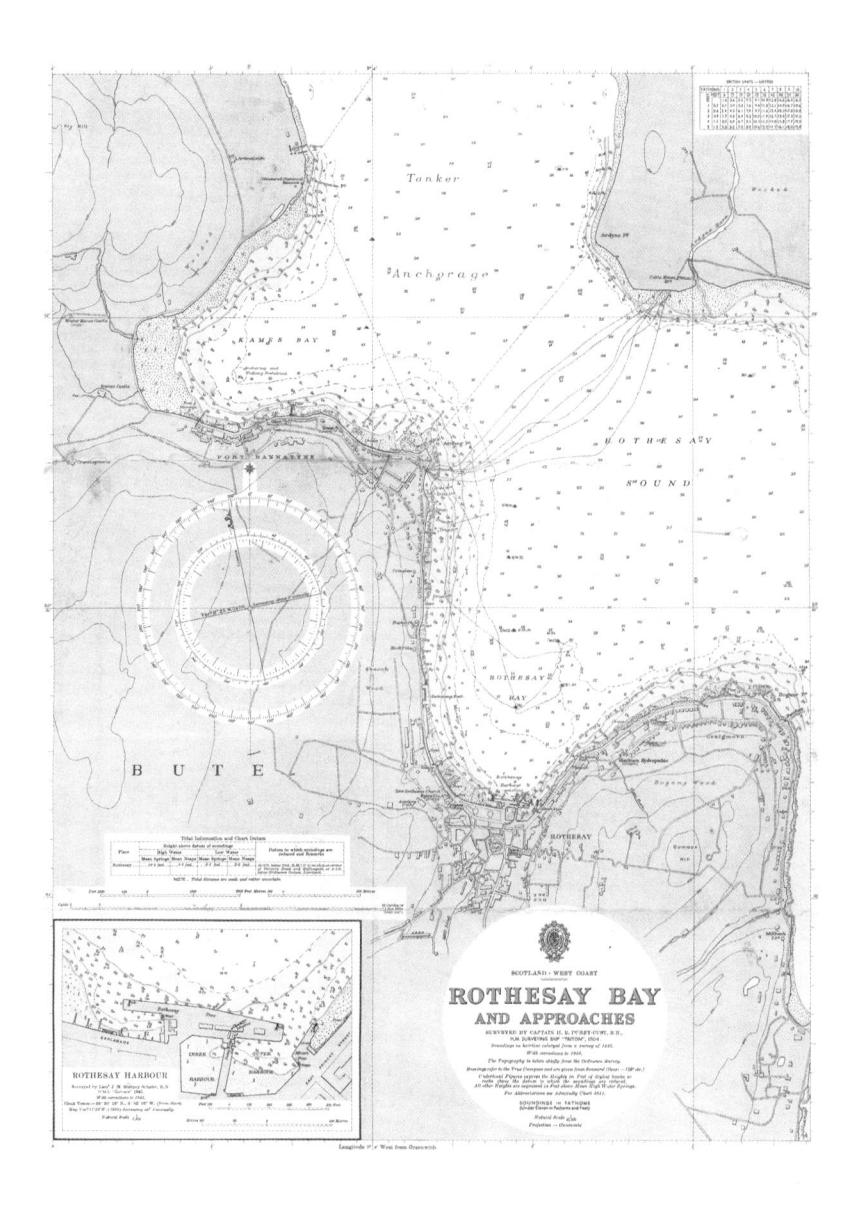

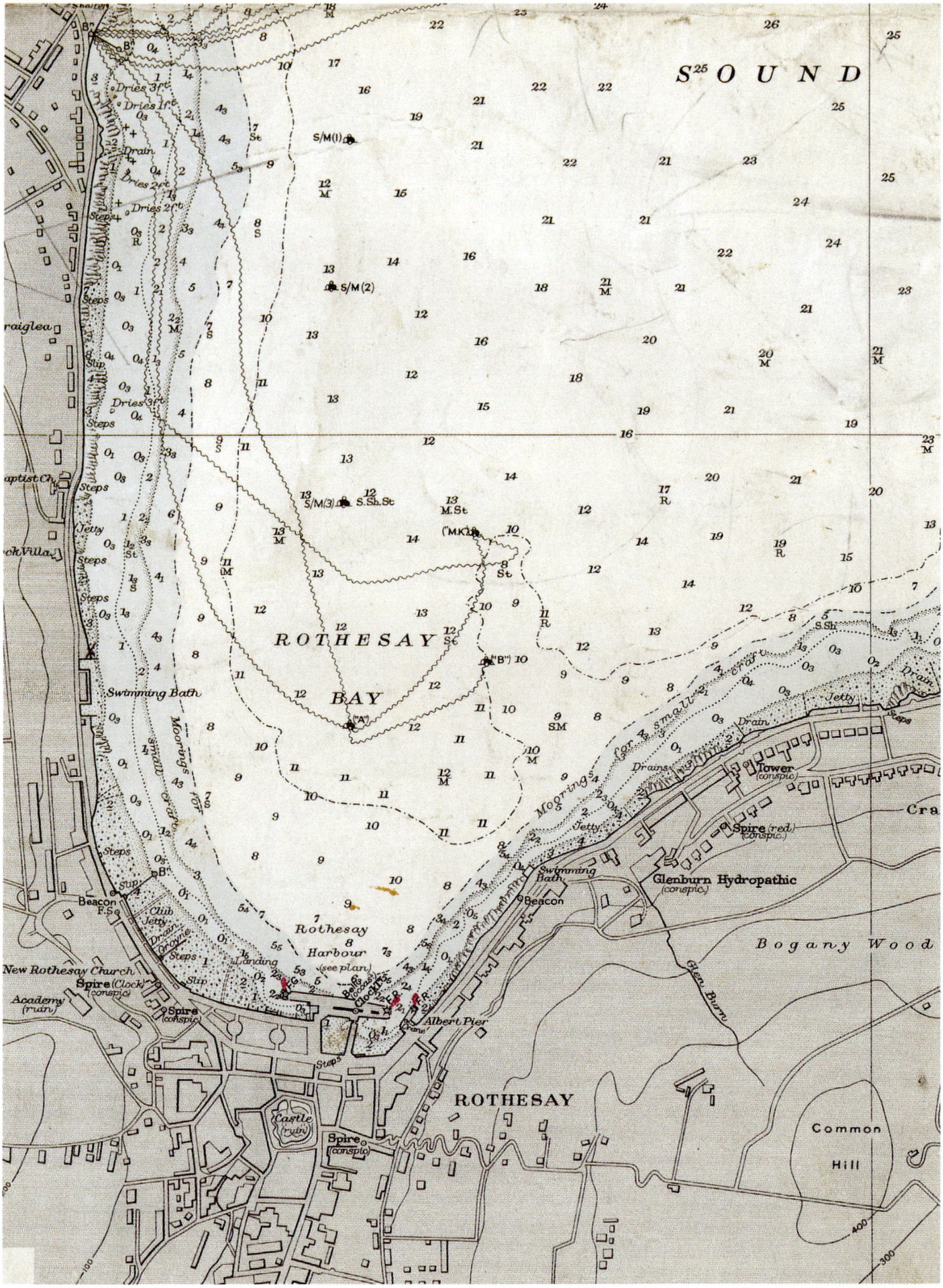
SOUND
ROTHESAY
BAY
Rothesay
Harbour
(see plan)
ROTHESAY
Swimming Bath
Moorings for small craft
Beacon
New Rothesay Church
Spire (Clock)
(conspic)
Academy
(ruin)
Castle
(ruin)
Albert Pier
Glenburn Hydropathic
(conspic)
Tower
(conspic)
Spire (red)
(conspic)
Bogany Wood
Glen Burn
Common
Hill
Baptist Ch.
Craiglea

*C*YCLOPS of the Seventh Submarine Flotilla was the first of the depot ships at Rothesay, arriving from Malta in 1939. She still had Maltese stewards on board, and a number of them married local girls. It was at this time the buoys S/m 1-2-3 were put in place. Buoy "A" was the depot ship buoy and the telephone cables shown on the Chart have now been removed.

"Warships of World War II" lists wartime submarines deployed in May 1944 as 4-"U", 2-"T", 1-"S", 1-"P", 1-"O", 4 Royal Netherlands Navy, 1 Royal Norwegian Navy and 1 ex-US Navy. *Forth* during the war was at Holy Loch with the Third Submarine Flotilla, and she replaced *Cyclops* at Rothesay in the early months of 1946 as depot ship of the Third Submarine Flotilla.

When submarines arrived, if they were not to go alongside the depot ship, they would be instructed to go to buoys 1,2 or 3. Buoy "B" indicated on the Chart was also used by a small depot ship. All these buoys have now been removed. Nowadays there are only two Admiralty buoys at Rothesay, buoy "A" and one far out in the bay, still used by submarines.

Below: Rothesay Harbour, Surveyed by Lieut. J.M.Sharpey Schafer, R.N., H.M.S. *Gulnare*, 1940, with corrections to 1955

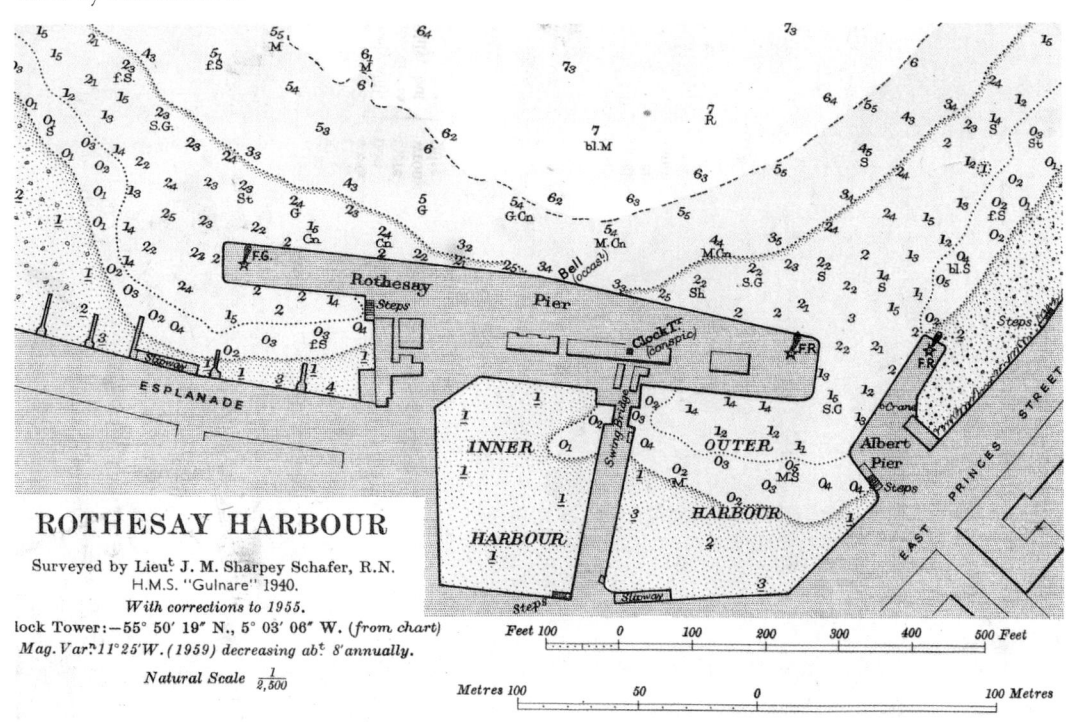

ROTHESAY HARBOUR
Surveyed by Lieut. J. M. Sharpey Schafer, R.N.
H.M.S. "Gulnare" 1940.
With corrections to 1955.
lock Tower:—55° 50' 19" N., 5° 03' 06" W. *(from chart)*
Mag. Var: 11° 25' W. (1959) decreasing ab: 8' annually.
Natural Scale $\frac{1}{2,500}$

I am very grateful to George Mackenzie, Administrator for Bute for the Argyll & Bute District Council for supplying this Chart which was published in London at the Admiralty, 13th July, 1956, under the Superintendence of Commodore K.St.B. Collins O.B.E., D.S.C., RN., Hydrographer (Crown Copyright reserved), and also to Commander I Hamilton for helping me with this caption.

Copyright Holders

I would like to thank the following Copyright holders for giving me permission to reproduce their material:

Associated Press Photo Library
Bute Newspapers—The *Rothesay Express* and *The Buteman*
Caledonian MacBrayne
City of Plymouth Museums & Art Gallery
Commander Ian Hamilton
Dennis Hardley, Scottish Photo Library
Ewan MacNaughton Associates
George G. Harrap & Co. Ltd.
Iain L. MacLeod
Ian McCrorie
Imperial War Museum
International Syndication, IPC Magazines Ltd
John Murray (Publishers) Ltd
Lt. Cdr. Ben Warlow
Maritime Books
Ministry of Defence Crown Copyright Administrator
National Maritime Museum London
News International Syndication
Nicolson of Largs
Paddle Steamer Preservation Society, Scottish Branch
Print Point (K.M.M. Limited)
Random House UK Limited
Scottish Media Newspapers
The Bute Museum
The Controller of Her Majesty's Stationery Office
The *Daily Mirror*
The Royal Navy Submarine Museum
Waverley Excursions Limited
Western Morning News
Whiteholme (Publishers) Ltd
Wright & Logan

Bibliography

Vice-Admiral J. E. Harper, C.B., M.V.O. *The Royal Navy at War*, 1941.
Christopher Chant. *Submarines of the 20 Century*, 1996.
Rear Admiral John Hervey, C.B., O.B.E. *Submarines*, Vol. Seven, 1994.
Jeremy Flack. *Today's Royal Navy in Colour*, 1996.
Commander J. J. Tall and Paul Kemp. *HM Submarines in Camera: An illustrated history of British Submarines 1901–1996.*
Captain John Wells. *The Royal Navy: An illustrated social history 1870-1982.*
Julian Thompson. *The War at Sea.* Imperial War Museum, 1997.
Lt. Cdr. Ben Warlow, RN(Retd). *The Royal Navy in Focus 1970-1979.*
Helen Long. *Change into Uniform*, 1978.
Peter Padfield. *War Beneath The Sea (Submarine conflict 1939-1945).*
Martin Middlebrook. *Convoy*, 1976.
Commander Edward Young, D.S.O., D.S.C., R.N.V.(S)R. *One of Our Submarines*, 1952.
Jane's Fighting Ships 1946-1947. Sampson Low Marston & Co. Ltd.
Lt. Cdr. M.A. Critchley, RN(Retd). *British Warships & Auxiliaries*, 1998.
Peter Brimacombe. *Drake's Drum. A history of the Devonport Naval Base and Dockyard*, 1998.
Irvin Block. *The Real Book of Ships*, 1960.
Sub-Lieutenant Ludovic Kennedy, RNVR. *Youth at War*, 1944.
Mark Arnold-Forster. *The World At War*, 1973.
Charles Owen. *No More Heroes*, 1975.
Harold F.B. Wheeler, F.R.Hist.S. *A Little Book of Naval Wisdom.*
Lord Strabolgi, RN. *Narvik and After.*
C.H. Wright, A.M.N.I. *The Efficient Deck Hand*, 1975.
Christopher Chant. *Submarines of World War II. An Illustrated Data Guide*, 1997.
Christopher Chant. *Battleships of World War II. An Illustrated Data Guide*, 1997.
Lt. Cdr. B. Warlow, RN(Retd). *Shore Establishments of the Royal Navy*, 1992.
His Majesty's Stationery Office. *A Seamans Pocket-Book*, 1943.
His Majesty's Stationery Office. *Combined Operations 1939-1942.*
His Majesty's Stationery Office. *Fleet Air Arm*, 1943.
His Majesty's Stationery Office. *East of Malta - West of Suez, 1939-1941.*
His Majesty's Stationery Office. *The Mediterranean Fleet, 1941-1943.*
His Majesty's Stationery Office. *Ark Royal*, 1942.
His Majesty's Stationery Office. *The Navy and the Y Scheme*, 1944.
His Majesty's Stationery Office. *Coastal Command, 1939-1942.*
Frank E. Dodman. *The Observer's Book of Ships*, 1966 & 1973.
Captain Ellison Hawks, R.A. *Britain's Wonderful Fighting Forces.*
Leo Walmsley. *Britain's Ports and Harbours*, 1946.

P.S. *Jeanie Deans* approaching Dunoon in August, 1963. Built 1931 by Fairfield, Govan. Withdrawn 1964 and sold 1965 for operation on the Thames where she was renamed Queen of the South. This venture was unsuccessful and she was towed to Antwerp for breaking up in late 1967. Postcard kindly supplied by Donald Ferguson. Copyright - Nicolson of Largs.

PERIODICALS-MAGAZINES-GAZETTES

Various copies of *The Sea Cadet*. 1944-1945 (Official Organ of the Sea Cadet Corps).

Various copies of *The Navy*, 1941-1942 (Official Organ of the Navy League).

Various copies of *The Cadet Journal* 1943 (Official Organ of The British National Cadet Association (INC) and of The Army Cadet Force).

Numerous copies of *The War Illustrated*, 1939-1945.

Caledonian MacBrayne, *Callmac's Gazette*.

Waverley Excursions Limited. *The Waverley Times*.

Maritime Books, *Warship World*.

NEWSPAPERS

The Daily Telegraph
The Times
The Glasgow Herald
The Scottish Daily News
The Rothesay Express
The Buteman

BOOKSELLERS

Maritime Books
Mainmast Books
Fisher Nautical

Index

A-class submarines, 80
Adamant, xxiv
Admiralty buoys, 221, 240
Aeneas building plans, 52-53
Aeneas, xvi, 51, 53, 63, 80, 91, 209
Affray building plans, 52-53
Affray, xvi, 50, 51, 52, 61, 63, 117, 213
Air Raid Precautions (ARP), 5
Air Training Corps (ATC), xxvii, 3, 5, 8
Aisne, xxix, 152
Alaric, 60, 105, 119, 140, 148, 209
Alcide, 80, 88, 91, 141, 148, 209
Alderney, xxvi, 105, 108, 119, 142, 148
Aldis lamp, 74
Alliance, 104, 107, 118 119, 148, 208, 211
Ambush, xvi, 119, 122, 202, 209
Amphion, 43
Anson, xxix, 20, 98, 125, 127, 146, 166, 207
Anzio, 133
Ardtaraig House, 229, 231
Ark Royal, xxxi, xxxii
Army Cadet Force (ACF), xxvii, 2
Astute, 43, 46, 209
Atlantic Wall, 223
Attlee, Clement, 151, 152
Auriga, 59, 114, 117
Aurochs, 118, 119, 209

Babur, 209
Bailey, A. W. xviii
Barrosa, 145, 152
Basic Disciplinary Training, 9, 21
Battle of Largs, vii
Beaufighters, 98
Belfast, 146, 203, 212, 238
Belson, D, xviii
Bennett, A. xx, 170, 175, 197
Beresford, C. Admiral Lord, xx
Berthing Plan, 131
Bicester, 126
Birch, Lt. 201
Birmingham, 91
Bismark, xxxi, xxxii, 146
Black Ranger, 88, 93, 95
Blackmore,
  Lt. Commander, L. E. 165

Bleasdale, 165, 207
Bonaventure, 229
Boxer, 134, 135
Bramble, 132
British Fleet Train, 114
British Pacific Fleet (BPF), 144
British Transport Commission, 217
Britannia, 218
Brooklyn Yard, x
Bryant, Commander B. 57
Bunty, 187
Burghead Bay, 125
Bushe, N, xviii
Bute Battery, viii
Bute Museum, xxiv, 189, 191
Bute Newspapers, xx, 178, 180, 182, 190
Bute road map, 172
Bute Volunteer Cavalry, vii
Buteshire Regiment & Local Militia, vii
Butlins, 2, 9, 10, 19

Cadiz, 145, 152
Caledonian Macbrayne, xxi, 215
Caledonian Steam Packet Co. Ltd, 169, 215
Caledonia, 181, 250
Cameron, Lt. D. 161
Canadian Pacific Railway, 113
Cannon House Hotel, 201
Cavalier, 212
Central Reception Depot, 202
Certificate of Registration, 7
Certificate of Service, 201
Chalets, 34
Changing ashore, 194-196
Chapelhill, 170
Charles, Prince of Wales, 170
Chatham Barracks (RNB), 39, 201
Chatham Ship, 146
Childrens corner, 175
Church of Scotland Huts, 192
Churchill, Sir, W. xxviii
City of Plymouth Archives & Records, xviii
City of Plymouth Museum, xviii
City of Plymouth, 109
Civil Defence (CD), xxvii

Civilian Clothing Depot, xxviii, 201
Clare, 186
Class 151, Royal Arthur, 18, 19
Class T/P15, Scotia, 33
Clegg, Kathleen, xxiv, 185, 189, 191, 232
Cleopatra, 70, 85, 88, 91, 95, 99, 146, 147, 209
Climbing the Mainmast, 67, 105
Cloch Lighthouse, 179
Clothing store (Slops), 15
Clyde Naval Review, xx, 167, 168
Clyde Visit Orders, 167, 168
Coastal Command, 81
Convoy Manoeuvres, 85
Cookham Mess, 39
Cooks to the Galley, 59
Cornwall, Colonel, R. F. 127
Corunna, 145, 152
Courageous, xxxi, xxvii
Cox, M. xvii
Creasey, Rear Admiral, G. E. 57
Creole, 154
Cripplegate, 110-111
Crispin, xxix, 88, 98, 154
Critchley, Lt. Commander, M. A. xx
Cross of Lorraine, 166
Cyclebox, 53
Cyclops Farewell, 54-57
Cyclops, viii, 52, 54, 189, 191, 195, 202

Daedalus, 24
Dalrymple-Hamilton, Vice Admiral, Sir Frederick, H. G. xx
Dance on board ship, 191
Dasher, ix
Davis, Jack, xviii
Decoy village, ix
Defender, 222
Defiance, 103
Devonport, 103, 109, 112, 113
Dewar, Duncan, 195
Diadem, 69, 72, 73, 78, 85, 91, 99, 147, 209
Dido, 70, 72, 85, 88, 81, 95, 99, 147, 209
Divisional Organisation, 237-238
Divisions, 11

Dolphin, xvi, 50, 211
Dorsetshire, xxxii
Down for the last time, 57
Dryland, M. xvii
Duchess of Fife, 181
Duchess of Hamilton, 182
Duchess of Montrose, 1, 41, 177, 180, 182, 217
Duke of Connaught, 11
Duke of Rothesay, vii
Duke of York, xxii, xxix, 83, 98, 124, 127, 146, 152, 166, 167, 207, 209
Dunkirk, 145, 152
Dwarf, 146

Eagle, xxxii
Easton, 165
Elizabeth, Queen, xxix, 149-150, 159
Enforcer, 151
Enlistment Notice, xxviii, 6
Euryalus, 147
Exercise on Guard, 117
Eyre, A. xvii

Fairey Albacore, 145
Fairey Barracuda, 30
Fairey Firefly, 217
Fairey Swordfish, 144
Fame, 86
Fancy, 132
Ferguson, D. xx, 1, 169, 170, 244
FEX9, 88-102
Fifth Destroyer Flotilla, 99
Fiji, xxxii
Finisterre, 145, 152
Firth of Clyde, 1, 118, 178, 223
Fisher, Ted, 119
Fishery Protection Flotilla, xvii, 151
Fitzroy, Captain R. O. xxix, 224, 225
Flag Deck, 70
Flags, 75
Fleet Air Arm Shore Establishments, 24
Fleet Air Arm, 23
Fleet Oilers, 93
Fleet Train, 87 93, 95, 98
Fleetwood, xvii
Flint castle, 128, 129, 138
Formidable, xxix
Formidable, xxix, xxxiv, 144
Fort Dusquesne, 130
Fort Rosalie, 130
Forth building plans, 42-43

Forth, xxix, xxxii, 1, 2, 39, 40, 41, 57, 61, 64, 67, 69, 88, 91, 93, 103, 111, 114, 115, 116, 117, 176, 187, 191, 194, 200, 201, 203, 204, 205
Fountain, E. xvii
Freebooter, xvii, 88, 93, 94, 95
Fyfe & Fyfe Entertainers, 174
Fyfe, Hamilton, xviii

Gabbard, 99, 102, 128, 152, 166
Gabriel Wade & English, Ltd, 218
Gathering of Submarines, 140-141
George Hotel, 187
George VI, King, xxix, 149, 150,155, 156, 159, 160
Gerrard, Harry, 188, 191
Gill, Deborah, xix
Glasgow Herald, 125, 149
Glasgow Orpheus Choir, 219
Glenburn Hotel, 197, 201
Glendower, 9, 19, 21-32, 202
Glorious, xxvii, xxxi
Glory, xxix
Gloucester, xxxii
Glyndwr, Owen, 21
Gordon Highlanders, vii
Grand Marine Hotel, 185, 201
Grog, 13, 86, 87

Hall, James, xxv, 166
Halsey, Rear Admiral, Sir Lionel, xx
Hamilton, Commander, I, xi, xxii, xxiii, 190, 192, 196, 227, 229
Hammocks, 48
Harbour Trust, 196
Hardley Photography, Dennis, 175
Hartland, x
Hawker Sea Furies, 206
Heads of Ayr, 34, 37
Hermes, xxxii
Hesperus, 58
Hickling, Rear Admiral, Harold, 127
Holloway Medical Board, 6
Holywell Isolation Hospital, 218
Home Fleet, 69, 70
Hood, xxx, xxxi
Hostilities only, 14
Hotspur, 86, 87, 98
Howe, xxix, 98, 124, 125, 127, 166, 207
Hygiene, 37

Illustrious, xxxiv, xxix, 103, 104, 123, 125, 145, 166, 206, 207, 216, 217
Imperieuse II, 103
Implacable, xxix, 83, 91, 95, 96, 97, 109, 144, 207
Indefatigable, xxix, 109, 144, 207
Indomitable, xxix, 144
Inglis, A&J, 184
Initial Training Base, 2
Instructors, 28-29
Invergordon, 88
Island of Bute, 169
Isobel, 13

Jamaica, 146
Jane's Fighting Ships, xxvi, 8, 20, 227, 238
Janette, 187, 188, 197, 219
Jean, 186, 187
Jeanie Deans, 244
Jonas, Commander, R. xxix
Jones, E. xvii
Jupiter, 180, 181, 182, 192, 193, 201, 216, 217
Jutland, 145

Karpinski, Bernard, E. xx
Kestrel, 24
King George V, xxix, xxxii, xv, 20, 69, 72, 80, 91, 101, 103, 146, 207, 209
King of Scots, vii
King Robert III, 169
Kit Layout, 27
Kit, 15, 28
Knots, hitches and bends, 26
Korean War, 204
Kyles of Bute Hydro, ix, 229, 230

Lairds Isle, 177
Lakin, Lt, Commander, R. B. 57
Larter, c, xvii
Last, Pilot Officer, RAFVR, M. J. 3
LCT4039, 138
Leeds Castle, 90
Lennox, xvii, 132
Liberty boats, 13, 42
Lines of ships, 130
Loch Arkaig, 88, 98, 138
Loch Cairnbawn, 229
Loch Fada, 88, 98, 138
Loch Striven, 230
Loch Tralaig, 138
Loch Veyatie, 88, 92, 98, 138
London & North Eastern Railway, 169, 184

London Midland & Scottish Railway, 169
Long Weight, 46
Lyle Hill, 137

MacLeod, Ian L, xx, 174, 183, 185, 186
Maidstone, 139, 150, 159, 160, 161, 162, 163, 166, 205, 209
Malabar, 24
Malaya, x
Marchioness of Lorne, 181, 182
Margeret, Princess, xxix, 149-150
Marmion, 132, 162
Marquess & Marchioness of Bute, 190
McMillan, 67
McNeill, Sir, Hector, 123, 127
Medical Grade Card, 7
Mediterranean Fleet, 145
Merlin, 24
Mersey, ix
Mess 33 *Forth*,
Mess 61 *Montclare*, 117
Mess Hall, 19
Mighty Armada, 127
Mines-Defence boom, 177, 179
Ministry of Defence Admiralty Library, xviii
Ministry of Labour and National Service, 5
Miss World, 189
MMS84, 157
Monice Square, Devenport, 112, 113
Montclare modification plans, 112-113
Montclare, xxiv, xxix, 63, 104, 111, 113, 114, 115, 116, 117, 118, 119, 123, 125, 139, 166, 176, 187, 188, 192, 193, 194, 195, 196, 200, 201, 206, 207, 210, 211
Montgomery, General, 223
Moore, Admiral Sir Henry, R. xxix
Morgan, Commander, 56
Morley, Eric, 189
Mosquitos, 81, 98
Mountbatten, Lt. 149-150, 152, 162, 165
Mrs. Miller, 188
MTB V2015, 236
MTB V2016, 155
Mull of Kintyre, 118, 121, 191, 209
Musical composition, 188
Myngs, 88, 91, 154, 163

NAAFI, 12, 19
Naiad, 147
Narvik, 136
National Maritime Museum London, 42-43, 52-53, 76, 112-113, 120-121
National Registration Identity Card, 7
National Service Acts, 6, 204
Naval Air Station, 98
Naval Bases, 103
Naval Discipline Act, 24
Naval fighters and bombers, 143
Naval Historical Branch, MOD, 91
Naval sleeve badges, 22
Navy Y Scheme, 5
Nelson, xxviii, xxx, 227
Nerissa, 132, 149
Norfolk, 146
Normandy, 223
North British Steam Packet Co. Ltd, 184
North Bute Cemetery, xi
Northern Lighthouse Commissioners, 157
Number 1165, Top Division, Glendower, 21
Number One's, 17

Ocean, xxix
O'Dell and family, 220
Oerlikon gun, 76
Offer, 91
Onslaught, 41, 58, 88, 91, 93, 95, 97, 99, 122, 125, 148
Onslow, 125, 148
Operation Blackcurrent, 105
Operation Exodus, 117
Operation Mainbrace, 217
Opportune, 63, 122, 125, 148, 207

Paddle Steamer Preservation Society, 185, 217
Paddle Steamer Preservation Society-Scottish Branch, 181, 183, 184
Palace cinema, 174
Palmer, Captain, I. M. 11
Parade ground, Scotia, 37
Parker, Rear Admiral, A. H. 127
Pay, 25
Peebles, A, 5
Pembroke, 24
Peregrine, 24
Petrobus, 152
Pluto, 132
Poems, 71, 198
Poliomyelitits, 218-219

Port Bannatyne, ix
Prince of Wales, xxxii, xxxiii
Promotion, 86, 87
Prudential building, Plymouth, 112
Pussers stores, 15
Pwllheli, 19

Qualifications, 38
Queen Street, Devonport, 112
Quota Acts 1795, vii

R.A.F. 24
Ranks, 23
Rapid, 161
Red Bay, Northern Ireland, 70
Reflector, 65, 74
Regal cinema, 174
Reggio, 133
Registration of Boys and Girls, 5
Renown, 8
Replenishing at sea, 93-95
Repulse, xxxii, xxxiii, 144
Returning to Portland, 100-101
Revellers Dance Band, 191
Rickmansworth Civil Defence (CD), 4
Rickmansworth School of Drama & Art, 7
Rickmansworth Urban District Council, 5
Ritz cinema, 174
Rodger, P. xix
Rodney, xxviii, xxix, xxx, xxxii, 91, 223, 226, 227
Romola, 132
Rosario, 132, 149
Rosneath, 138
Rothesay (Minesweeper), x, 170, 171
Rothesay Advertising Association, 186
Rothesay Castle, vii
Rothesay Entertainers, 191
Rothesay Harbour, 241
Rothesay street map, 173
Rothesay Town Council, 185
Rothesay Tramways Company, 174
Rothesay Welcome Home Fund, 190
Rothesay, ix, xxii, xxiii, xxix, xxxii, 1, 2, 41, 169, 170, 173, 175
Route map, Glasgow to Rothesay, 44-45
Royal Army Service Corps, x

Royal Arthur, xxviii, 1, 2, 6, 7, 9-20, 202
Royal Burgh of Rothesay, 169
Royal Fleet Auxilliaries, 130
Royal Marines, 24
Royal Norwegian Navy, 63
Royal Oak, xxxi
Rycroft, E. xvii

Safari, 56, 57
San Demetrio, ix
Sanguine, 88, 89
Satyr, 146
Saucy, 151, 157
Scharnhorst, 146, 147, 212
Scilly Islands, 207
S-class submarines, 79
Scotia, 9, 31, 33, 204
Scotsman, 105
Scottish Tourist Board, 135
Scythian, 105
Sea Cadet, 9
Sea Devil, 88, 89, 105
Seaman's Manual, 48
Seawanhaka Cup, 123
Selection officer, 15
Selene, 105, 107
Seneschal, 88, 105, 144, 146
Seraph, 105
Sheffield, 146
Shell Display, 186, 194, 201
Shifting *Montclare,* 195
Ship under Sailing Orders, 69
Shipbuilding, xxx
Short Magazine Lee-Enfield Rifle, 2
Sick Bay, 63
Signal History Sheet, 201
Sinbad The Sailor, 189
Sirdar, 146
Sirius, 126
Skegness, 1, 2, 7, 10
Skipper Woods, 169, 170
Slaughter, Captain, J. E. 111, 117, 191
Sluys, 102, 127, 152, 166
Snort, 117, 214
Soldiers, Sailors and Airmen's Families Assoc, 175
Solebay, 85, 88, 91, 99, 152, 153, 207
Spanker, 132
Spartan, viii, x
Spirit, 146
Spiteful, 79, 88, 105, 146
Splice the Mainbrace, 164
Springer, 88
Spur, 105, 108
Spurrier, J, xvii

St. Andrews Day, 191
St. James, 88, 91, 99, 100, 101, 145, 152, 166, 207
St. Kitts, 71, 88, 91, 99, 100, 101, 128, 152, 166
Starling, 158
Station Card, 13
Steamy mugs, 70
Stevenson, Lt. J. C. 2
Stork, 151
Sturdy, 105, 142, 144
Submarines foiled, 95-99
Sunday Divisions, 28
Superb, xxix, 84, 85, 88, 91, 99, 102, 161, 162, 166, 209
Suvla, 135
Swimming off the side, 119
Syfret, Admiral, Sir Neveille, 69, 127, 167

Taciturn, 105, 106, 119, 132, 209
Tactician, 132
Tail of the Bank, 126
Tantalus, 117
T-class submarines, 79
Teleprinters, 33, 38
Teredo, 63, 80, 120, 209
Teredo/Talent building plans, 120-121
Tetrach, 77
The Clyde at War, 178-179
The Daily Mirror, xx
The Daily Telegraph, xviii, 81, 210, 211, 213
The Evening News, 191
The Rickmansworth Players, 4
The Rothesay Express, 118, 123, 124, 165, 189, 191, 195
The Rothesay Tramways Co. Ltd, 174
Theseus, xxix, 141, 215
Third Submarine Flotilla, 103
Thorough, 132
Thrasher, 78
Three Scates, 36
Thring, Captain, G. A. 127
Thule, 132
Tiddley suit, 110, 186
Tiptoe, 162
Tirpitz, 77
Titania, 189
Tobacco, 12, 24
Toilet block, 195
Token, 32, 105, 117, 132
Top Division, Glendower, 21
Tradewind, 90, 105, 109, 132
Training Battleship Squadron, 20, 149
Training Establishment Ships, 103

Trespasser, 132
Tribune, 65, 66, 67, 68
Triumph, xxix, 47, 117
Truculent, 228
Trump, 132
Turpin, 132
Twentyfourth Herts Cadets, 2

Ulster, 155
Uncle Phil's Punch and Judy Show, 175
Uniform, 15-17
Utstein, 63, 64

Vanguard, xxix, xxxi, 35, 36, 117, 161, 238
Varbel, ix, 230
Varley Marine Works, 229
Venerable, xxix
Vengeance, xxix, 123, 125, 128, 161, 212
Venturer, 62, 63
Victorious, xxix, xxxii, xxxiv, 24, 104, 144
Victory, 24
Visitors enjoy concert, 188
Volendam, ix

Wakeful, 137
Walker, Anthony, 1, 200
Walker, David, 1, 200
Wallace, vii
Walney, x, xi
Warden (tug), 210
Warlow, Lt. Commander, B. xix
Watches, 11, 13, 21, 25
Waterbourne Training Centre, 190
Watford Grammar School, 1, 2, 3
Watford swimming baths, 219
Waverley Excursions, Ltd, 217
Waverley, Edward, 184
Waverley, xxi, 169, 180, 183, 184, 185, 201, 217
Wemyss Bay, 1, 201, 217
Wemyss, Admiral Sir Rosslyn, xx
Whirlwind, 136, 137
White Ensign, 11, 24
Williams, Captain, A. M. 21
Winter Garden, 174
Wizard, 137
Woodbridge Haven, 56, 57, 58, 118, 125, 209
Wooden, 67
Woods, W. S. Captain, 51
Wrangler, 137
WRNS, 30, 31

X-24, 232
X-3, 229, 230
X4-X10, 230
X-6, X-7, 230
XE-3, 233

Young, Ian, 181
Youth Training Service, 7

Zach, 119
Zealous, 88, 91
Zenith, 88, 91, 92
Zephyr, 88, 91, 154, 163, 207
Zest, 88, 91, 163

Shipbuilders included throughout the book are scheduled below:-

A & J.Inglis, Ltd, Glasgow.
Ailsa Shipbuilding Co, Ltd, Troon.
Alex Stephen & Sons, Ltd, (Linthouse, Govan, Glasgow).
Blyth Shipbuilding & Dry Dock Co, Ltd.
Caledonian Shipbuilding & Engineering Co, Ltd, Dundee.
Cammell Laird & Co, (Birkenhead).
Camper & Nicholson.
Charles Hill & Sons, Bristol.
Chatham Dockyard.
Cochrane & Sons, Selby.
Davie.
Devonport Dockyard.
Fleming & Ferguson, Ltd, Paisley.
Harland & Wolff, Ltd, Belfast.
Henry Robb, Ltd, Leith.
John Brown & Co, Ltd, (Shipbuilding & Engineering Works, Clydebank, Glasgow).
John I.Thorneycroft & Co, Ltd, (Woolston, Southampton).
J. Samuel White & Co, Ltd, (Cowes).
Philip & Son, Ltd, Dartmouth.
Port Arthur Shipyards.
Portsmouth Dockyard.
R & W Hawthorn Leslie & Co, Ltd, (Hebburn-on-Tyne).
Redfern Construction Co.
Scotts' Shipbuilding & Engineering Co, Ltd, (Greenock).
Swan, Hunter & Wigham Richardson, Ltd, (Wallsend-on-Tyne).
The Fairfield Shipbuilding & Engineering Co, Ltd, (Govan, Glasgow).
United Shipyards, Monteal.
Vickers-Armstrong, (Barrow-in-Furness).
Vosper, Ltd, Portsmouth.
West Coast Shipbuilders.
Wivenhoe.
Wm.Denny & Bros, Ltd, (Leven Shipyard, Dumbarton).
Wm.Hamilton & Co, Ltd, Port Glasgow.
Wm.Pickersgill & Sons, Sunderland.
Yarrow & Co, Ltd, (Scotstoun, Glasgow).

Hotspur, built by Scotts' Shipbuilding & Engineering, Co, Ltd, Greenock, launched 23 March, 1936, and completed 29 December, the same year.

Jane's Fighting Ships, 1946/1947, with the kind permission of Random House UK Limited.

In this tranquil setting, P. S. *Caledonia* is seen making headway in the Firth of Clyde.

CLYDE PADDLE STEAMERS

P.S. *Jeanie*

Tr.S.S. *King Edward*, built 1901.

T.S.M.V.

Tr.S.S *Saint Columba* (ex *Queen Alexandra*), built 1912 renamed on conversion 1936.

Tr.S.S. *Duchess*

P.M.V. *Talisman*, built 1935.

0   50   100